THE UNIQUE AND ULTIMATE GUIDE TO STARTING

THE CREDIT COUNSELING BUSINESS

LAUNCH YOUR OWN PROFITABLE AND RECURRING REVENUE BUSINESS

Contents

Chapter 04   The Basic of Starting Credit Counseling and Repair Business..87

Chapter 07   Credit Terminologies **175**

★ Contents ★

Acknowledgments

This is the proudest moment for us to work on this book as it is our third book. After the success of our previous books, "The Indian Credit Reporting System" and "Improove Your Credit Health," we have put in even more effort into this book to provide you with insight into business opportunities in the credit counseling and repair industry.

We would like to express our sincere gratitude to each member of our Apoorvaa Foundation who supported us in the successful publishing of this book.

We are delighted that we have created a well-designed and user-friendly book for those who aspire to own a business and are seeking unique business opportunities. We firmly believe that our efforts will undoubtedly assist them in achieving success.

Preface

Credit counseling and repair is still an unknown or foreign concept to many due to a lack of knowledge. Credit reports and credit scores now seem familiar to a few at this point. We have provided in-depth knowledge of credit reports and credit scores in our previous book "The Indian Credit Reporting System."

Credit counseling and repair is simply the process of restoring bad to good in your credit report to boost your credit score and rebuild your credit to be healthy. Whether you choose to undertake credit counseling and repair on your own or hire credit counseling and repair organization for professional services is entirely up to you. However, it is wise to seek expert help as credit counseling and repair involves numerous processes, paperwork, knowledge, time, and patience to achieve positive results. We have provided enough insight into credit repair for restoring credit in our previous book "Improove Your Credit Health."

This book now specifically focuses on credit counseling and repair in terms of starting a business or pursuing a career. It explores the scope and opportunities in credit counseling and repair, how to establish it as a business, and how it operates in India and globally. Whether you are genuinely seeking opportunities in the credit counseling and repair field or simply seeking information, this book will help you understand the ins and outs of credit counseling and repair.

The unfortunate reality is that credit repair is not widely recognized as a solution to credit issues, and the same applies to credit counseling and repair business, which remains an untapped opportunity. The door to credit counseling and repair business is open to all, given the soaring credit requirements in everyday life for personal and business expansion. It can be considered recession-free, with limited competition to handle and expand.

There are numerous reasons to pursue a credit counseling and repair business, but people are unaware of its importance and have their own doubts, such as the belief that credit counseling and repair has no concept in India, that those who offer these services are fraudsters, or that credit counseling and repair companies are scams. However, these are mere myths.

The potential and scope are vast in the credit counseling and repair field, especially in densely populated countries like India. Surveys indicate that eight out of ten people face challenges in their credit reports and are unable to pursue credit repair on their own. Furthermore, banking terminologies, dispute handling, letter or email drafting, follow-up processes, etc., are not everyone's expertises, as each query may require a different approach.

Previously, people spent as much as they could handle. But now the situation has changed, as individuals tend to spend more on their lifestyle using credit and accumulate more debt. When they struggle to maintain their credit, the need for credit counseling and repair arises.

Engaging in the credit counseling and repair business also allows you to fulfill a social responsibility, as helping others repair their credit history and rebuild their financial lives is incredibly rewarding.

If you approach the credit counseling and repair business with diligence, hard work, and perseverance, you can achieve a good income and reputation in your life. The book "The Credit Counseling Business" is written in an easy-to-understand language accessible to all. It contains all the necessary resources for a comprehensive understanding of the credit counseling and repair business.

The book is written to provide you with insight into whether to pursue credit counseling and repair as a business, address doubts or concerns, guide you on how to establish it as a business, and offer valuable advice. Credit counseling and repair is a distinct vertical within the banking and finance industry that indirectly impacts the country's industry and economy.

In a nutshell, this book will be a valuable tool for those embarking on their entrepreneurial journey and seeking a unique and different business opportunity.

– Apoorvaa Foundation
www.apoorvaa.co.in

Credit Counseling and Repair – Should You Do It as a Business or Not?

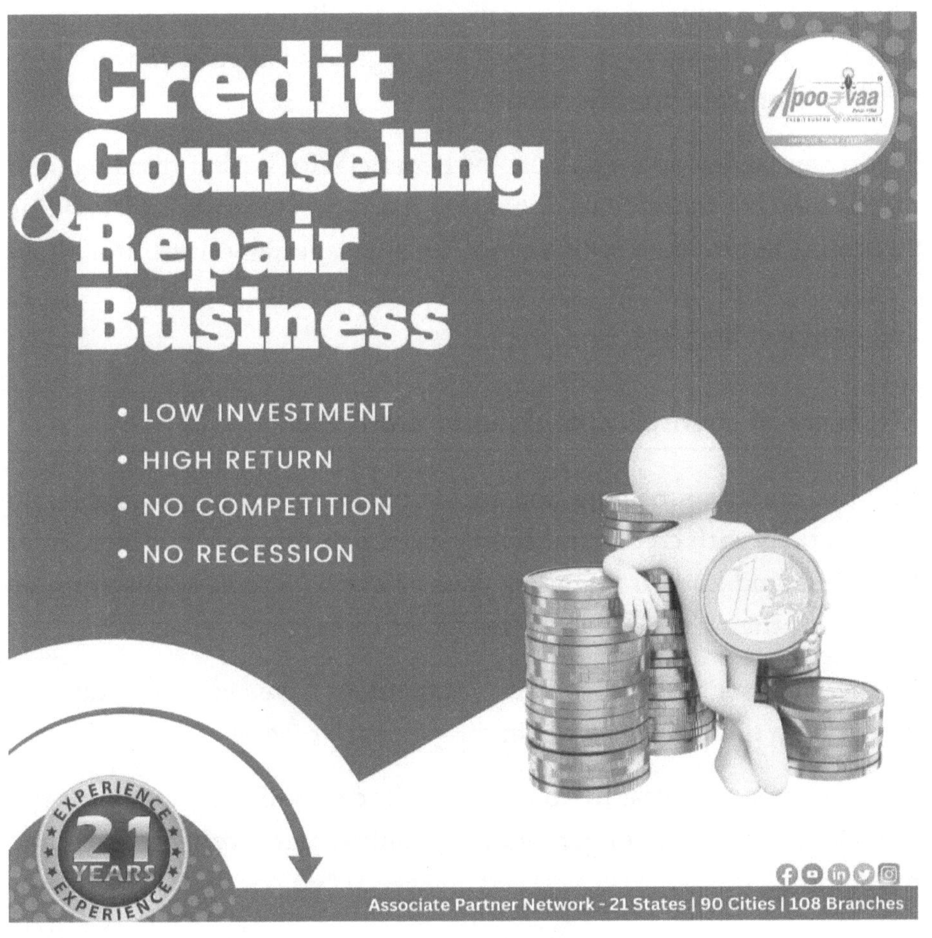

> **WHAT'S INCLUDED IN THIS CHAPTER**
>
> - **Is credit counseling and repair profitable?**
> - **The nobility of credit counseling and repair**
> - **The correct way to do credit counseling and repair**
> - **The final words**

Credit counseling and repair is a service that helps people improve their credit scores. The goal of this type of assistance is to support individuals who are facing credit issues.

The process begins when you contact a credit counselor or company that offers these services. You will be assigned an advisor to work with you based on your specific needs.

Credit counseling and repair can be beneficial for both individuals and businesses. For individuals, it helps in managing finances by providing advice on improving credit scores. This is especially useful for those struggling with debt or loan repayments. For businesses, it helps in addressing delinquencies.

1.1 Is credit counseling and repair profitable?

Yes, the credit counseling and repair business can be profitable. To make money with credit counseling and repair services, it is important to understand how to monetize your offerings. Credit counselors can charge for their time or for the results of their credit repair work.

Credit counseling and repair companies have various ways of monetizing their services, depending on each case.

However, it is essential to note that credit counseling and repair is not a quick scheme for making money. It requires hard work, patience, and dedication.

If you possess an entrepreneurial spirit, are willing to work hard, and have a passion for helping people, you can achieve significant growth in the credit counseling and repair industry.

But if you are looking for shortcuts, unwilling to follow the proper process or system, the business will not yield results. Focus on learning, sharing, and helping others to succeed in this field.

1.2   The nobility of credit counseling and repair

Credit counseling and repair is a noble business because it assists individuals and businesses facing financial distress.

Credit counseling and repair are crucial for the financial health of individuals and families. The benefits include:

- Improved credit scores
- Lower interest rates on loans
- Improved access to loans for those in need

Credit repair not only helps individuals enhance their credit scores but also contributes to the overall economy of the country. The economy relies on the responsible financial behavior of citizens in maintaining creditworthiness.

In summary, credit counseling and repair businesses help individuals, businesses, the banking industry, and the economy. This business offers the opportunity to earn both money and respect through noble actions.

1.3   The correct way to approach credit counseling and repair

To ensure success in credit counseling and repair, several steps can be taken. The most important is to thoroughly research your options and prepare for the process. Additionally, understand the time commitment required and the marketing efforts needed.

- If you are unsure about taking on a customer, become your own first customer and work on improving your own credit. Start by analyzing your own credit reports.
- Learn about credit bureaus, credit reporting systems, how to import credit reports, and different terminologies.
- Familiarize yourself with the dispute process with credit bureaus, as each credit bureau has its own procedure.
- Determine how much you will charge for credit counseling and repair services. Create a simple business model that delivers what you promise at affordable pricing.
- Stay updated with industry trends, new laws, and amendments. Also, learn techniques to scale your business.
- Develop effective customer and affiliate relationship-building skills.
- Utilize various tools to promote the scalability of your business, such as business cards, flyers, brochures, newspaper ads, etc.
- Establish a well-defined business website, business email, and contact information for prompt services.

Jumping into the credit counseling and repair business without proper preparation is likely to result in failure. Just as you need to learn how to swim before jumping into a river, the same applies to business. Learn the basics and plan accordingly for maximum output.

1.4   The final words

Credit counseling and repair is a profitable business venture. It is crucial to develop a well-defined plan that aligns with the needs of both you and your clients. While there are numerous benefits to entering the credit counseling industry, it is important to acknowledge and address the challenges that come with starting this type of business.

If you are considering establishing your own credit counseling or repair practice, there are essential factors to consider before diving into the field. Firstly, ensure that you have sufficient capital to initiate your business operations. You will need funds for advertising campaigns, such as Google Ad Words, as well as essential office equipment like computers, training materials, and other expenses associated with running an independent business.

By adequately preparing yourself and understanding the requirements of the credit counseling industry, you can set yourself up for success and make a positive impact on the financial well-being of individuals and businesses.

Summary of Chapter 1

This chapter delves into the subject of credit counseling and repair comprehensively. It seeks to answer the fundamental question: Is credit counseling and repair a profitable venture?

While this chapter is concise, it serves as the foundation and essence of the entire book, encapsulating the core principles and virtues of the credit counseling and repair business. It also highlights the numerous benefits associated with credit counseling and repair.

For aspiring entrepreneurs in the field, this chapter provides well-defined steps and guidelines for starting a credit counseling and repair business.

In summary, if you are considering entering the credit counseling and repair industry and are uncertain about the viability of such a business, this chapter provides all the necessary information to dispel any doubts and guide you in your journey.

Chapter 02

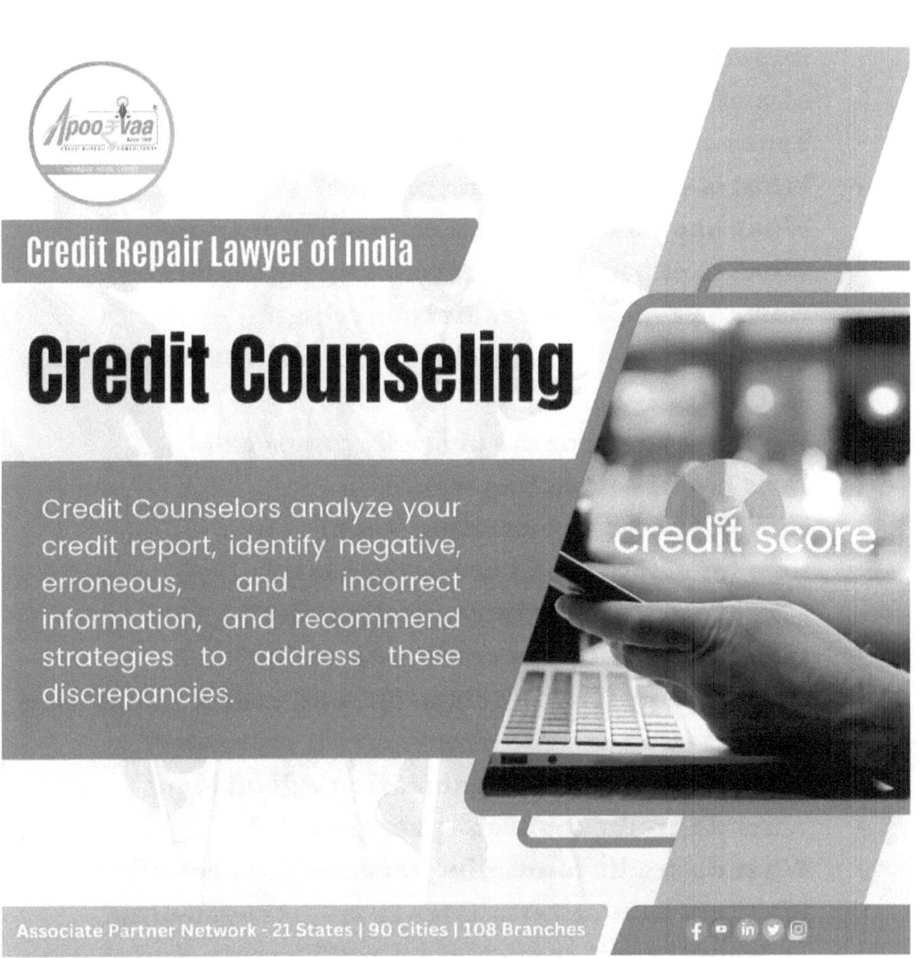
Credit Repair Lawyer of India
Credit Counseling
Credit Counselors analyze your credit report, identify negative, erroneous, and incorrect information, and recommend strategies to address these discrepancies.
credit score
Associate Partner Network - 21 States | 90 Cities | 108 Branches

WHAT'S INCLUDED IN THIS CHAPTER

- **What is credit counselor?**
- **What skills and competencies credit counselor posses?**
- **What does a credit counselor do?**
- **What does a credit counselor do with my personal information?**
- **How do I choose which credit counselor is right for me?**
- **What is credit counseling?**
- **Understanding credit counseling**
- **Importance of credit counselling**
- **Aim of credit counselling**
- **Types of credit counseling**
- **What is credit counseling process?**
- **What happens in a credit counseling session?**
- **What to expect in a credit counseling session?**
- **How to prepare for credit counseling?**
- **Impact of credit counseling on credit score and credit history**
- **What are the benefits of credit counseling?**
- **Does credit counseling work?**
- **How does credit counseling work?**
- **How long does credit counseling last?**
- **How much does credit counseling cost?**
- **When should you use credit counseling?**
- **Help finding credit counselor and credit counseling organization/How to choose credit counselor?**
- **Is credit counseling organization a good idea?**
- **What do credit counseling services do?**
- **What do credit counseling services does not offer?**
- **What are some alternatives to credit cousneling?**
- **To whom credit counselor or credit counseling session help?**

- **What does a credit counselor do if I need general information about credit repair?**
- **What does a credit counselor or credit counseling organization do if I am not located near in office?**
- **Watch out for credit counseling scam**
- **What are the sign of reputable credit counseling or repair organization?**
- **The final words**

Credit counseling is a term commonly used in the banking and financial sector, encompassing various forms of counseling from different perspectives. These include counseling for budgeting, financial planning, debt management, and credit repair.

This chapter focuses specifically on credit counseling from a credit repair standpoint.

2.1   What is a credit counselor?

Typically, a credit counselor can offer guidance on budgeting, debt repayment, and other aspects of money management. They can help you improve your credit by assessing your financial situation and creating a debt management plan to make your unsecured debt payments more manageable.

However, in the context of credit repair, credit counselors have a different role. They analyze your credit report, identify negative, erroneous, and incorrect information, and recommend strategies to address these discrepancies. Certified credit counselors possess the necessary expertise and can provide personalized advice, addressing both immediate credit report issues and underlying causes.

If you are struggling to maintain a healthy credit report or experiencing a low credit score, a credit counselor can be instrumental in helping you navigate these challenges.

2.2 What skills and competencies does a credit counselor possess?

In addition to relevant qualifications and formal training, credit counselors should possess specific skills and competencies to effectively address credit-related issues during counseling sessions. These include:

- Strong communication skills and prompt response time
- Proficiency in analyzing credit-related information
- Excellent customer service
- Active listening skills
- Interpersonal skills
- Knowledge of relevant laws and regulations
- Problem-solving abilities
- Observational skills
- Reasoning skills

Furthermore, counselors should be non-judgmental and unbiased, avoiding jumping to conclusions prematurely.

2.3 What does a credit counselor do?

Credit counselors offer a range of services, from basic budgeting advice to debt management plans. However, credit counselors specializing in credit repair can provide specific services such as credit report and credit score checks, credit report analysis, credit score building, credit report rectification, commercial credit report checks, commercial rank rectification, and credit monitoring. Working with a credit counselor can yield the following outcomes:

2.3.1 Personalized advice

The credit counselor will discuss your credit analysis and help you develop a personalized plan to improve your credit score and resolve any negative items on your credit report. Areas of focus can include:

- Creating a personalized plan based on credit report analysis
- Assisting you in accessing your credit reports and scores
- Improving financial and credit literacy
- Providing tips for credit score improvement
- Offering best practices for maintaining a good credit score
- Providing credit monitoring services

If you are unsure about how to handle issues with your credit report and credit score, seeking help from a credit counselor is recommended.

2.3.2 Credit awareness seminars

Credit awareness seminars may be unfamiliar to many people in India, as credit reports and credit bureaus are relatively new concepts. While most Indians are aware of financial workshops or seminars on budgeting, managing finances, and debt management, knowledge about credit management is often lacking.

You can attend workshops on various topics, including:

- Understanding the credit reporting system
- Learning how to check your credit report and credit score
- Managing credit cards effectively
- Maintaining a healthy credit history
- Understanding loans and credit scores

If you have specific questions or issues, you can check with credit counseling organizations or credit rectification organizations to see if they offer seminars or workshops that can help you.

2.4 What does a credit counselor do with my personal information?

We understand the importance of protecting your personal information. Your credit counselor will handle your details with the utmost confidentiality.

2.5   How do I choose the right credit counselor for me?

Here are some questions to consider when selecting a credit counseling service that suits your needs:

What services do you offer? Look for an organization that provides a comprehensive range of services, including credit analysis, credit report retrieval, credit counseling, credit rectification, and credit score building. Be cautious of organizations that offer unusual services, such as removing DPD cycles or promising immediate credit repair or score improvement within a few hours or days, without addressing underlying issues or payment dues to banks.

2.5.1   How is the service offered?

Look for an organization that offers services through multiple channels, such as online, in-person, or over the phone. You may also want to check if they have a head office or branch office setup.

Do they provide free educational materials? Avoid organizations that charge you for basic information or educational materials.

2.5.2   What are the fees?

Keep in mind that nothing is truly free, so be cautious of organizations that claim to offer a free credit report or credit score but later push you to avail of their other paid services. Before availing any service, carefully review their fees and details, such as agreements or validity periods.

2.5.3   What if I cannot afford to pay the fees or make contributions?

If you are unable to afford the full payment upfront, check if the organization offers a part payment option or flexible payment plans.

2.5.4   Will I have a formal written agreement or contract with you?

Legitimate organizations usually have formal written agreements or contracts in place, as they understand the importance of legal compliance and accountability. Be cautious of organizations that refuse to provide a written contract or agreement, as this could be a red flag for fraudulent practices.

2.6   What is credit counseling?

Credit counseling aims to assist consumers in understanding and addressing their credit issues. It involves one-on-one sessions between a credit counselor and an individual or business facing credit-related challenges. These sessions can take place over the phone, in-person, or via video conferencing.

Credit counseling is not limited to individuals; it can also be provided to companies or businesses experiencing credit discrepancies or issues. The primary goal of credit counseling is to help individuals or businesses identify and resolve their credit-related problems.

During a credit counseling session, a thorough review of the customer's credit report is conducted to identify the factors that contributed to their credit issues and unhealthy credit status. The resolutions offered vary depending on the unique circumstances of each customer.

Every credit counseling session is completely confidential, and the advice provided is tailored to the specific needs of each individual or company. Meeting with a certified credit counselor allows individuals to receive expert guidance on overcoming credit-related issues and rebuilding their credit.

2.7   Understanding credit counseling

Reputable credit counseling organizations employ trained and certified staff who can assist clients in developing a personalized plan for their credit issues. These organizations should provide information about their services without requiring clients to disclose specific details about their situation.

It is important to note that credit counseling is distinct from debt management, debt consolidation, or debt settlement. While credit counseling focuses on understanding credit report discrepancies and providing credit rectification services, debt settlement involves negotiating to reduce the total amount of debt owed. Debt settlement can be done independently, but it can have negative consequences for your credit score, even though it helps eliminate debt for less than the owed amount. Debt consolidation, on the other hand, involves obtaining a consolidation loan to pay off existing loans but does not involve paying less than the owed amount towards your debt.

2.8 Importance of credit counseling

Credit-related issues can affect individuals of all ages and income levels, particularly during financial crises or instances of identity theft or late payments. Credit counseling is crucial for understanding these issues, identifying the causes of negative items in your credit report, understanding why your credit score has declined, developing a credit repair plan, and receiving guidance on the credit rebuilding process. It is essential to find a reputable credit counseling and repair organization to address your credit issues effectively.

If you are experiencing financial distress and are unsure why your credit score has suffered, seeking the assistance of a credit counselor can be beneficial. Here are some key reasons why credit counseling is important:

2.8.1 Help you understand your credit report

To address credit issues, it is important to have a clear understanding of credit report analysis, what aspects to check, the impact of negative items on your credit score, and more. Credit counseling can help you comprehend credit reports and the reasons behind your credit score decrease.

2.8.2   Provide recommendations to eliminate negative items

Credit counselors possess the knowledge and expertise to handle negative items on your credit report and offer personalized, legal, and genuine solutions to remove them. They can provide recommendations tailored to your specific situation to help eliminate negative items from your credit report.

2.8.3   Maintaining a good credit score

Having a good credit score is essential if you plan to obtain a loan at a lower interest rate. Credit counseling services can assist you in maintaining a good credit score. If you currently have a bad credit score, don't worry, as credit counselors can help you build it back up.

2.8.4   Providing credit literacy

Credit counseling services offer financial education and practical solutions to improve your credit literacy. You will gain knowledge on how to maintain your credit score and credit history. Credit counselors can provide valuable insights to help you rebuild your credit score after credit rectification.

2.9   The aim of credit counseling

The main objective of credit counseling is to help individuals and companies address their credit-related issues, particularly if they are struggling to access credit. Credit counseling organizations assist in resolving credit report issues, including:

- Assisting financially distressed individuals in resolving negative credit report issues.
- Helping MSMEs (Micro, Small, and Medium Enterprises) overcome delinquencies to access financial resources for business expansion.
- Assisting individuals in rebuilding their credit.
- Supporting individuals in maintaining their credit scores.
- Providing genuine credit repair resolutions.

Credit counseling organizations aim to provide comprehensive credit repair solutions that benefit individuals, society, the banking industry, and the overall economy.

2.10 Types of credit counseling

Credit counseling is a valuable resource for individuals seeking to regain control of their finances. It offers guidance on money management, better spending decisions, and improved financial outcomes. Various types of credit counseling services can be tailored to meet specific needs, including debt management plans, budgeting advice, credit report reviews, and more. Understanding the different types of credit counseling services available can help you choose the best solution for your financial situation.

Here are some examples:

2.10.1 General budget counseling

Budgeting is a crucial aspect of financial planning, enabling you to make the most of your money. General budget counseling provides personalized advice on managing your finances effectively. Counselors can assist you in creating a budget plan, setting up automatic payments, and understanding the fundamentals of budgeting. By leveraging their expertise and experience, they can help you identify areas where adjustments are needed to reach your financial goals.

2.10.2 Debt management counseling

Debt management counseling is a common type of credit counseling that is typically offered by approved organizations. With this option, you make one monthly payment for a specified period (usually three years) to pay off all your debts. It's important to note that you may be charged interest on top of your existing debts, so it's essential to inquire about any fees before committing to this option.

Debt management counselors can provide valuable guidance on budgeting, saving money, and optimizing available resources. They can also advise on negotiating with creditors, consolidating debts, and, if necessary, considering bankruptcy. With the right guidance, individuals can regain control of their finances and avoid being burdened by debt for an extended period.

2.10.3 Bankruptcy counseling

Bankruptcy counseling is a crucial process that assists individuals and families in financial distress. It equips them with the necessary knowledge and resources to make informed decisions about their finances. The goal of bankruptcy counseling is to help individuals understand their rights, responsibilities, and options when filing for bankruptcy. It also aids in developing a plan for managing debts and rebuilding credit. Bankruptcy counselors can provide guidance on budgeting, debt management, credit repair, and other strategies that help individuals recover financially.

2.10.4 Credit repair counseling

Credit repair counseling is a service that helps individuals improve their credit scores and overall financial situation. It involves identifying the causes of bad credit, finding solutions to those problems, and assisting individuals in creating a plan for credit improvement. Credit repair counselors offer advice on debt management, budgeting, and enhancing creditworthiness. They also help individuals understand their rights regarding credit report accuracy and debt collection practices. With proper guidance and support, individuals can take steps towards repairing their credit scores and achieving better financial health.

2.11 The credit counseling process

The credit counseling process aims to help you achieve your financial goals by improving your credit score and addressing credit report issues. It involves understanding and identifying your credit-related issues and receiving comprehensive recommendations from a credit counselor. The process typically begins with a consultation, which can last between 30 minutes to an hour. Prior to the consultation, it's important to have your credit report readily available.

Credit counseling sessions can take place in a one-on-one setting, over the phone, or via video conference.

2.12   What happens in a credit counseling session?

If you are struggling to get a loan or credit card, it's important to be proactive. Chances are the situation will worsen financially, and the longer you wait to address it, the more challenging it will be to overcome.

Credit repair or credit counseling organizations offer services over phone calls, in-person meetings, or video conferences for credit analysis. During credit counseling sessions, they typically ask open-ended questions about your loans, credit cards, missed payments (if any), settlements (if any), and other relevant information to identify the root causes of your credit issues. Before starting a credit counseling session, it's beneficial to gather details about your loans or credit cards, any missed or delayed payments, and any conversations you may have had with the bank or lenders.

Counselors will inquire about the circumstances that led to your credit issues, such as financial crises, medical issues, job changes, or other common causes. Based on this information, credit counselors can design credit rectification plans and provide recommendations to address the issues you are facing.

2.13   What to expect in a credit counseling session?

Once you have chosen a credit counseling organization, they will pair you with an experienced, professionally certified credit counselor to begin the process.

During the session, you can expect to meet with the credit counselor either in person or by telephone. They will treat you with respect and dignity while reviewing your credit report and discussing negative items found within it.

The credit counselor will first review your credit report to identify the specific areas of concern, and then they will ask you some questions to gain a better understanding of your financial situation. This allows them to have a good idea of the best options to help you move forward.

Next, the credit counselor will discuss the various credit repair options available to you.

Once your counseling session is complete, you can rest assured knowing that you are not alone. There are resources available to help you address your credit-related issues. While it may feel like a long journey to overcome your credit problems, seeking credit counseling will make the process of credit rectification easier, faster, and less burdensome.

2.14   How to prepare for credit counseling?

Preparing to speak with a credit counselor may not be anyone's idea of fun, but focusing on the benefits it can bring will help you make the most of the session. The more prepared you are, the better your chances of devising a successful plan.

Credit counselors will need information regarding:

- Whether you have a credit report or not
- Whether you have previously settled any loans or credit card accounts
- Whether you have properly closed any loans or credit card accounts
- Whether you have obtained a No Objection Certificate (NOC) for any closed loan or credit card account

- Whether your current ongoing loans are being regularly paid or if you are experiencing repayment difficulties
- Whether you are a co-borrower or guarantor for any loans

Based on this information and an analysis of your credit report, the credit counselor will provide you with a roadmap to rectify the credit issues you are facing.

2.15   Impact of credit counseling on credit score and credit history

If you are struggling with a low credit score or a tarnished credit history, seeking the guidance of a credit counselor or credit counseling organization can be beneficial. They can provide you with specific steps to rectify discrepancies and improve your credit score.

It's important to note that meeting with a credit counselor does not have a negative impact on your credit score. The strategies they advise may temporarily impact your credit score if you opt for credit rectification, but ultimately, it will lead to improvement once the rectification work is complete.

During a credit counseling session, counselors typically begin by reviewing your credit report. They will pull your credit report, explain how to read it, and address any questions you may have. It's important to be aware that while your rectification process is ongoing, the credit bureau may add a temporary note to your credit report.

2.16   What are the benefits of credit counseling?

In simple terms, credit counseling can help you overcome credit-related issues and lead you towards a financially healthy life.

2.16.1   Reviewing your credit report

A credit report review is a crucial step in rectifying errors. However, many people lack knowledge about what to look for in their credit reports. Credit counselors assist you in analyzing your credit report to identify potential issues that have impacted your credit score.

2.16.2   Offering rectification services

Having a good credit score is essential for obtaining favorable interest rates on credit cards and bank loans. Credit counselors thoroughly examine your credit report to identify inaccuracies that, if corrected, could boost your credit score.

2.16.3   Building credit scores

When you have experienced a lower credit score, it can be challenging to obtain desired loans. Credit counselors can guide you on how to effectively build your credit scores.

2.16.4   Building credit history

If you are new to the credit line and have no credit history, it can result in a lack of credit score and an empty credit report. A good counselor can help you build your credit history properly.

2.16.5   Gaining financial education

In addition to assisting, you with rectifying your credit report, credit counseling organizations also provide financial education to their clients.

There are numerous benefits to credit counseling. Whether you need assistance with credit analysis, eliminating negative items from your credit report, or resolving discrepancies in commercial credit reports, credit counseling provides a holistic view of your credit report and credit score. It helps identify the underlying causes of credit problems. The fact that you are researching your options indicates that you are already on the right path.

2.17   Does credit counseling work?

The effectiveness of credit counseling may vary depending on the specific queries or problems you are facing. If you lack knowledge in credit analysis to identify errors or the root causes of low credit scores, or if you are overwhelmed by credit-related issues and unable to handle them, credit counseling and repair services can be beneficial. Engaging professional credit repair services can increase the likelihood of achieving the desired results with less hassle. Similar to hiring professionals to manage retirement funds or assist with buying or selling homes, professional credit repair can make the process easier for you.

Here is how professional credit counseling services generally work:

1. Find a reputable credit counseling or repair organization (note that in India, credit counseling and credit repair services are often offered by the same organization).
2. Authorize the credit repair organization to pull your credit reports if you don't have them. This typically involves fees or charges.
3. The credit counseling or repair organization's team reviews your credit report to identify erroneous, incomplete, and incorrect information.
4. After the credit counseling team completes the review of your credit report, they conduct a counseling session with you through phone, in-person, or video conferencing to understand each credit account from your perspective. They will guide you on the need for credit repair and provide recommendations. However, credit repair services are chargeable, and the decision to take up these services is up to you.
5. If you decide to proceed with credit repair, the credit counseling or repair organization will handle the entire process on your behalf and keep you updated on the progress. Once all the work and disputes are completed, they will provide you with an updated copy of your credit report so you can review and compare it before and after the process.

2.18   How does credit counseling work?

When you are facing overdue issues, written-off accounts, or collection notices, it can quickly become overwhelming. One common problem people face when dealing with credit-related challenges is a lack of awareness about available credit counseling and repair solutions. Many individuals only start exploring these options when they are already in the worst situation with their credit.

2.18.1   Contact a credit counseling service

Credit counseling service providers or credit repair service providers have certified and trained credit counselors who specialize in credit repair and handling credit-related issues. Credit counseling sessions are typically conducted over the phone, but consultations can also take place in person or through video conferencing.

2.18.2   Authorize a credit check

To gain a complete understanding of your financial situation, the counselor will ask to run a credit check. This allows them to review your credit report and identify any collections or other noteworthy items. It's important to note that this is a "soft" inquiry and does not impact your credit score. However, please be aware that checking your credit report is not a free service if you don't have a credit report with you.

2.18.3   Analysis of your credit report

To initiate the credit counseling process, the counselor will request basic information about your past and current loans or credit cards. Be prepared to provide details such as:

- Your current debts, including secured loans like your mortgage or auto loan
- Current balances on your credit cards and the APR for each account
- Other obligations, such as loans from an app, being a guarantor for someone else's loan, or being a co-applicant or co-borrower in a loan

For credit counseling to be effective, it is crucial to be completely honest and transparent in providing this information. Withholding any relevant details could significantly impact the recommendations they provide.

2.18.4   Credit counselor's recommendation

Once the credit counselor has a comprehensive understanding of your credit history and financial situation, they will make recommendations based on what would be best for you.

In summary, the credit repair process can be tedious and time-consuming. That's why credit counseling is the recommended approach to finding a solution for your credit-related issues and rectifying them. With credit counseling, you can receive unbiased, expert opinions on what steps you need to take to address the issues on your credit report, how to rebuild your credit, ask questions about different solutions, and learn how to minimize further credit damage.

2.19   How long does credit counseling last?

The duration of a credit counseling session varies depending on the complexity of your credit-related issues. Typically, credit counseling sessions can last at least half an hour or more. It may require multiple sessions based on the extent of your queries and concerns.

2.20   How much does credit counseling cost?

Credit counseling is often available free of charge or at a lower cost. However, if you opt for credit repair or rectification services, there may be charges involved. The specific fees vary depending on the nature of your problems, but paying for these services can be worthwhile as it helps you avoid the lengthy credit repair process.

2.21   When should you use credit counseling?

Credit counseling can be a valuable option if you feel overwhelmed or anxious about loan rejections due to credit report and credit score issues. Additionally, if you have experienced challenges like job loss, medical issues, or financial difficulties that led to the settlement of your loans or credit cards, credit counseling can help alleviate the stress. Credit counseling organizations offer personalized and tailored plans to help you rectify these issues.

In general, credit counseling is a suitable choice for anyone who needs assistance in addressing credit-related issues or wants to improve their credit score.

2.22   How to find a credit counselor and credit counseling organization/How to choose a credit counselor?

Not all credit counseling organizations are the same, so it's important to choose one that meets your needs. Selecting a reputable credit counseling service is similar to any other shopping endeavor.

To ensure a positive experience, consider the following steps to find a good credit counseling service or counselor:

- Determine your needs: Understanding your specific requirements can help narrow down your options from the start.
- Seek recommendations: Ask friends and colleagues who have used credit counseling services for their recommendations.
- Use a reputable starting point: Conduct online research to learn about the organization's practices and history before making a decision.
- Schedule an initial consultation: Before finalizing your choice, ask important questions to gauge the credibility of the credit counseling organization. Some essential questions to ask include:

  1. What services do you offer?
  2. How is credit counseling conducted at your organization?
  3. Do you offer services online, in person, or via telephone?
  4. How frequently will we meet or communicate?

5. Do you provide free educational resources?
6. What fees, if any, do you charge?
7. Will I need to sign a contract that outlines fees, services, and a timeline for completing the work?
8. Do you offer credit counseling and credit rectification as separate services or together?

Asking these questions will help you make an informed decision about which credit counseling organization is the best fit for your needs.

2.23   Is a credit counseling organization a good idea?

Whether or not a credit counseling organization is a good idea depends on your individual circumstances and needs. Here are some factors to consider:

2.23.1   Save you from the lengthy credit repair process

If you are unfamiliar with credit repair processes and find them overwhelming, credit counseling can be a valuable resource. Credit counselors are knowledgeable about the steps involved in credit repair and can guide you through the process, potentially saving you time and effort.

2.23.2   Help you understand the root cause of your credit issues

Credit counseling can provide insights into the factors that have negatively affected your credit score. By understanding the root causes of your credit issues, you can make more informed decisions and take appropriate steps to improve your credit.

2.23.3   Provide guidance on credit building

If you need assistance in building or rebuilding your credit, credit counseling can offer valuable guidance. Credit counselors can provide you with strategies and advice on how to effectively improve your credit score and maintain a healthy credit profile.

2.23.4   Help with credit monitoring service

Many credit counseling organizations also offer credit monitoring services. These services can help you stay informed about changes in your credit report, detect any potential fraud or identity theft, and maintain a vigilant approach towards your credit health.

2.24   What do credit counseling services do?

Credit counseling services offer various assistance and resources to individuals or companies facing credit-related issues. These services typically include:

- Answering questions and providing guidance on strategies to resolve credit-related issues.
- Assisting in identifying appropriate solutions for delinquencies and credit challenges.
- Reviewing credit reports to identify negative, incorrect, or incomplete information.
- Providing educational resources to improve credit literacy and understanding.
- Offering guidance on maintaining a healthy credit life.
- Assisting in credit rebuilding efforts.
- Providing credit repair services if desired to address credit-related issues.
- Offering credit monitoring services to help maintain credit health after credit rectification.

Overall, credit counseling services aim to support individuals in navigating their credit challenges, improving their credit scores, and achieving financial well-being.

2.25   What do credit counseling services not offer?

Credit counseling services do not provide the following options:

- They do not offer debt forgiveness.

- They do not assist with debt settlement negotiations with your creditors.
- They do not provide assistance with other services such as debt management, debt consolidation, or obtaining loans.
- They cannot stop any ongoing court action related to your debts if a lawsuit has already been filed by the bank.

Please note that for services like debt management or debt consolidation, it is recommended to consult a financial consultant or advisor who can guide you on budgeting, managing finances, and handling debt issues.

2.26   What are some alternatives to credit counseling?

If you are uncertain about whether credit counseling is the right choice for you, there are a few alternatives you may consider. One option is to handle credit repair on your own.

However, please keep in mind that undertaking credit repair on your own can be time-consuming, tedious, and involves lengthy processing. It requires significant communication with lenders and credit bureaus, each with their own processes and procedures. If you are not familiar with financial and banking terminology, it can be challenging to navigate on your own.

Before attempting credit repair on your own, it is important to thoroughly educate yourself about the entire process, which in itself can be time-consuming.

Another alternative is to choose not to pursue credit repair solutions and leave the negative items on your credit report as they are. However, this approach will likely limit your options for obtaining loans, and any available loans may come with higher interest rates that may not be affordable.

Credit counseling can be an excellent choice when your credit report is burdened with numerous negative, incorrect, or inaccurate items. Credit counselors can assist in removing negative items from your credit report more efficiently while providing you with the knowledge and tools to better manage your credit score in the future.

2.27 To whom do credit counselors or credit counseling sessions help?

Credit counselors or credit counseling sessions are helpful to those:

- Who feel overwhelmed by credit-related issues and want someone to help and guide them towards a better resolution while educating them about their issues.
- Who are unsure how to analyze their credit report and tackle credit-related issues and seek assistance with that process.
- Who are unfamiliar with the credit repair and credit rebuilding process and want a professional to handle the matter on their behalf.
- Who are facing challenges with discrepancies in their company or business credit report and are seeking a better resolution to address the issues.

If you find yourself in any of the above situations, consulting with a credit counselor can help you identify the root cause. Following the consultation, credit counselors provide recommendations based on credit analysis and counseling to rectify credit issues.

2.28 What does a credit counselor do if I need general information about credit repair?

Credit counseling organizations also work to provide education on credit awareness. If you need general information, you can directly contact them through their helpline or the contact details available on their website. You can also find blogs, articles, or videos on the topics you would like to gather information about.

2.29   What does a credit counselor or credit counseling organization do if I am not located near their office?

Credit counseling sessions can be conducted over the phone or via video conferencing if you are unable to visit their office in person. The credit counseling session can be scheduled during working hours.

2.30   Watch out for credit counseling scams

Unfortunately, there are some counselors who may take your money without providing the necessary help for your credit report. Credit counseling scams are prevalent, and they can have a detrimental impact on both your credit and finances. Some companies may make false claims, guaranteeing specific increases in your credit score or the removal of negative credit information from your credit report, even if the information is accurate and up-to-date.

When seeking credit counseling or credit repair organizations, it is important to be cautious as not all organizations are problem solvers; some may create additional problems. Legitimate organizations can provide assistance, but there are also scammers who should be avoided.

Before considering any organization, watch out for the following signs that indicate a scam:

2.30.1   Guarantee of improving your credit score by a specific number

It is impossible to guarantee a specific increase in your credit score after credit rectification. Results vary on a case-by-case basis. Be cautious of false promises that are impossible and outside of legal boundaries.

2.30.2   Advising you to engage in illegal activities

A certified credit counselor will never suggest creating a new identity to escape from your existing debts. Those who advise obtaining a new PAN Number and forging documents are scammers. Counselors should not encourage running away or hiding from creditors or collectors; instead, they help you find ways to face your challenges directly.

2.30.3 Offering to remove accurate information

No one can do this. If a negative mark is accurate, it cannot be removed. Do not fall for such claims.

2.30.4 Refusing or avoiding explanations about services/issues

If an organization refuses to provide precise details about credit repair or credit analysis and tries to manipulate you, consider it a red flag. Scammers may overpromise on things that are not even possible.

Ask the credit counseling organization for free information about their services and what they provide. A reputable credit counseling organization should be willing to send you free information about themselves and their services without requiring you to provide any details about your situation. If they fail to do so, consider it a red flag and seek help elsewhere.

2.31 What are the signs of a reputable credit counseling or repair organization?

Not all organizations are scammers. Some operate legally and provide genuine services. Look for the following signs that indicate a reputable organization:

2.31.1 The organization does not make unrealistic promises

Promising to raise your credit score by a specific number of points is an example of a false promise. A credit repair organization can show you results from previous customers but should not guarantee specific outcomes.

2.31.2   The organization discusses your situation before developing a credit strategy

A legitimate company cannot determine how they can help you until they understand your credit history. Expect them to ask questions and review your credit reports before formulating a game plan.

2.31.3   The organization provides advice based on your best interests

They work for your benefit and will suggest what is right for you rather than pushing you towards dubious solutions.

It is wise to be skeptical and exercise caution when making such decisions. However, reputable organizations do exist. Choose the one that best fits your needs.

Credit counseling, if conducted by a reputable organization, can be a lifesaver in addressing financial problems. A trusted credit counselor can offer personalized advice to help resolve credit-related issues.

2.32   The final words

It is advisable to consider credit counseling and seek help from a credit counselor when you notice your credit score deteriorating and impacting your overall credit health. For other aspects of your financial life, such as budgeting, investment, or debt management, you can consult a qualified credit counselor for assistance in improving your financial well-being.

Summary of Chapter 2

The chapter focuses on everything you want to know about credit counseling in detail. The chapter starts with the basic definition of a credit counselor. Further, it defines what skills make your credit counseling session successful:

- Good communication and prompt response time
- Strong analytical skills
- Great customer service
- Good listening skill
- Interpersonal skill
- Knowledge of law and regulations
- Problem-solving skills
- Observational skills
- Reasoning skills

The credit counselor generally provides a variety of services that range from basic budgeting advice to debt management plans depending on the nature of the industry. The credit repair counselor will provide you:

- Personalized plan based on credit report analysis
- Gaining access to your credit reports and scores
- Improving financial and credit literacy
- Provide credit score improvement tips
- Provide best practices to maintain a credit score
- Provide credit monitoring

Apart from that, the credit repair counselor conducts credit awareness seminars on topics like:

- Credit reporting system
- How to check credit report and credit score
- Credit card management

- Maintaining a healthy credit history
- Loan and credit score

The chapter further gives answers to many questions like what they do with my personal information and how to choose the right credit counselor. To know that you can check some criteria like:

- How is the service offered?
- What are your fees?
- What if I cannot afford to pay your fees or make contributions?
- Will I have a formal written agreement or contract with you?

These can help you get the right credit counselor to help you with your credit-related issues.

The chapter further provides a glance at defining credit counseling and its importance to know how it helps individuals:

- Help you understand your credit report
- Provide recommendations to eliminate negative items
- Maintaining a good credit score
- Provide credit literacy

If you are unable to do credit rectification on your own, you should consider opting for credit counseling. The chapter clearly defines the aim of credit counseling:

- Help financially distressed people to get rid of their negative credit report issues.
- Help MSMEs to extend their finances to expand their business by tackling delinquencies.
- Help people rebuild their credit.
- Help people maintain their credit scores.
- Provide genuine credit repair resolution.

However, there is a variety of credit counseling people can take depending on their financial problems as each type of counseling is meant for the specific problem, and the counselor conducting the credit counseling session is an expert in that domain. There are various types of credit counseling:

- General budget counseling
- Debt management counseling
- Bankruptcy counseling
- Credit repair counseling

Furthermore, the chapter has defined the credit counseling process, what happens in the credit counseling session, and what customers can expect in the credit counseling session. As a customer, if you are planning to take credit counseling sessions, you should have some information handy as credit counselors may want that:

- Whether you have a credit report or not
- If you have done any loan or credit card settlements in the past
- If you have properly closed your loan or credit card
- Whether you have the NOC (No Objection Certificate) of a closed loan or credit card
- Whether your current ongoing loans are regular or if you are missing repayments
- If you are a co-borrower or guarantor in a loan

The credit counseling session aims to understand the viewpoints of customers and discuss pain points to define strategies to get out of discrepancies and improve your credit score. Meeting with a credit counselor does not negatively impact a person's credit score.

The benefits of credit counseling are also discussed in this chapter to help customers understand why they should go for credit counseling sessions:

- Review your credit report
- Offer rectifying services

- Credit score building
- Credit history building
- Gaining financial education

The answer to the question "Does credit counseling work?" may vary because it depends on the specific queries and problems you are facing. Opting for professional credit repair services can often yield the desired results and make the process less cumbersome. Just as people hire professionals to manage their retirement funds or assist with real estate transactions, professional credit repair can make the process easier for you.

When seeking a credit counseling session to address your credit-related issues, you should follow these basic steps:

- Contact a credit counseling service.
- Authorize a credit check.
- Analyze your credit report.
- Receive recommendations from a credit counselor.

Your credit counseling session may last from half an hour to one hour or more, and you may require multiple sessions depending on the complexity of your problems. While some credit counseling services may be free of charge or have lower fees, it is generally worth paying for their expertise, as it frees you from the tedious credit repair process.

It is important to note that not all credit counseling organizations are equal, so it is essential to research and find one that best suits your needs.

If you are considering credit counseling, there are a few points to consider:

- Credit counseling services can save you from the lengthy credit repair process.

- They help you understand the root cause of your credit issues.
- They provide guidance on credit building.
- They assist with credit monitoring services.

Credit counseling services can help individuals and companies understand credit-related issues by:

- Answering questions about different strategies to resolve credit-related issues.
- Assisting in identifying the right solution for your delinquencies.
- Identifying negative, incorrect, and incomplete information on your credit report.
- Providing resources to improve credit literacy.
- Teaching you how to maintain a healthy credit life.
- Helping you rebuild your credit.
- Offering credit repair services if you choose to address your credit-related issues.
- Providing credit monitoring services after credit rectification.

Credit counseling services do not offer the following options:

- They do not provide debt forgiveness.
- They do not assist with settlements with your creditors.
- They do not offer assistance with debt management, debt consolidation, or other loan facilities.
- They cannot stop existing court action related to your debt if you have already been sued by the bank.

If you are considering alternatives to credit counseling organizations, there are two options you can consider:

- Attempt credit repair on your own
- Keep the negative items in your credit report as they are.

Both options are unlikely to lead to a satisfactory resolution. Credit repair requires extensive communication, time, and patience, making it overwhelming to undertake on your own. Keeping negative items in your credit report is not a solution, as it hinders your ability to obtain future finances.

A credit counselor or credit counseling session can be helpful for individuals:

- Feeling overwhelmed by credit-related issues and seeking guidance and support.
- Unsure about how to analyze their credit report and address credit-related issues.
- Unfamiliar with the credit repair and credit rebuilding process and seeking professional assistance.
- Facing challenges with discrepancies in their company or business credit report and seeking resolution.

For general information, you can contact credit counseling organizations directly through their helpline or the contact details available on their websites. Credit counseling sessions can be conducted over the phone or via video conferencing if you are unable to visit their office.

Additionally, the chapter highlights the essence of credit counseling and warns about credit repair scams. Before engaging with any organization, watch out for the following signs of a scam:

- Guaranteeing to improve your credit score by a specific number.
- Advising you to engage in illegal activities.
- Offering to remove accurate information from your credit report.
- Refusing or avoiding explanations about their services or issues.

Legitimate organizations demonstrate openness and communicate clearly. Here are a few signs of a reputable credit counseling organization:

- They do not make promises they cannot keep.
- They discuss your situation with you before developing a credit strategy.
- They advise you based on what is right for you.

In summary, credit counseling is essential when facing financial issues and dealing with a credit report containing negative, incorrect, or incomplete information that hinders access to new financing from banks.

Chapter 03

Credit Counseling and Repair Business

WHAT'S INCLUDED IN THIS CHAPTER

- **What is credit counseling and repair business?**
- **Why start credit counseling and repair business?**
- **What does a credit counseling and repair business really do?**
- **How a credit counseling and repair business really works?**
- **What does a credit counselor and credit repair professional do?**
- **Credit repair works because of the law**
- **What is credit counseling and repair company & How do credit repair company work?**
- **What if your customer has bank report or third party reports?**
- **How to read credit report?**
- **Basics of dispute process**
- **Adapt the five attitudes of credit counseling and repair**
- **Difference between credit counseling and credit repair**
- **The final words**

The credit counseling and repair business is part of the banking and financial vertical. It has an indirect impact on the banking system, but it directly impacts people because if people are credit unhealthy, the chances of rejection for loans and credit cards are high. The chapter is going forward with the entire concept of credit counseling and repair business.

3.1   What is a credit counseling and repair business?

A credit repair business is a third-party service that resolves your credit report issues by contacting your lenders or banks and credit bureaus on your behalf.

If you are looking to buy a home, a car, or even get a credit card, your credit score will be a crucial factor influencing the rates and terms you receive. So, if your credit score is lower than you would like, a credit repair organization can help you clean it up.

Of course, this is not a free service. In exchange for professional fees, the organization will remove inaccurate or negative information and help you improve your credit over time.

A good credit score means better interest rates on homes, cars, and credit cards. But if the credit score is bad, everything will turn against the consumer. However, the door is open to joining the good credit score club for those who are lacking it.

Credit counseling and credit repair are two routes to enter the good credit score club. The perspectives of both are different; the only real similarity between them is that both work to scrub and clean some of the smudges on a credit report.

They cannot remove accurate stains such as late or missed payments, but they can try to wipe away negative activity that was not the consumer's mistake, like identity theft or accounts that were mistakenly mismatched with yours.

They can even help you rectify delinquencies as per banking norms and the CIC Act. However, do not expect any quick relief like removing settled or written off dues without payment to the bank.

Their approach to achieving that end, however, is vastly different, and unfortunately, not all credit counseling and repair organizations that operate in this section of debt relief are trustworthy.

Be careful which door you knock on, and be sure you know what you are getting into before you enter.

3.2 Why start a credit counseling and repair business?

If you are in a hurry to make money or want to take a shortcut, you should not consider this business. This business demands patience to grow, dedication to work, and a cooperative attitude because you are going to handle financially distressed people who are looking for help to tackle their credit report issues.

The concept of credit counseling and repair business may seem foreign to many, but it is not unusual in India; the concept is still in its early stages. Thousands of people have poor credit, and most do not understand the credit reporting system or find it difficult to handle it on their own. Therefore, they need help to rectify their credit and improve their credit scores.

From both earning and helping perspectives, the credit counseling and repair business fit well. When people in a country have healthy credit and hold little to no debt, the economy of the country grows. Conversely, if people are burdened with lots of debt, it can damage the economy of the country, as the economy relies heavily on the responsible credit behavior of its citizens.

Unfortunately, the credit reporting system is designed to disadvantage consumers. You may wonder why such a system exists if it harms people. Banks have devised the system as a way to keep people in poverty. Once you fall behind, it becomes nearly impossible to recover. It is no accident. If you are late on a payment, they can raise your interest rate, making it even harder to pay off the debt. They lower your credit score in the process, increasing interest rates on your other accounts. It is a secret that banks earn a lot of money and become richer and richer.

Most credit reports contain mistakes. Nearly eight out of ten people face challenges with their credit reports. The system can feel overwhelming for those who lack knowledge in this area. Fortunately, there is something you can do to help people get rid of credit issues and make them credit-healthy again.

A credit counseling and repair business is one of the most prosperous businesses, even in the most troubling economy, as people tend to rely more on debt and fall behind in maintaining their credit during challenging times.

The credit card culture and high-rise lifestyle push people towards impulsive buying and a lifestyle that accumulates a lot of credit card debt and damages their credit when they miss even one or two EMIs. It quickly takes a toll on their creditworthiness. You can help them and earn a good income in the process.

A credit repair business:

- Is recession-proof.
- Is competition-free.
- Is easy to handle.
- Can make you money.
- Creates passive income.
- Is better for prospering in a tough economy.
- Provides an opportunity to serve the nation and society.
- Is a great supplement to your existing business and customers.
- Has recurring revenue.
- Does not require a formal degree.

Learning the basics of credit counseling and repair will enable you to start a new business immediately. Helping others repair their credit history and rebuild their credit is extremely rewarding. It is also true that people can do their credit repair, but most lack the skills to communicate with credit bureaus and deal with their banks or lenders. This is where you can help them handle the entire credit repair process. With the right tools and approach, you can help people effortlessly overcome credit issues and rebuild their creditworthiness.

3.3   What does a credit counseling and repair business do?

You might be wondering what credit counseling and repair business does and how it can earn you money.

In Chapter One, you learned about credit counseling and credit repair. Both are different terms with one common word, 'credit.' However, the purpose of both is to help people resolve their credit report issues and rebuild their credit.

Let's break down the steps involved:

- You receive a lead from a person seeking credit counseling and repair solutions.
- Begin with basic counseling to understand what they are looking for and request credit bureau reports based on their needs. In India, there are four credit bureaus: TransUnion CIBIL, Equifax, Experian, and CRIF High Mark.
- Once you have the credit bureau report, analyze it to identify any negative items. Credit analysis is a powerful sales tool if done diligently.
- After the credit analysis, you can start the actual credit counseling process. Use the credit report to gain further insight from the customer and explain the evaluation and recommendations.
- Once the credit counseling is complete, move on to credit repair.
- Onboard new customers by having them sign an agreement and kick-start the credit repair work.
- Work with the customer's banks or lenders, as well as the credit bureaus, to dispute any issues. It may seem easy at first, but it is complicated and time-consuming, though not impossible.
- Continue working until the negative items are successfully removed. Your customers will see the results and can compare before and after.

- Ask your customers to provide feedback or testimonials expressing their satisfaction once they receive updated credit bureau reports.
- Lastly, ask for referrals or encourage your customers to recommend your services to their friends, family, colleagues, and relatives.

I hope these steps clearly define what credit counseling and repair business entails, and by following them, you can earn both money and blessings.

3.4   What if your customer has a bank report or third-party reports?

There is no need to panic in such situations. However, it is important to help your customers understand the difference between bank reports, third-party reports, and authentic master credit bureau reports.

Explain to them that it is crucial to obtain fresh, current, and up-to-date reports in order to identify erroneous and inaccurate information. Additionally, inform them about the consequences of using a bank report, as it can generate hard inquiries on their credit report. On the other hand, a master credit bureau report is considered a soft inquiry and has no impact on their credit score.

3.5   How does a credit counseling and repair business work?

It is not rocket science, but many people are unaware of its existence, which leads them to believe it is not their area of expertise. Scammers or those with partial knowledge of credit repair create doubts for others.

You can put your doubts to rest. This book is designed to provide you with knowledge about credit counseling and repair. Keep in mind that there are no quick fixes when it comes to building or repairing credit. Therefore, avoid promising quick fixes to your customers.

3.6   What do credit counselors and credit repair professionals do?

It is quite simple. As a credit counselor and repair professional, you handle the entire credit rectification process on behalf of your customers and teach them how to better manage their credit. In return, they pay you professional fees.

There are several simple steps involved in the work of a credit counselor and credit repair professional:

- Obtain credit bureau reports.
- Perform credit analysis on the reports.
- Recommend credit repair solutions.
- Carry out the credit rectification work.

3.7   Credit repair works because of the law

You may have questions about the legality of credit repair. The Credit Information Companies (CIC) Act grants individuals the right to dispute any inaccurate and incorrect item on their credit report.

The CIC Act was designed to regulate the credit reporting system and protect consumers from the inclusion of inaccurate information in their credit reports, whether intentional or negligent. It ensures the accuracy, fairness, and privacy of consumer information in credit reports.

Under the CIC Act, consumers have the right to access and obtain all the information in their credit files, including their credit scores. They also have the right to dispute incomplete or inaccurate information with the credit bureau, which is required to act upon the dispute and resolve it.

Credit bureaus in India are regulated and licensed by the Reserve Bank of India, and they must adhere to the provisions of the CIC Act in their operations.

Further details about the CIC Act can be found in our book "Improve Your Credit Health."

3.8 What is a credit counseling and repair organization, and how do they work?

By now, you have learned about credit counseling, the role of credit counselors, what happens in credit counseling sessions, and the credit repair business. Now, let's delve into what a credit counseling and repair organization is and how they operate.

A credit counseling and repair organization is a third-party service that identifies negative credit information and contacts credit reporting bureaus on behalf of individuals seeking assistance. In exchange for a fee, the organization works to remove inaccurate or negative information from credit reports and helps individuals improve their credit over time.

Here are the basic steps followed by a credit counseling and repair organization to carry out credit rectification work:

3.8.1 Acquire and analyze the customer's credit report

The first step is to obtain a copy of the customer's credit report from one or all four credit bureaus (TransUnion CIBIL, Equifax, Experian, and CRIF High Mark). Analyze the reports to identify inaccuracies, delinquencies, and unverifiable information that can be disputed. Once you have identified negative items, discuss the course of action with the customer and educate them about expectations and required information.

3.8.2 Proceed with credit rectification

This step involves the meticulous process of handling credit rectification, including disputing negative issues with banks and credit bureaus. It requires patience, effective communication, and perseverance. Familiarity with banking and credit bureau report terminologies is crucial for navigating this process successfully.

Follow-up, addressing counter-questions, and providing replies are integral parts of the process. Credit counseling and repair organizations are domain experts in this field and handle these tasks seamlessly.

3.8.3   Update customers on their progress

This step involves tracking the progress of credit repair work and providing regular updates to customers. Most credit counseling and repair organizations have a system in place or develop one to ensure transparency and maintain customer trust throughout the credit repair process. This communication continues until the rectification work is complete, and customers have their before and after reports.

3.8.4   Follow-up

This step involves ongoing follow-up with banks and credit bureaus to ensure the completion of credit repair work for customers. Depending on the specific case, customer follow-up may also be initiated. The extent of follow-up varies on a case-by-case basis. However, it is an essential part of completing the credit repair process.

In summary, patience and persistence are key to handling credit repair successfully. It is important for any credit counseling or repair organization to inform customers about the expected time frame for the entire credit repair process. This helps prevent panic situations and ensures that customers understand the credit repair process. When customers are well-educated during counseling sessions about the issues, recommendations, and processes involved, and receive timely updates on their ongoing work, it reduces the chances of customers creating any unpleasant situations themselves.

3.9   How to read a credit report?

Credit reports are important tools that help you manage your finances and make informed decisions. Understanding how to read a credit report is essential for anyone who wants to take control of their financial future. It can help you identify errors, spot potential identity theft, and ensure the accuracy of your credit score.

It can be challenging when you are unfamiliar with credit reports and their terminologies, especially if you are looking at a credit report for the first time. Here are some steps to help you read a credit report:

- Take time to review the credit reports carefully.
- Mark the items you wish to dispute.
- Choose which item to dispute first.

Once you have identified the credit reports with errors, start by addressing the easiest error disputes. Keep in mind that most credit reports contain errors.

Common credit report errors include false delinquencies, loan accounts or credit cards that do not belong to you, multiple loan or credit card accounts, and closed loans or credit cards shown as open. These errors can potentially lower your credit scores. Some errors may be due to identity theft, while others may be the result of data entry issues. It is important to carefully evaluate the credit reports and make every effort to correct, update, or delete any incorrect or inaccurate information.

A credit report typically contains the following sections of information:

1. Credit Score –

The credit score represents your creditworthiness and is based on an analysis of your credit history and other relevant factors.

2. Identification Information –

This section includes your name, date of birth, gender, addresses (both residential and office), contact numbers (mobile and landline), emails, and government identities provided to banks or financial institutions. Sometimes, your employment information may also be included.

3. Account Details –

This section provides information about your accounts, including

- the bank or lender's name,
- type of loan or credit, account number,
- loan amount, interest rate,
- current balance, start date,
- highest credit limit,
- highest amount of credit used,
- close date (if applicable),
- current status (open/closed/written off/settlement), and
- repayment history for the last 36 months.

This section makes up the bulk of the report. The repayment history is usually shown as numbers indicating your payment history.

4. Inquiries –

This section lists

- all the banks or lending institutions that have requested your credit report, along with the product inquired for (such as personal loan, credit card, home loan, etc.) and
- the amount applied for.

These are the basic sections found in a credit report. By carefully reviewing and understanding each section, you can gain valuable insights into your credit history and take appropriate actions to manage your credit effectively.

Look for the following delinquencies in your credit report:

- **Incorrect or incomplete personal identification information** – Credit bureaus may confuse your name, address, date of birth, phone number, or PAN card information. You may also find missing, incorrect, or outdated employment information.

- **Account details and their status** – Your account information may be incorrect, such as wrong account balances, credit limits, closed accounts shown as open, or incorrect account numbers. The payment status of accounts may also be reported inaccurately, which can lower your credit score.
- **Accounts you do not recognize** – You may find accounts listed on your credit report that you did not open. This could be a sign of identity theft and should be taken seriously.
- **Duplicate accounts** – You may come across accounts that are listed more than once, indicating duplicate entries. These can easily be identified as they will appear identical, but they can contribute to the total number of active accounts.
- **Inquiries you do not recognize** – There may be credit inquiries listed on your report that you do not recognize. These could be the result of comparison shopping for loans or credit cards.

If incorrect, incomplete, inaccurate, or outdated information remains on your credit report, it can hinder your credit score from increasing. Analyzing your credit report is crucial to identify these errors. If you suspect any signs of identity theft, immediate action should be taken to rectify the situation.

3.10 Basics of the dispute process

After analyzing your credit report, it is time to rectify the errors you have identified. Disputing with a credit bureau can be a stressful and demanding process. Understanding the basics of the dispute process is important in order to navigate it effectively and achieve the best possible outcome. Under the CIC Act, individuals have the right to dispute any incomplete, inaccurate, or untimely items on their credit reports.

As a credit repair organization, it is important to be transparent about what you can and cannot remove from the credit report. Remember that negative items that are accurate cannot be removed. There are several reasons to dispute negative items, including:

- The account does not belong to the customer.
- The current balance is inaccurate.
- The credit line amount is incorrect.
- The account numbers are incorrect.
- The original creditors are listed incorrectly.
- The open date is listed incorrectly.
- The close date is listed incorrectly or not listed at all.
- The credit limit is listed incorrectly.
- The account status is inaccurate.
- The account appears as a duplicate.

Being a successful credit counseling and repair organization requires skill, experience, and patience. When following ethical practices, credit counseling and repair organizations or counselors review credit reports with their customers to identify inaccuracies, errors, or incompleteness.

Before providing recommendations to your customers, it is important to thoroughly check all the information based on,

- Is it accurate?
- Is this correct?
- Is it complete?

Once you have ensured that the information is accurate and correct, you can proceed with your recommendations and explain how the credit repair process will work.

3.11   Adapt the five attitudes of credit counseling and repair

Before venturing into the credit repair business, it is essential to develop the right attitude to handle it. Lack of knowledge in credit repair will lead you nowhere and hinder your ability to assist your customers. Additionally, possessing strong analytical skills, problem-solving skills, and communication skills are crucial for successfully carrying out credit counseling.

3.11.1 Understanding credit scores

Credit scores are numerical representations of an individual's creditworthiness. They are based on information in the credit report, which includes records of loans taken out and the repayment history. A higher credit score can lead to lower interest rates on loans and better credit card offers.

3.11.2 Monitoring credit reports

Monitoring credit reports is a crucial step in the credit repair process. A credit report provides a record of an individual's financial activity, including loans, mortgages, and other types of debt. It also indicates the payment history and whether the debts are current or delinquent.

After obtaining copies of credit reports from TransUnion, Experian, Equifax, and CRIF High Mark, carefully review them for accuracy. If any errors are found, such as incorrect information or someone else's name appearing as yours, notify the banks or lenders immediately to correct the error before it affects future borrowing opportunities.

3.11.3 Developing a credit repair strategy

A credit repair strategy is a plan of action designed to help individuals reduce debt and improve their credit scores. Having a well-defined strategy in place can bring several benefits, such as saving money on interest rates, reducing the time to pay off debts, and minimizing financial stress.

3.11.4 Educating your customers

Go the extra mile in credit repair by educating your customers about how credit works, how to improve credit scores after the repair process, and the importance of avoiding unnecessary credit applications. This personalized approach will not only make your customers happy but also contribute to the growth of your business.

3.11.5 Creating awareness

As a credit counseling and repair business, it is important to create awareness about the concept and importance of credit repair. Taking steps to educate others about credit repair will help foster growth in your business.

3.12 Difference between credit counseling and credit repair

Credit counseling and credit repair are two distinct services that assist individuals in managing their finances. Credit counseling involves working with a counselor to develop a budget and repayment plan, while credit repair focuses on improving credit scores by disputing errors on credit reports. Both services can help individuals improve their financial situation, but they have different approaches and outcomes. Credit counseling primarily focuses on understanding and managing one's financial situation, while credit repair focuses on correcting errors in credit reports to enhance overall creditworthiness.

3.13 The final words

Credit counseling and repair organizations identify errors in credit reports and dispute them with the credit bureaus. These errors may include misspelled names, incorrect addresses, or more serious issues such as identity theft or fraudulently opened accounts. The organization will work with the bureaus to correct these errors and monitor future updates to prevent further problems.

Summary of Chapter 3

The chapter focuses on credit counseling and repair businesses in depth. A credit repair business is a third-party service that aims to resolve credit report issues by contacting lenders, banks, and credit bureaus on behalf of clients.

Moreover, the chapter highlights why starting a credit counseling and repair business can be advantageous. Some key points include:

- It is recession-proof.
- It faces less competition.
- It is easy to handle.
- It offers the potential to generate income.
- It can create passive income streams.
- It is conducive to prospering in a tough economy.
- It provides an opportunity to serve the nation and society.
- It can complement your existing business and customer base.
- It offers recurring revenue opportunities.
- It does not require a formal degree.

If you have the desire to help others and earn income, a credit counseling and repair business may be suitable for you. Given that most credit reports contain errors, and not everyone is well-versed in the credit repair process, the need for credit counseling and repair services is evident.

The steps involved in what credit counseling and repair businesses do are as follows:

- You receive a lead from a person seeking credit counseling and repair solutions.
- Begin with basic counseling to understand their specific needs and request credit bureau reports accordingly. In India, there are four credit bureaus: TransUnion CIBIL, Equifax, Experian, and CRIF High Mark.

- Once you have the credit bureau report in hand, analyze it to identify any negative items. Thorough credit analysis is a powerful sales tool if conducted diligently.
- After the credit analysis, initiate the actual credit counseling process, utilizing the credit report to gain further insights from the customer and provide evaluation and recommendations.
- Cover credit repair options with the customer following credit counseling.
- Onboard new customers by having them sign the agreement and commencing the credit repair work.
- Work with the customer's banks or lenders, as well as credit bureaus, to dispute any issues. While initially it may seem simple, this process can be complex and time-consuming, but not impossible.
- Continue working until negative items are successfully removed. Customers will be able to observe the results and compare their credit bureau reports before and after the credit repair process.
- Request that customers express their satisfaction by providing a feedback letter or testimonial once they receive updated credit bureau reports.
- Finally, ask for referrals or recommendations from customers to their friends, family, colleagues, and relatives.

It also provides an overview of how to handle customers when they have bank reports or third-party reports. There are simple process steps involved that a credit counselor and credit repair professional handle:

- Pulling out the credit bureau report
- Conducting a credit analysis of the credit report
- Providing credit repair solution recommendations
- Carrying out the credit rectification work

The credit reporting system in India is regulated by the Credit Information Companies (Regulation) Act, and all credit bureaus licensed and regulated by the Reserve Bank of India must adhere to this act. The act grants customers the right to dispute any incorrect information and have it corrected.

For more details on the Credit Information Companies (Regulation) Act, you can refer to the book "Improove Your Credit Health."

The basic steps that a credit counseling and repair organization follows to proceed with credit rectification work are:

- Acquiring and analyzing the customer's credit report
- Moving forward with the credit rectification process
- Providing updates to customers on their progress
- Following up on the credit repair process

Furthermore, the chapter provides a glimpse of how to read a credit report, as it is an important tool for initiating credit counseling and proceeding with credit repair. If you are reviewing a credit report for the first time, consider the following points:

Take time to carefully review the credit reports

Mark the items you wish to dispute

Prioritize which items to dispute first

Your credit report contains various sections with different types of information:

1. Credit Score
2. Identification Information
3. Account Details
4. Inquiries

When reviewing your credit report, look for the following delinquencies:

- Incorrect or incomplete personal identification information
- Account details with incorrect status
- Accounts that you do not recognize
- Duplicate accounts
- Inquiries that you do not recognize

The chapter provides a basic dispute process, which you should consider using if you encounter any of the following issues:

- The account does not belong to the customer
- Current balance is inaccurate
- Credit line amounts are incorrect
- Account numbers are incorrect
- Original creditors are listed incorrectly
- Open date is listed incorrectly
- Close date is listed incorrectly or not listed at all
- Credit limit is listed incorrectly
- Account status is inaccurate
- Account appears as duplicate for multiple times
- Account ownership is listed incorrectly

Before providing any recommendations to your customers, ensure that the information in the credit report is accurate, correct, and complete.

When starting a credit counseling and repair business, it is important to develop the following attitudes:

- Understanding credit scores
- Monitoring credit reports
- Developing a credit repair strategy
- Educating your customers
- Creating awareness

If you are confused about the difference between credit counseling and credit repair, the chapter lists the distinctions between the two.

In summary, to start a credit counseling and repair business, you should understand the role of such a business, how it operates, the responsibilities of a credit counselor and repair professional, how to read credit reports, the basics of the dispute process, and develop five key attitudes for success.

Chapter 04

The Basic of Starting Credit Counseling and Repair Business

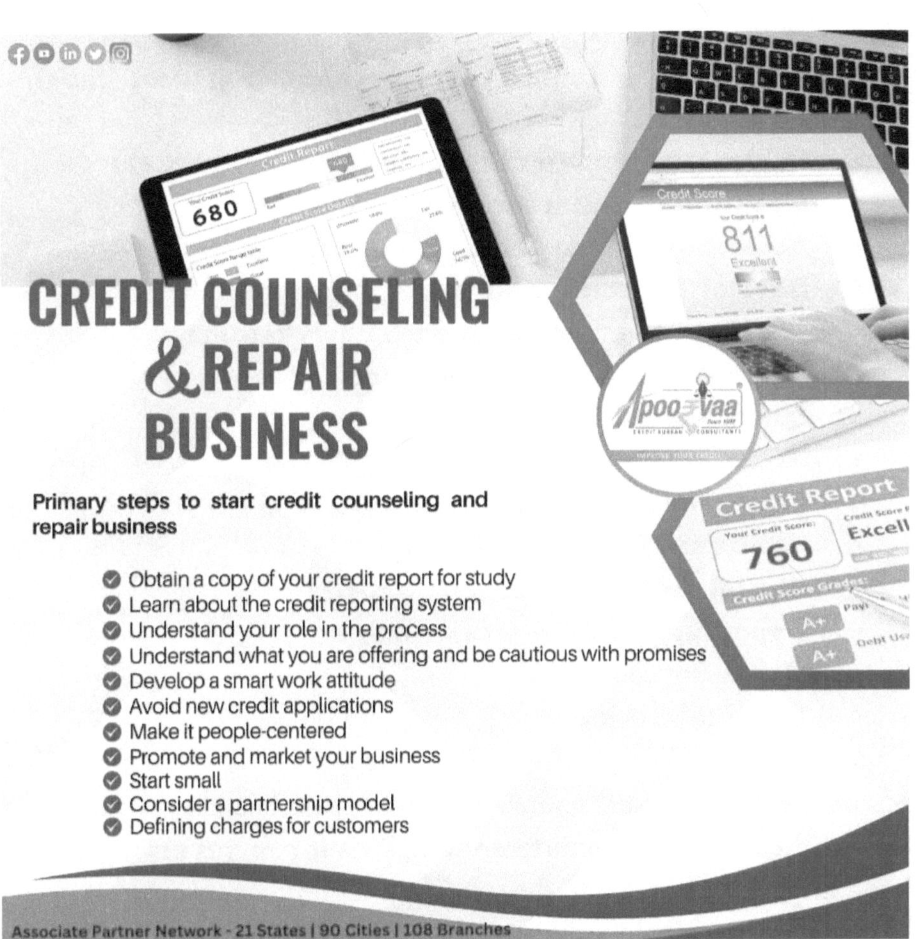

WHAT'S INCLUDED IN THIS CHAPTER

- **Nine tips to start credit counseling and repair business**
- **Primary steps to start credit counseling and repair business**
- **Simplify the sales through a sales funnel**
- **Managing the leads**
- **The pro sales pitch to acquire customers**
- **Building trust and integrity for business growth**
- **Learn about business credit**
- **Steps involved in launching credit counseling and repair business**
- **Checklist to launch credit counseling and repair business**
- **Dealing with customers (building relationships)**
- **Maintain transparency with your customer**
- **Accessing and importing credit reports**
- **Develop listening skill**
- **Three questions to start with new customers**
- **Dealing with the first customer**
- **Educating customers**
- **Exceptional customer service**
- **The best way to grow your business**
- **Define marketing strategies**
- **Digital presence with your website**
- **Opportunity lies in affiliation**
- **Managing team**
- **The final words**

Before starting a credit counseling and repair business, you should look at the basics from a different angle, as it requires prior industry knowledge and insight into the law. The chapter focuses on what needs to be included while looking ahead to the credit counseling and repair business.

4.1   Nine tips to start a credit counseling and repair business

Here are some tips that can help you understand the credit counseling and repair business:

4.1.1   Give time and involvement

If you think of credit counseling or repair as part-time work or something you can do sporadically, it may not be suitable for you. Building trust with your customers requires time and involvement. Without dedicating enough time, it will be challenging to generate more business. If you are serious about this business, you should consider giving it your full time and involvement.

4.1.2   Proper planning

No business can survive without proper planning. Before reaching your first customer, it is crucial to have well-developed plans. This doesn't mean you have to spend a lot of money on marketing, sales, or operations. However, you should know your target audience, have ideas for lead generation, and understand what to include in your marketing strategies.

4.1.3   Identify your target audience

Before starting the business, it is important to identify your target audience – potential customers in your locality. Your target audience consists of individuals who have lower credit scores and face challenges with their credit reports. Taking on customers whom you cannot help achieve their goals will only hinder your success.

4.1.4   Learning attitude

Continuous knowledge gain is essential in credit repair, including strategies, industry updates, and amendments in the law. Becoming an expert in your domain allows you to educate your customers effectively on what they need to know.

4.1.5   Utilize delegation

Thinking that you can handle the entire credit counseling and repair business alone may lead to fatigue and frustration. As a small business owner, it may be difficult to give up control, but attempting to do all tasks alone can impede the growth of your business. It is wise to hire someone who can assist you with business operations, customer follow-up, and day-to-day tasks. This allows you to focus on the broader vision and scale your business.

4.1.6   Build relationships to create affiliates

When you incorporate relationship-building into your business planning, you are more likely to receive a lot of referral business. Creating affiliate relationships is a wise idea to generate ongoing business. Identify potential affiliate partners who can refer customers to you and start building relationships with them. You may even consider offering them a commission. Focus on nurturing these relationships right from the start of your business.

4.1.7   Educate your affiliates

Having affiliates is a valuable resource for generating new business. However, their potential can be wasted if they are not properly educated about your offerings and services. Therefore, the first step is to educate your affiliates to ensure maximum output from them.

4.1.8   Plan out an operational system

Any business without a well-planned operational system is likely to face failure or end up in chaos. Before acquiring your first customer, it is crucial to establish a solid operational system that encompasses every aspect, from customer pitch to customer intake processes to follow-ups. This will make your work easier in the long run.

4.1.9   Educate your clients

Your customers look up to you as an expert and place their trust in you. Consider educating your clients on maintaining credit scores and rebuilding credit from scratch. Going the extra mile will increase the likelihood of receiving referrals and turning your clients into brand ambassadors for your business. This personal touch will contribute to the growth of your business.

4.2 Primary steps to start credit counseling and repair business

Every business has primary or basic steps to get started, and the same applies to credit counseling and repair businesses. Here are some primary steps:

4.2.1 Obtain a copy of your credit report for study

If you are uncertain about obtaining credit report copies from customers or are starting a business, the best way to understand credit reports is to obtain your own copy from all four credit bureaus: TransUnion CIBIL, Equifax, Experian, and CRIF High Mark.

4.2.2 Learn about the credit reporting system

Gaining industry or business knowledge is crucial before starting your business. Educate yourself about the credit reporting system in India, including its working pattern and other details. This knowledge will enable you to better manage your customers' issues.

4.2.3 Understand your role in the process

It is important to know the specific role you play in the credit counseling and repair process. Understand that after obtaining a customer's credit report and identifying errors, you will be responsible for rectifying them through mediation with credit bureaus or banks.

4.2.4 Understand what you are offering and be cautious with promises

Exercise caution when offering your services and avoid making unrealistic promises. Keep in mind that many negative items on a credit report may be accurate and cannot be removed. Also, remember that credit repair or building a credit score is not an overnight process. Avoid overpromising regarding timeframes or credit score increases.

4.2.5   Develop a smart work attitude

One common mistake business owners make is trying to handle all the work themselves instead of delegating tasks to a team. By taking on everything alone, your earning potential may be limited and your time may not be utilized efficiently. Invest in good tools, equipment, and manpower to free up more time to focus on your vision for growth.

4.2.6   Make it people-centered

Don't forget that your customers are your top priority. Build a strong rapport with them and be a good listener. Additionally, maintain good relationships with your affiliates who refer customers to you.

4.2.7   Promote and market your business

Promoting and marketing are significant parts of any business to gain visibility. You can utilize traditional marketing methods, such as distributing flyers and pamphlets, placing ads in local newspapers or on TV channels. However, remember not to provide excessive information in your ads. Instead, provide brief information about your offerings and contact information.

You can also leverage digital platforms like Facebook, Twitter, Instagram, and LinkedIn to promote your business. Run campaigns or ads to enhance your brand presence. Consider visiting different locations in your area to promote your business or organize seminars to educate potential customers.

4.2.8   Start small

Taking one step at a time will help your business establish a strong foundation. By gradually building credibility and gaining customer satisfaction, you will be better positioned for future expansion. The credit repair concept can be confusing to many, so ensure you provide clear information about your services and address their specific needs. Being honest and transparent with customers about what you can and cannot do is crucial. Investing in a solid foundation will contribute to a sustainable business model.

4.2.9 Consider a partnership model

If you are unsure about how to start credit counseling and repair business or what to include and exclude, consider partnering with an existing credit counseling and repair business through a franchise. Opting for a franchise offers benefits such as a proven working model, established brand recognition, and an existing customer base. With a franchise, you can save time on branding and promotion as you leverage the existing reputation of the franchise.

Starting from scratch would require building your own brand and customer base, which can be time-consuming. By joining a franchise, you benefit from recognizable branding and the assurance of being part of a successful network. Franchisees often receive support and guidance, minimizing the risk of failure.

When you opt for a partnering business i.e., franchisee business, the chances of failure are very low or not at all compared to a solo business. Because you become part of a successful brand, as well as a network that will offer you support and advice, making it is less likely you will go out of business.

One of the hardest parts of starting any new business is finding your first customer. Hence, by choosing a franchise over a solo business, you get access to an established, loyal customer base and potential employee pool.

Ultimately, whether to start a business from scratch or opt for a franchise partnership is a decision that depends on your preferences and circumstances. Consider the benefits and drawbacks of each option before making a choice.

4.2.10   Defining charges for customers

Defining charges for offering your services is a crucial part of any business as you cannot charge too high or too little. To finalize charges, you should look at your competitors' price models for research purposes. But do not copy them. It is just for research. When you have reasonable pricing and good service, you will have a flood of customers, and your business will grow beyond your expectations.

But the question is still there, "How much should I charge?"

Well, charges can be different ways. You can charge per query or have a package system. When you are a franchise partner for credit counseling and repair business, you do not have to consider the pricing side as they have a well-established charges plan.

Determining the exact fees or charges depends on your clientele, but every query is different, and the procedure is also different. So, deciding charges is viewed from every angle.

4.3   Simplify the sales through a sales funnel

Before managing sales, it is important to know what a sales funnel is.

A sales funnel is a tool for any business to understand and optimize its customer journey. It helps businesses identify potential leads, nurture them into customers, and ultimately convert them into loyal customers. The sales funnel also helps companies measure the effectiveness of their marketing efforts in terms of lead generation and conversion rates. By understanding the different stages of the sales funnel, companies can better target their marketing strategies to increase conversions and maximize profits.

It is also known as an "acquisition channel" or a "conversion funnel."

A successful salesperson knows that sales is a numbers game. A sales funnel is simply a process by which you guide potential customers through your business from initial contact to purchase. There are four main parts of this process:

Introduction (also called the "top of the funnel")

Funnel Middle (also called the "middle of the funnel")

Sales Closing (also called the "bottom of the funnel")

4.3.1   The top of the funnel

The top of the funnel is where you attract new potential clients. This can be done through organic search, paid ads, and other marketing channels. The goal is to get people who have never heard of you before into your sales funnel so that they can become leads for further nurturing and conversion.

The best way to do this is by creating content that solves a problem or answers a question for your target audience.

4.3.2   The middle of the funnel

The middle of the funnel is where you provide information to potential customers. You can do this by offering something in exchange for contact information, such as a free e-book or webinar registration. The goal here is to nurture leads until they become customers.

In addition to providing content that helps people decide whether or not they want what you're selling, this section also includes sales funnels that offer demos or trials of products before purchasing. This is a popular strategy among many SaaS companies (software-as-a-service).

4.3.3   The bottom of the funnel

The bottom of your funnel is where you follow up with clients, retain customers, and ensure their satisfaction. This is an important part because it can make or break your business. If you don't have a system in place for following up with clients and keeping them happy, there's no way they'll buy from you again.

You should also be looking for ways to improve the time it takes for someone to move from the top of the funnel down into this area. One approach is to automate processes as much as possible, so salespeople don't have an overwhelming workload when trying to close deals or make sales calls (which could potentially result in lost opportunities).

Typical sales funnel looks like this:

- You have a lead at the top of the funnel (e.g., someone who has just visited your website).
- The lead progresses through each stage of the funnel until they reach their ultimate goal (e.g., becoming a paying customer).

4.3.4 The benefits of a sales funnel

Sales funnels are powerful marketing tools that can help you generate leads, convert leads into customers, and retain those customers.

The first step of a sales funnel is to attract new potential clients by creating content that directly addresses their needs. The second step is to convert these visitors into leads by offering them something (like an ebook or webinar) in exchange for their contact information. The third step is to nurture those leads until they become paying customers, and then continue nurturing them to ensure their loyalty.

4.3.5 The different components of a sales funnel

A sales funnel is a marketing tool that helps you attract new customers and turn them into repeat buyers. It is made up of five stages:

4.3.5.1 Awareness

The first stage in your sales funnel is awareness. In this stage, people are just becoming aware of your brand and what it offers them.

4.3.5.2 Consideration

Once they have learned about your business, they will want to know more about what it can do for them before making any decisions about whether or not they want to buy from you (or at least talk with someone from your company).

4.3.5.3 Evaluation

This is where you have an opportunity to evaluate your customer's needs and determine if they are a good fit for your product or service. If they aren't, you can move on without wasting time on them. If they are, then it is time to move into the next stage: the purchase decision.

4.3.5.4 Decision

Now that potential customers have gotten all the information they need on their terms, it is time for them to decide whether or not they should buy from you based on their preferences and needs – not yours!

4.3.5.5 Post-Purchase

After purchasing something from you (or having you help them find another solution), you make sure that everything goes smoothly by following up with your clients regularly until their issue has been completely resolved.

4.3.6 How to create a sales funnel

4.3.6.1 Attracting new potential clients

The first step in creating a sales funnel is to attract new potential clients. You can do this by using social media, content marketing, and advertising campaigns.

4.3.6.2 Converting visitors into leads

Once you have attracted potential customers, it's time to convert them into leads who are interested in what you have to offer. This can be done by offering them something for free (like an eBook or video) so they can learn more about what you do before making any sort of commitment with their time or money.

4.3.6.3   Nurturing leads until they become customers

Once someone has become a lead, it's important that you nurture them until they become customers by continuing communication with them via email or phone calls until they make their final decision about whether or not they want your product/service enough to make a purchase. It's important to build trust and provide value during this nurturing process.

4.3.7   Using technology to optimize your sales funnel

There are many ways to optimize your sales funnel, but one of the most effective is using technology. Here are some examples:

4.3.7.1   Automation

This can be done with email marketing or social media automation software. It allows you to set up rules that automatically send emails based on certain conditions, such as when someone visits a specific page on your website or signs up for an email list. You can also use automation tools to schedule posts on Facebook or Twitter so they go out at specific times during the day, which helps ensure they get seen by as many people as possible (and don't get lost in the shuffle).

4.3.7.2   Analytics

By monitoring how customers interact with different parts of your website and other digital properties (like social media), you'll gain insight into what content resonates best with them and where there might be room for improvement in terms of conversion rates or overall engagement levels.

4.3.7.3   Personalization Tools

These allow marketers to personalize everything from emails sent via automated campaigns down to landing pages used during lead generation activities like webinars.

In addition to these technical aspects, it's important to keep certain points in mind while handling sales:

- Your lead is just a lead until you start communication with them.
- Keep track of all communication and note down their interest or follow-up needs.
- Utilize CRM or Excel sheets to streamline your sales funnel process.
- Focus on filling the top of your sales funnel with leads to increase conversion ratios.
- Build referrals and network with loan providers and credit card providers to generate more leads.
- Educate your customers about credit repair and the credit reporting system to create a positive impact and provide excellent service to encourage referrals.
- Employ different tactics to generate new leads and keep your sales funnel active.

Remember that acquiring new business may require contacting many leads, so don't be discouraged. With time and a strong brand establishment, your sales figures will gradually improve. That's how the sales funnel works.

4.4   Managing the leads

Lead management is the process of managing leads and converting them into customers. It involves nurturing the relationship with each lead until they make a purchase. Lead management is crucial for salespeople to prioritize their efforts and utilize their time effectively.

The goals of lead management are:

- Increase sales opportunities by identifying potential customers who show interest in your business or product (prospecting).
- Nurture prospects until they are ready to make a purchase (qualification).
- Provide an excellent customer experience to encourage repeat business.

4.4.1   Gathering leads

Leads are individuals who have shown interest in doing business with you but have not yet become customers. There are various ways to gather leads, including:

- Google ads
- Social media marketing (such as Facebook ads)
- Email marketing

It is important to keep in mind that not all leads will convert into customers. A successful lead management process typically achieves a conversion rate of around 5%.

4.4.2   Qualifying leads

Lead qualification is the process of assessing whether a lead is ready to make a purchase. Lead qualification criteria are used to determine which leads are worth pursuing and which ones should be ignored.

Lead qualification can be time-consuming, but it is essential for ensuring that your sales team focuses on high-quality prospects. By qualifying leads, you can allocate more time and resources to those who are more likely to convert into customers or clients.

4.4.3   Organizing leads

Organizing leads is a crucial aspect of lead management. Being able to quickly find and access your leads enables you to follow up with them promptly and smoothly integrate them into your sales funnel. Here are a few effective ways to organize your leads:

By Source – Categorize leads based on where they originated from, such as ad campaigns, email sign-ups, or referrals.

By Status – Track the engagement level of each lead, distinguishing between active conversations, leads awaiting more information, or general browsing.

By Interests – Identify the specific interests or preferences of each lead to tailor your communication and offerings accordingly.

4.4.4   Engaging leads

- **Creating Engaging Content** – Develop compelling content that resonates with your leads, providing value and capturing their interest.
- **Automating Lead Engagement** – Utilize automation tools to streamline lead engagement, such as automated email sequences or personalized follow-up messages.
- **Tracking Lead Engagement** – Monitor and analyze how leads engage with your content and communications to gain insights into their level of interest and potential conversion readiness.

4.4.5   Nurturing leads

Lead nurturing involves fostering relationships with leads who have expressed interest but are not yet ready to make a purchase. This is achieved through targeted and personalized communication, such as sending relevant emails, providing helpful resources, and offering exclusive incentives. The goal is to build trust and loyalty, ultimately converting leads into paying customers in the future.

Lead nurturing helps you:

- Build trust by delivering valuable information about your product or service.
- Cultivate loyalty among existing customers through exclusive offers and incentives.

4.4.6   Analyzing leads

Analyzing leads is a critical component of managing your sales funnel. Here are three key aspects to consider when analyzing your leads:

4.4.6.1   Analyzing lead performance

Lead performance refers to how well a lead has performed in the past or present. This information is used to determine the value of a particular lead, whether it should be considered high-value or low-value, based on the revenue it has generated for your business over time. If you have an existing customer base, it is relatively easy for them to provide feedback on the ROI they have received from working with you. However, if you do not have data on the spending habits of each customer, it becomes more challenging. You will need alternative methods to measure these factors so that when new prospects come along, they can be automatically categorized as high-value leads based on their potential value rather than their actual performance thus far, which may be zero.

4.4.7   Tracking leads

Tracking leads is an important part of the sales funnel. Utilizing a CRM (customer relationship management) system can assist you in effectively keeping track of your leads. However, there are also alternative methods to accomplish this.

Here are some tips for tracking your leads:

Use a CRM system to manage all your contacts and interactions. This will enable you to easily monitor which leads have been contacted and the actions taken for each one.

If you do not use a CRM, you can create an Excel spreadsheet. Each column can represent a stage in the sales process, such as prospecting, qualification/assessment, presentation/demonstration, and closing deals. Additionally, include columns for notes on each contact's interests, follow-up dates, and more.

4.4.8   Converting leads

Converting leads is the final and most important step in the sales funnel. The success of your business relies on effectively converting leads into customers.

To convert leads into customers, you need to establish a process that aligns well with the skills and personalities of your team members. This process should also be easily replicated by any staff member who may be involved in customer interactions.

Understanding the benefits of lead management in the credit counseling and repair business is crucial, particularly in this relatively new field. Effective lead management is an essential component of your marketing strategy and can contribute to the growth of your business by increasing sales and fostering customer loyalty.

Lead management software is constantly evolving to meet the ever-changing needs of businesses. As technology advances, we can expect innovative solutions to further enhance our ability to serve clients and simplify their lives.

When it comes to converting leads into customers in the credit counseling and repair business, it is important to have a smooth and seamless process in place.

4.4.8.1   Step 1 - Understand the prospect's interest and timeframe

This is a fundamental step in any sales process. Start by providing basic information about your services and actively listen to the prospect's story. Understand the main issue the prospect wants to resolve and why they are seeking credit repair. It is important to also grasp the prospect's timeframe for resolution.

4.4.8.2   Step 2 - Obtain a copy of the credit report

Obtaining a copy of the credit report is a crucial step in order to analyze the issues. The sooner you obtain the credit reports, the faster you can convert the prospect into a customer. It is also a necessary step for conducting credit counseling sessions.

4.4.8.3   Step 3 - Conduct a credit counseling session

After acquiring the credit report, the next step is to conduct a credit counseling session. During this session, you can assess the number of derogatory accounts, inquiries, and instances of incorrect personal information on the credit report.

Once you have a basic understanding of the negative items on the credit report, the next step is to explore why the prospect is seeking credit repair. Determine if they are planning to apply for a loan in the near future and, if so, what their timeframe is.

Avoid delving too deep into excessive details during the session, but rather focus on covering the main points and discussing the essentials.

4.4.8.4 Step 4 - Assess the prospect's eligibility

It is time to evaluate whether the prospect is a good fit for your services. Assess the reasonableness of their desired timeframe and expectations. At this stage, the prospect is likely ready to become your customer. Therefore, it is also an opportune moment to proceed with further document processes and discuss your professional fees.

4.4.8.5 Step 5 - Gather additional details, if necessary

Once the work and other document processes have been finalized, if you require any additional details, you can proceed with a second credit counseling session to gather more information. This session can also be used to discuss the workflow and how the process will proceed to complete the work.

Creating and implementing a clear process will help you efficiently convert prospects into customers. The outlined steps and lead management details are designed to facilitate the sales process.

4.5 The pro sales pitch to acquire customers

A pro sales pitch is a concise presentation used to sell your product or service. The goal of pro sales pitch is to convince prospects that they need what you're offering and persuade them to make a purchase.

The key to creating an effective sales pitch is by understanding your audience and their specific needs.

4.5.1 Research your prospects

Before you begin crafting your pitch, it is essential to research your prospects. Who are they? What are their needs? How much are they willing to invest in credit repair work? This information will help you tailor your pitch to be most effective for them.

Additionally, keep in mind that prospective customers may feel embarrassed discussing their credit issues. Convincing them that your credit repair service can help them rectify these issues requires a softer and more engaging approach.

4.5.2 Develop your pitch

As you develop your pitch, consider the following points:

- Craft a concise and compelling narrative for your pitch.
- Highlight the key benefits of your services and how they can assist customers.
- Avoid using excessive jargon or terminology that may confuse or overwhelm prospects.
- Focus on creating opportunities rather than solely aiming to close the sale.
- Structure your pitch in a linear manner, starting with an opening, followed by a presentation of your services, and concluding with a strong close.
- Keep your pitch flexible, allowing room for engagement with prospects to build trust.

4.5.3 Steps to build a sales pitch like a pro

4.5.3.1 Start by building rapport

Focus on engaging with a prospect. So, start by building a rapport and showing that you care about them. Use context to start your conversation rather than creating a fuss or pushing on closing the sales.

4.5.3.2   Inquire about their goals

You can start by asking, "How did you find our services? Did you come to us through one of the ads we posted on Facebook, or did you find our contact information from the website chatbot?" This basic information will guide us through the rest of the conversation.

4.5.3.3   Identify their problems

Identify the prospect's problems and acknowledge the reasons behind their current credit issues. This is where sales are made. If they are in urgent need of a solution, they are more likely to take action.

4.5.3.4   Determine the decision maker and time frame

This will help you understand who will be the key decision maker to take your service or if you need to discuss it with someone else. It is crucial that you cannot move ahead until the prospect is ready.

4.5.3.5   Budget

Everyone has a budget when it comes to purchasing a service or product. Be clear and specific about the cost, as there is no point in delivering your presentation if they cannot afford your service.

4.5.3.6   Soft close

A soft close involves action-oriented steps, such as offering a discount if they take action today or within a specific time frame. This approach highlights the benefits of your service using low-impact questions.

4.5.3.7   Close

Conclude your pitch by reiterating the benefits of your services and mentioning the fees. Focus on how you can assist and help the prospect.

If, after all your efforts, the prospect is not interested in your services, it may indicate that you failed to establish trust in yourself, your service, or your company. Ask questions to identify which aspect requires further explanation. If objections are handled well, there is a chance to convert the prospect into a customer.

The purpose of a pitch is to streamline the sales process and effectively convert prospects. Your primary focus should be on demonstrating how you can assist them.

4.6 Building trust and integrity for business growth

Success can be attributed to having a solid marketing and sales strategy. You need to gain the trust of your customers to grow your business, and at the same time, you should demonstrate integrity.

4.6.1 Identify the problem

Almost 8 out of 10 people face issues with their credit reports and have low credit scores. Consequently, most people are unable to access their finances in the way they want to. The primary concern is finding a solution to this problem, rather than assigning blame. As a credit counseling and repair consultant or organization, your role is to provide adequate counseling, credit repair solutions, and educate your customers.

4.6.2 Ask the right questions

Customers are discerning and can tell whether you are approaching them solely for monetary gain or if you genuinely want to help them. To establish the right relationship with customers, it is crucial to have the right intentions. Building trust is key, and one way to achieve this is by asking the right questions. These questions should be a mix of open-ended and close-ended ones.

4.6.3 Discuss their goals

Convince people of your authenticity, and they will trust you. It is important to understand why they need credit repair and what their plans are for credit in the near future. This helps in building rapport and trust. People with credit repair problems will benefit from your services, but you should also educate them with your resources on maintaining and rebuilding credit.

4.6.4 Creating your marketing strategy

When building your marketing and sales strategy, prioritize building trust by asking the right questions. Many people face credit issues, but they also need to be educated about potential solutions. It is important to recognize that every business is unique, but the basic sales and marketing funnel follows a similar structure: attract, engage, nurture, sell, and deliver.

4.6.5 Closing the deal

Follow up with your customers through phone or email to build trust, but be mindful not to frustrate them. If a prospect doesn't become your customer, ensure that you remain on top of their needs for credit repair or if someone in their circle requires credit repair in the future.

Be realistic and honest with your customers. Never make promises you cannot deliver on, but instead, educate them on how credit bureaus work, how to rebuild credit, and how to maintain a good credit score.

4.6.6 Be transparent

Acknowledge that customers have the ability to pursue credit repair on their own. However, gain their trust by demonstrating that you can handle it in a more organized manner and possess a better understanding of relevant laws, making you a trusted expert.

Maintain transparency in all aspects, from your professional fees to the completion of the work.

In addition to earning your customers' trust, demonstrating integrity is crucial due to the prevalence of credit repair scams in the market. Many individuals pose as credit repair consultants or coaches without the necessary knowledge of the Consumer Information Act and other relevant regulations.

To counter negative public perceptions, operate your business in the most ethical, transparent, and honest way possible. Educate your employees to uphold honesty and integrity, establishing strong ethical standards. This will help you build trust among customers and enhance your reputation in the market.

Furthermore, you can change people's opinions about credit repair by actively engaging with them, maintaining a presence on social media, sharing your knowledge, and spreading the message of integrity.

4.7   Learn about business credit

Business credit refers to the credit associated with a business, such as business loans, working capital loans, or any other form of credit required for business purposes. It is important to familiarize yourself with business credit since many of your customers may have their own businesses. In the future, they may require credit repair services for their businesses as well.

Assessments for loan approvals in business loans are based on commercial credit reports and CMR ranks. As a credit repair professional, you should have knowledge about business credit and understand how to handle commercial credit reports and CMR ranks.

4.7.1   Business credit is separate from individual credit

Business credit is separate from individual credit and has different parameters for getting approved for business credit. However, being associated with a business, an individual's profile may also be checked. The credit reports for both individuals and businesses are different. Individual creditworthiness is measured through a credit score, which is a three-digit numerical expression from 300 to 900, reflecting their past repayment history and financial management. In contrast, business creditworthiness is measured through a rank, which is a single-digit number between 1 and 10, indicating the ability to repay business debts and how well past credit facilities were managed.

4.7.2   Banks can see delinquent accounts

Banks have access to a special dataset for businesses that is only shared among them. Banks can see every delinquent account associated with a business. This can have a significant impact on bank loan approvals and interest rates.

4.7.3   Banks check individual credit along with business credit

This doesn't mean that banks won't check your credit if you are applying for a business loan or working capital loan. When you apply for a business loan, the bank will also perform a credit check on all directors or partners, depending on the loan amount.

Most customers are not aware of the difference between individual and business credit and how they can impact each other. As a credit counseling and repair business, it's important for you to understand the distinction and address both aspects separately.

Remember, business credit repair involves a different process and timeframe compared to individual credit repair. When promoting your business, don't forget to highlight business credit repair as one of your services.

4.8   Steps involved in launching a credit counseling and repair business

Credit counseling and repair is a service that helps people with their finances. It can be used to assist those struggling with debt or individuals who want to improve their credit scores. In this chapter, we will explore how you can start your own credit counseling and repair business.

However, many people face challenges when starting and understanding the ins and outs of this field. Here are the steps involved in launching a credit counseling and repair business.

4.8.1   Business plan

Launching a credit counseling and repair business involves several steps, including defining the business model, creating a business plan, assessing the market, and securing financing.

The first step in any new venture is to define your goals. What do you want to achieve? Are there specific problems or challenges you aim to address? How will you approach this? Answering these questions is crucial before considering the feasibility of opening a business in this field, even without prior experience. As an entrepreneur offering services related to helping people improve their credit scores, secure loans at reasonable rates, and manage their monthly payments to avoid bankruptcy, building trust and fostering cooperation are essential for success.

4.8.2   Research and analysis

Before launching your credit counseling and repair business, it is important to conduct thorough research and analysis. You need to collect customer data and analyze trends to understand your target audience and their needs.

The first step is to identify the type of information that will be most useful for analyzing customer trends. This may include:

- Demographic information such as age, gender, location, and income level.
- Psychographic data, which includes attitudes towards money management or levels of financial stress.

4.8.3   Defining the business name

Choosing the right business name is not just a formality but a critical aspect of how customers and affiliates perceive your business. The name should be clear, concise, memorable, professional, and relevant to your industry. Once you have decided on a name, it is important to check for any existing businesses with similar names and ensure the availability of a domain for your business.

4.8.4   Legal requirements

Before launching your credit counseling and repair business, you must meet various legal requirements, if applicable. These requirements may include:

- Licensing
- Registration
- Compliance with legal regulations

4.8.5   Financial resources

While starting a credit counseling and repair business may not require substantial financial investment, it is important to have adequate financial resources for basic operations and day-to-day expenses. If you are considering a franchise for credit counseling and repair, you may need initial funding for it.

Consider the following aspects related to financial resources:

- Sources of capital
- Budgeting and financial forecasting

4.8.6   Business website

In today's digitalized world, having a website is essential for your credit counseling and repair business. It not only adds credibility but also serves as a primary resource for providing information about your services to potential customers.

When creating your website, ensure that it contains sufficient and unique information that helps potential customers understand your services. Avoid copying and pasting content from other websites and focus on presenting your unique value proposition.

4.8.7   Designing the pricing structure

Determining how much and how you will charge customers for your credit repair services is an important decision. You can opt for a one-time charge, offer installment payments, or create package plans based on your business model. However, if you are operating under a credit counseling and repair franchise, the pricing structure may already be defined by the main franchisor.

4.8.8   Hiring and training

Hiring and training competent staff is crucial for the success of your business. Seek individuals who can provide high-quality services and invest in their training to enhance their skills and efficiency.

Consider implementing ongoing training programs for your employees to continually improve their expertise and enhance customer satisfaction.

4.8.9   Customer service

Customer service plays a vital role in the success of any business. It is the backbone of your credit counseling and repair services. Without excellent customer service, it becomes difficult to retain existing customers and attract new ones. Neglecting customer needs and wants can quickly lead to business failure.

Ensure that you prioritize exceptional customer service by understanding and addressing your customers' needs promptly and effectively.

4.8.9.1   Developing customer service policies

This includes everything from how long someone should wait before calling back after leaving a message (if at all) or whether or not employees should take personal calls while working on behalf of clients.

4.8.9.2   Customer relations

This refers specifically to dealing with those who have been unhappy with something done by your company.

4.8.9.3 Customer retention

This refers specifically to keeping clients happy so they stick around longer than just one session.

4.8.10 Data security

The first step in securing your business is to have a strong data security policy. This will help you protect the information of your customers, as well as prevent any breaches of personal or financial data. Your policy should include things like:

- How long you keep customer records for.
- What kind of security measures are used to protect customer data from hackers, malware, and other threats (e.g., firewalls).
- Whether or not employees have access to customer files.

4.8.11 Marketing strategies

You should have clear and well-defined marketing strategies to boost credit counseling and repair sales.

- Create a brand
- Design a website
- Implement digital marketing
- Utilize PR and media relations
- Produce print materials like business cards, flyers, brochures, etc

You can choose marketing strategies that align with your business goals and target audience to effectively grow your sales.

4.8.12 Affiliate partners

Affiliations are crucial relationships for the growth of your credit counseling and repair business. These can include local businesses like loan providers, credit card companies, and collection agencies. It is important to build strong relationships with these professionals to expand your business to the next level.

4.9   Checklist to launch credit counseling and repair business

Starting any new business can seem difficult at first. However, breaking it down into small achievable goals can make the process easier. Here is a checklist to help you launch your credit counseling and repair business:

Business plan – Create a simple business plan outlining the necessary steps to start your credit counseling and repair business.

Research and analysis – Conduct market research to understand the potential of the business and analyze your target audience.

Define business name – Choose a professional and relevant name for your business.

Legal requirements – Check if you need any licenses or permits to fulfill legal requirements.

Financial resources – Assess your financial resources and allocate a budget for different business operations.

Business website – Develop a professional website with comprehensive information about your services.

Design pricing structure – Determine the pricing for your credit counseling and repair services.

Merchant account and gateway – Set up a merchant account and payment gateway to facilitate easy payment collection.

Hiring and training – Hire skilled employees for various operational roles and provide them with necessary training.

Business cards and brochures – Create professionally designed business cards and brochures to make a strong first impression and serve as initial contact points.

Customer service – Establish effective customer service strategies to attract and retain customers.

Data security – Implement a system to ensure the security and confidentiality of customer data.

Marketing strategies – Develop effective marketing strategies to promote your business and increase sales.

Customer agreement – If required, create a legal agreement for customers to sign up for your services.

Professional email – Set up a professional email address using your domain to enhance credibility and reliability.

Helpline – Provide dedicated helpline numbers for customer support and assistance.

Affiliate partners – If you plan to collaborate with other professionals, create strategies to develop affiliate relationships.

By following this checklist, you can systematically launch your credit counseling and repair business. Remember to adapt and customize these steps according to the specific needs and goals of your business.

4.10   Dealing with customers (building relationships)

You need to find ways to differentiate yourself from your competition. One way you can do this is by building relationships with your customers, which will help them see that you are the best choice for them when it comes time for them to choose a company that can help them get out of credit-related issues.

4.10.1   Communication with customers

- Communication is the key to building relationships.
- Establish trust by being honest, open, and transparent.
- Provide customer service that goes beyond expectations by listening to their needs and providing solutions that meet those needs.

From your initial conversation with customers, remember that you are building a long-term relationship, not just aiming for a single sale. Do not start a conversation solely for the purpose of making a sale, but instead aim to genuinely help customers.

Customers should always feel that you will take care of their issues well, even if it also benefits your business.

4.10.2 Developing a strategy

The first step in developing a strategy is identifying your customers' needs. This can be done through surveys, focus groups, and interviews with customers. You can also ask them what changes they would like to see in your business or product.

Once you know their needs, develop a plan to meet those needs by setting realistic yet challenging goals for yourself and your company to stay motivated.

4.10.3 Use marketing automation

Utilize high-end marketing automation systems to build and maintain customer relationships. Automation can be scheduled to provide regular updates or educate customers without direct individual contact. You can use automated emails or WhatsApp messages to add a personal touch and deliver genuine information.

4.10.4 Provide value

To enhance your value and establish yourself as a trusted expert, focus on providing resources that educate customers about the credit industry and beyond. Regularly offer tips and guidance on improving and maintaining credit scores. This helps customers see you as someone they can trust.

4.10.5 Collect testimonials

It is important to collect testimonials from your happy and satisfied customers. These testimonials can be in the form of a few written sentences or even a small video. They serve as powerful marketing tools for your services.

Remember, customers prefer to work with professionals whom they trust and respect. Building a strong relationship with your customers is key to success in your business. By following these steps, you can cultivate high-quality relationships with your customers.

4.11   Maintain transparency with your customers

In the age of online fraud and scams, maintaining transparency is essential in the credit counseling and repair industry. Building long-lasting relationships with your customers requires a commitment to transparency. Be clear about what your customers can expect from working with you and provide them with a realistic timeframe for achieving results. Ensure that they have all the necessary information before making decisions about your services. It is crucial for everyone on your team to be aligned and focused on the same goal: helping people overcome credit issues.

Additionally, it is necessary to consistently track and update your customers on the progress of their credit repair work. Maintaining transparency about the status of their case builds trust and keeps them informed. During the initial counseling phase, provide comprehensive information with transparency and avoid overpromising results that cannot be guaranteed.

In all communications, strive to be specific, clear, and concise to avoid any misunderstandings. Ensure that all your employees are aligned in their communication approach when interacting with customers.

4.12   Accessing and importing credit reports

The main question that arises is how to access and import credit reports from different credit bureaus for your customers. In India, there are many third-party websites that provide credit reports, but the authenticity of the data can be questionable. Banks also pull credit reports when they receive loan applications, but these reports may not provide all the necessary details. Additionally, such reports are considered hard inquiries and can potentially impact credit scores.

To ensure the credit reports you access are authentic, genuine, and up-to-date, it is best to obtain them directly from the credit bureau. However, always ensure that your customer authorizes you to pull their credit report before doing so. Accessing and importing credit reports is the first step in starting a credit counseling session followed by credit repair.

4.13   Develop listening skills

As a credit repair counselor, your first role is to be a listener for your customers. Many people come to you with specific needs regarding their credit repair or loan planning. It could be related to a home purchase, business loan, or simply the desire to rectify their credit issues. Often, financial difficulties have led them to face credit problems.

When working with such customers, ask questions in a way that puts them at ease and conveys your understanding of their struggles. Allow them to share their stories and avoid interrupting or dismissing them. Being a good listener and providing emotional support are key elements of a successful credit counseling and repair business.

By engaging in interactive and two-way credit counseling sessions, you increase the likelihood of prospects becoming customers. The focus should not solely be on earning money or closing sales, but on genuinely helping the customer. Even if a prospect does not immediately become a customer, if you have acknowledged their concerns, understood their perspective, and paid attention to their story, they may become a future customer.

Therefore, develop strong listening skills and utilize both open-ended and close-ended questions during credit counseling sessions.

4.14   Three questions to start with new customers

You cannot assume that one solution fits all customers. The nature of providing credit services is different on a case-by-case basis. It is crucial to understand each case by discussing it with each customer to know their current credit standing and issues. The approach to handling each query is also different.

There are three basic questions to ask a customer to determine what types of services best fit them.

4.14.1   What made you contact me today?

This is the first question that is normally asked to customers to understand their mindset, financial goals, pain points, and timelines. Most people have limited knowledge about credit repair, and your role is to listen to their problems and provide the best recommendations to take action against their credit issues.

Many customers think that they only need a basic dispute process or believe it is just a matter of contacting a bank or credit bureau. During credit counseling sessions, as a counselor, you should explain how the entire process will be carried forward and how you will assist them in resolving their credit issues.

4.14.2   Why do you want to go ahead with credit repair?

Most people seek out credit repair services when they are about to apply for a loan or have already been rejected due to errors on their credit reports. Many people approach you when they are facing numerous credit issues and see no solution to obtaining a loan. As a credit repair professional, you will not only offer credit repair but also provide advice on dealing with collection agents, managing credit scores, and rebuilding credit after credit rectification.

Identifying the breaking point will give you an idea of whether they have multiple issues in their credit report that need to be addressed or not.

4.14.3   Are you a business owner?

Many customers approach you to resolve their personal credit issues, unaware of the fact that you can also help with their business credit rectification. Asking this basic question can help identify additional revenue streams and provides assistance to customers who require business credit rectification.

Implementing these practices and starting with relevant questions will help you provide the best credit repair service to your customers and create additional revenue streams for your business.

4.15   Dealing with the first customer

When you are ready to start your credit counseling and repair business, you have advertised well, set up your website, and started visiting affiliates to get referrals. Now, it is time to deal with your first customer by scheduling an appointment to conduct a credit counseling session.

4.15.1   The simple free credit counseling

If customers only want to know about your services, impress them with detailed information, but do not push them to take your services. Ask them relevant questions to understand their pain points and acknowledge them. Provide enough information so that customers feel good, but it should not seem like you are aggressively selling your service. Instead, show them that you are there to help them. By doing so, the chances of turning that initial inquiry into a prospect and eventually a customer will increase.

4.15.2   Create a step-by-step process

Initially, customers are interested in getting details about your services. This is where you guide them towards the point where they are ready to proceed with credit reports and further information. By creating a step-by-step process and maintaining proper interaction, you can effectively close the sales deal on a positive note.

4.15.3   Don't be pussy to close the deal

Avoid rushing to close the sale without proper closure. If you are too pushy with your services without gaining the trust of the customers, you risk losing potential customers. It is your duty to help customers understand the entire credit repair process step-by-step and provide them with a credit analysis, demonstrating how you will help them resolve their pain points.

4.15.4   Give them time to think

Many customers require some time to think about whether they want to proceed with credit repair or not. Give them the space and time to think, while gently following up to highlight the benefits of getting credit repair done. Remember, solely focusing on revenue can result in losing potential customers now and potential referrals in the future.

A sale is an art, so focus on creating a positive impression on your customers. Gain their trust and respect, and don't reach out to them only when you want their business. Find ways to continuously show them that you care. Connect with customers through customized interactions and active responses.

4.16   Educating customers

In addition to credit repair, it is equally important to educate your customers. This ensures that they don't fall back into the same bad patterns that led to their credit troubles in the first place. Some common practices that negatively impact credit scores include missing repayments, delaying EMIs, or applying for new credit indiscriminately, regardless of whether they actually need it or not.

You can educate them through the following tips:

4.16.1   Do not apply for credit

Each time you apply for new credit, it is considered a hard inquiry and can lower your credit score.

4.16.2   Do not co-sign

When you co-sign on someone else's loan, you are agreeing to be responsible for it. If that person doesn't pay the bill, your credit score will suffer.

4.16.3   Pay your bills on time

A single past due payment can decrease your credit score. Make sure to pay your credit card bills on time. If you have trouble remembering, set a reminder.

4.16.4   Pay your credit card balance in full

Paying your credit card bill with a lower amount will increase your debt. It is best to make a habit of keeping your credit card balance as low as possible, and when it comes to paying the bill, pay the full amount.

4.16.5   Monitor your credit report

It is a wise decision to periodically monitor your credit report to detect any signs of identity theft or negative information on your report.

4.16.6   Do not overpromise on quick results or quick credit score increase

It is important not to overpromise anything regarding credit repair. Explain to your customers that credit repair is a time-consuming process and credit scores do not change overnight. Credit bureaus and banks have their own processes for reporting data.

4.16.7   Ask them to forward any correspondence they receive from the bank or credit bureau

Although you are handling everything on behalf of your customers, banks or credit bureaus may contact them directly. Ask your customers to forward any correspondence they receive from banks or credit bureaus to you.

4.17 Exceptional customer service

You can create a positive customer experience by providing exceptional customer service:

- Making customers feel valued
- Emphasizing customer satisfaction
- Ensuring customer loyalty

Customer service is a critical aspect that can make or break your business. By developing a customer service strategy, you can provide exceptional service that will benefit you in many ways. To develop a customer service strategy, you must first identify your customers' needs. This can be done through surveys or direct communication with them to understand what they expect from your business. Once you know their needs, create a plan that will help you meet those needs and exceed their expectations.

Once the plan is in place, set goals for yourself and your team so that everyone understands what success looks like when it comes to providing exceptional service. Providing exceptional customer service is one of the best ways to ensure that your customers are satisfied with their experience. It can also help improve customer retention and loyalty, ultimately leading to more sales.

The benefits of providing exceptional customer service include:

- Higher customer satisfaction
- Increased customer loyalty
- Improved customer retention

However, implementing exceptional customer service can be challenging. With the following hands-on tips, you can provide exceptional service to your customers:

4.17.1 Know your service

To gain the trust of customers, it is crucial to have exceptional knowledge of your service. As a credit counseling and repair professional, you should be well-versed in relevant laws, handling different queries, staying updated with the latest amendments, and understanding the ins and outs of the industry.

4.17.2   Maintain a positive attitude

Attitude is everything. Maintaining a positive attitude will help you provide exceptional credit repair service to your customers. Your customers should feel that you are enthusiastic about helping them. Your tone and attitude can make a significant difference in how your customers respond to you.

4.17.3   Personalize your service

To make your customers feel valued, provide a personalized touch in your service. Customers don't want to be treated as just another transaction or receive generic responses. They want to interact with a person, not just a company. That's why many companies send birthday or festival greetings to their customers.

Going the extra mile and acknowledging special occasions can give your customers a wow feeling, and this small gesture helps your company retain customers for a longer time.

4.17.4   Respond quickly

Resolving customer queries as quickly as possible is a cornerstone of exceptional customer service. Customers do not want to wait in a ticket queue. There is a difference between the time it takes you to respond and the speed at which you resolve their problems. Customers understand that more complex queries take time to resolve. Get back to your customer quickly, but do not be in a rush to get off the phone without resolving their query.

4.17.5   Listen to them

Listen to their issues and relate to them. Remember that the most important part of the job is to educate your customers on how to better manage their credit and finances so they can maintain their credit long after your rectification work is done. Do not be in a hurry to give a baffled reply.

Listen to what they have to say without pushing your agenda. Don't assume that you know what your customer is going to say.

Tips for Improving Customer Service:

- Listen to your customers.
- Invest in customer service training for your employees.
- Use customer service technology to improve the way you interact with customers, such as chatbots and live chat software that can help you respond quickly so they don't have to wait for a response from a human being (which can take days).
- Create a positive company culture.
- Foster a customer-centric environment where everyone is focused on providing the best service possible. Make sure your employees are trained in the latest techniques and tools for providing exceptional customer service, including how to handle difficult situations with empathy and grace.
- Prioritize customer service over other business goals, such as profit or growth targets. This can be done by offering incentives for employees who go above and beyond their job descriptions (e.g., "best customer service" awards).
- Be friendly and polite when interacting with customers.
- Listen to their concerns and address them promptly.
- Offer solutions that fit each customer's needs and budget (if applicable).

In addition, you must be able to recognize when someone is having trouble understanding something or has questions about how something works, and then help them out.

Remember, the customer wants to be treated like a human and not a ticket or waiting number. If you provide exceptional customer service, customers will stay with you for a longer time and refer you to new customers by spreading the word about your services to their friends and family.

4.18   The best way to grow your business

Before we get into the nitty-gritty of growing your business, let's start with some basics.

Growing your business is important because it allows you to make more money and have more freedom in your life. It can also help you build a legacy for yourself and your family and give back to the world around you.

The benefits of growing your business include:

- More customers (and more revenue)
- Better relationships with clients/customers
- A better lifestyle for yourself and those around you

To grow your business, you need a growth strategy. A growth strategy is a plan that outlines how you will get new customers and keep them coming back. It is more than just a marketing plan: it includes all the steps needed to achieve your goals, including identifying your target market, setting achievable goals, and creating an action plan.

When customers love your service, they will spread its benefits to their friends and family. Word of mouth is the best advertising to grow your business.

Here are some ways through which you can be truly awesome with your credit counseling and repair business.

4.18.1   Be a trusted expert

When you lack industry knowledge, customers and affiliates may not trust you. To be trustworthy among your customers and affiliates, you need to handle their issues and educate them on credit repair properly.

4.18.2   Be customer-focused

When you provide amazing customer service, with quick responses and a problem-solving attitude, customers feel valued and special. Do not treat your customers like outsiders; consider them as part of your business.

4.18.3   Be transparent

Transparency is often overlooked in business. However, being transparent can attract more customers. Share updates on their files and how you will proceed. Do not hide anything just for the sake of getting customers. Be clear about what you can do for them and provide specific timelines.

4.18.4   Know your customers

Knowing who your customers are and what they need is vital. This is possible when you have developed good listening skills. Before starting your business, be involved in customer surveys and analysis to identify your target market.

Tips for growing your business:

- The best way to grow your business is by ensuring your customers are happy.
- Avoid being greedy with fees.
- Never promise what you cannot deliver.
- Never engage in anything that is illegal or unethical, no matter how profitable it may seem.
- Stay focused on what you can offer to customers.
- Provide exceptional customer service.

4.18.5   Money-back guarantee

Remember, in the credit counseling and repair business, you cannot guarantee that all negative items will magically vanish from customers' credit reports. It is important to clearly explain to your customers what can be removed and what cannot be. Offering a money-back guarantee can benefit your business.

Find out why you should have a money-back guarantee in your credit counseling and repair business.

4.18.5.1 Promoting a money-back guarantee will bring you more business

With a money-back guarantee, potential customers will feel more comfortable taking your services because they perceive no risk with this guarantee. This can help scale your business by attracting more customers.

4.18.5.2 Unhappy customers get their money back

If a customer is unhappy and dissatisfied with your service for any reason, a money-back guarantee allows you to refund their payment without engaging in unpleasant arguments and conflicts.

4.18.5.3 Refunds save time, protect reputation, and reduce stress

While most customers may not request a refund, there will always be a few challenging individuals. In such cases, it is better to provide a refund promptly and peacefully, without disrupting your business operations and reputation. When you are new to this business, it may be difficult to issue refunds. However, maintaining a positive reputation and image are crucial.

It is not just the credit counseling and repair business that faces such challenges; many businesses encounter difficult customers. Therefore, having a money-back guarantee and refund policy is beneficial for your business.

4.19 Define marketing strategies

It is important to have well-defined marketing strategies to grow your business. Without promotion and the right marketing strategies, you cannot achieve your desired growth.

Here are some marketing strategies you can consider for your business:

4.19.1   Social media

Social media is a great way to connect with your customers and grow your business. It is also one of the most effective ways to market your brand since it allows you to reach potential customers directly without having to pay for advertising space. If you want to target people who are interested in what you do and how you do it, then social media should be part of your marketing strategy.

4.19.2   Content marketing

Content marketing involves creating valuable content that attracts new customers while also educating them on what makes your brand different from others in the industry. This can include blog posts or videos featuring tips or advice related specifically to businesses like yours. If done correctly and consistently, this type of strategy will help establish credibility among potential clients and increase traffic through search engines such as Google, which often show results based on their ranking algorithm called PageRank (or PR).

4.19.3   Print marketing

Create flyers, pamphlets, and brochures to spread information about your services and distribute them wherever possible. These are excellent and affordable ways to advertise your business. Consider hanging posters in restaurant and shop windows, grocery stores, banks, light poles, bulletin boards, etc. You may also want to place small ads for your services in local newspapers, newsletters, and periodicals.

4.19.4   Direct mail marketing

Direct mail marketing can be a bit challenging to manage and track, but you can try it in small quantities. Create 5-10 email marketing scripts and send them to potential customers. You can also use a third-party mailer service.

4.19.5 Mini billboard

Traditional billboards can be very expensive, but a mini billboard can be a cost-effective option for advertising. It can be seen every day by drivers passing by, helping to increase brand visibility.

4.19.6 Start small and slowly expand

Avoid rushing to expand your business too quickly. Take small steps to start and grow your business. Plan your marketing and advertising efforts, and focus on cost-effective yet impactful strategies to scale your business.

4.19.7 Networking

The banking and financial industry is vast, offering great potential for business growth. One way to tap into this potential is through networking and partnering with professionals in different segments. You can network with an insurance agent, stock agent, or mutual fund agent also to get referral business.

4.19.8 Know online marketing

It is important to learn how to market your business online through different social media platforms. If you are unable to focus on multiple platforms at once, at least create a Facebook page dedicated to your business. You can launch ad campaigns on various social media platforms to generate leads for your business.

4.19.9 Customer testimonials

Customer testimonials are one of the best marketing strategies you can use to grow your business and acquire new customers both online and offline. Since many people are unfamiliar with credit repair, testimonials can help establish you as a trusted expert in the credit counseling and repair business. When potential customers research the best credit counseling and repair services, your testimonials will show them that you can be trusted.

Make effective use of customer testimonials to take your business to the next level. Ask your customers for brief testimonials regarding your work ethic, trustworthiness, or commitment to success.

You can collect testimonials in various formats, including video, audio, and text. Of these options, video testimonials tend to be the most impactful because they allow potential customers to see and hear your satisfied clients speaking about their experiences with you. You can ask a satisfied client if they would be willing to shoot a brief video using their cell phone camera or send one from their laptop. These videos are easy to create and serve as powerful marketing tools. Alternatively, you can ask clients if they would be open to participating in an interview session where they can share their thoughts and experiences with you.

If a customer is not ready for video testimonials, you can ask them to write about their experience with your services. Pairing their written testimonial with a genuine photo of the client adds authenticity.

Audio testimonials can also be effective, although not as impactful as video or text. If you are meeting with a client in person, you can record a brief audio snippet on your cell phone, lasting around 15-30 seconds.

4.20   Digital presence with your website

If you want to scale your business faster than you think, you need a professional website that represents your credit counseling and repair business. It will help customers see you as a legitimate and trustworthy service provider.

Avoid using ready-made templates for your website. Instead, opt for a customized website that includes all the relevant information about your business. Choose appropriate colors and visuals to give your website a professional and credible look.

Creating an effective website with an impressive homepage is an art that can greatly contribute to your online business growth.

Your website serves as a valuable source for lead generation and engaging potential customers. If your homepage is confusing, lacks information, or if your website takes too long to load, you risk losing potential customers.

Here are some tips to create an effective website for your credit counseling and repair business:

4.20.1 Design an engaging homepage

Your homepage is the first thing visitors see when they arrive on your website, and it's crucial to make a good first impression. An engaging homepage design should accomplish three things:

- Attract attention and engage users through visuals or compelling copy
- Provide clear calls to action
- Create a sense of trust by demonstrating your expertise

4.20.2 Create quality content

Use high-quality, relevant content that is error-free and easy to understand. Consider the following:

- Create content that is directly relevant to your website and business
- Write well-crafted and engaging content tailored to your target audience
- Keep your content up-to-date and timely, taking your target audience into consideration

4.20.3 Make the website mobile-friendly

In the digital era, having a mobile-friendly website is essential as most people use mobile devices frequently. Consider the following:

- Test your website on multiple devices to ensure compatibility
- Optimize your website for mobile users

- Ensure easy navigation on mobile devices
- Pay attention to the loading speed of your site, as mobile users have less patience for slow-loading pages

4.20.4   Keep it clean

Keep your website attractive, crisp, and clutter-free. Avoid excessive text or unnecessary elements. Get straight to the point and be concise in your content.

4.20.5   Make the website accessible

Ensure that your website is accessible to people with disabilities. Consider the following:

- Make sure your website is compatible with assistive technologies.
- Include alt text for images.
- Use high-contrast colors and provide transcripts for audio and video content, if applicable.

4.20.6   Monitor the website performance

Once you've launched your website, it's important to monitor its performance. This can be done using analytics software and other tools that help you measure the loading speed of your site, check for any downtime, and identify broken links.

4.20.7   Keep the website updated

To keep your website fresh and relevant, ensure that it is always up-to-date. This includes adding new content, fixing broken links and images, and removing outdated information.

The goal of your marketing efforts is to generate leads and scale your business. By creating an effective, clean, and goal-oriented website, you can increase leads and grow your business.

Additionally, you can leverage SEO to improve the visibility of your website. Search Engine Optimization (SEO) involves optimizing your website's content, structure, and other elements to improve its ranking in organic search results. This helps your website appear higher in search engine listings and drives more organic traffic.

Lastly, creating a sitemap for your website enables visitors to easily find what they're looking for without having to navigate through multiple pages. This improves user experience and increases overall website traffic.

4.21   Opportunity lies in affiliation

Getting referrals from affiliates is one of the best ways to generate leads for your credit counseling and repair business. While managing and engaging affiliates can be challenging, it is not impossible.

Identify your target audience and search for potential affiliate partners who can refer customers to your business. Even if they are not directly related to the banking and finance industry, they may still have the potential to refer customers. Consider developing an affiliate program that offers payouts or commissions for successful referrals. Engage in activities to build strong relationships with your affiliates.

Educate your affiliates about credit counseling and repair and its benefits so they can effectively communicate with their customers. Provide them with concise and easy-to-use scripts to pitch your services.

Make the referral process as seamless as possible for your affiliate partners, so they are motivated to provide you with more referrals. Regularly communicate with them via email, phone, or messaging apps to maintain your relationship.

When an affiliate refers a prospect, act quickly to convert them into a customer. Your initial conversation is crucial as it may be your only chance to close the deal. Be sincere and engaging, understand the prospect's pain points, goals, and expectations, and recommend suitable solutions accordingly.

Building mutually beneficial relationships with affiliates is vital for taking your credit counseling and repair business to the next level. Maintain professionalism and transparency in all your interactions with affiliates.

You can use the following tips to establish strong relationships with your affiliates:

- Help affiliates understand the long-term benefits of the relationship. When they see that the business comes back around, they will be eager to send more referrals your way.
- Building a high level of trust with a client also helps build trust between that customer and your affiliates.
- Affiliates do not want to turn down customers. Providing excellent customer service as an advisor builds trust and positive word-of-mouth, with each client becoming an ambassador for your business and your affiliate's business.

If your affiliates see that you can add value to their business, you will be able to develop strong relationships with each other and with clients.

4.22 Managing the team

As a business owner, focusing on internal growth is crucial. It's not just about external business growth, but also about building a functional and cohesive team that engages employees.

When building a team, assess the skills, experience, values, and cultural fit of potential team members. If you have a specific role in mind, look for individuals with the required skills or the ability to learn quickly. If necessary, consider hiring someone with less experience but who possesses other qualities that can benefit the business, such as being personable.

When hiring new employees for credit repair businesses, look for candidates who are passionate about helping consumers resolve their credit issues by repairing their credit scores.

4.22.1   Set clear goals and expectations

As a manager, it is crucial to ensure that everyone on your team is working towards the same goals and expectations. This can be achieved through the following approaches:

4.22.1.1   Define roles and responsibilities

Not all employees have the same skills or capabilities, and that's perfectly fine. It's important to clearly define each person's job responsibilities so that everyone understands their role within the company and what they need to do to succeed in their position.

4.22.1.2   Establish deadlines and metrics for success

Setting clear deadlines and performance metrics is essential for employees working on teams or projects. This helps them understand how much time they have to complete tasks and ensures effective communication and coordination among team members. Additionally, having clear expectations from the beginning helps manage workloads and prevent overwhelming situations during busy periods.

4.22.2   Create a collaborative environment

Fostering a collaborative environment in the workplace contributes to employee happiness and satisfaction. You can achieve this by:

- Encourage open dialogue and feedback
- Foster a culture of trust and respect
- Provide resources and support for team members

By creating a collaborative environment, you can enhance teamwork, communication, and overall productivity within your team.

4.22.3   Smothering bosses

Remember, micromanagement is one of the top de-motivators for employees. If your employees feel that you don't trust them to make simple decisions, they will quickly start feeling unimportant and disrespected. Give them the freedom and trust to make their own decisions, as it will make your life easier and your employees happier.

4.22.4   Encourage continuous learning

Learning is a vital part of the credit repair process. Your team members should constantly strive to expand their knowledge and stay updated on new regulations and best practices in their field.

To foster continuous learning, provide opportunities for team members to attend conferences or seminars that can enhance their knowledge and skills. Consider offering incentives like bonuses or extra vacation days for those who participate in these learning events.

4.22.5   Promote open communication

Creating a safe space for open dialogue is crucial. Encourage team members to ask questions, provide feedback, and share ideas. Facilitate regular check-ins where everyone can discuss their work, express their feelings, and address any challenges they may be facing.

This will ensure that everyone feels comfortable speaking openly about successes, areas for improvement, and any concerns within their respective roles or departments.

4.22.6   Monitor progress

Once your team is established, it is important to monitor progress and performance. This will help you identify areas for improvement and make necessary adjustments. Some team members may be more effective than others, and you can consider reassigning roles to maximize their strengths and provide development opportunities for those in need of additional support or training.

4.22.7   Implement performance reviews

Performance reviews are an essential part of managing a team. They provide the opportunity for managers and employees to discuss goals, progress, and potential areas for improvement. Performance reviews can also be used to reward good performance or recognize outstanding achievements.

Performance reviews should be conducted regularly, at least once per year, but they don't need to be time-consuming. Keeping them short and concise allows you to quickly return to your day-to-day tasks.

4.22.8   Avoid meeting overload

Meetings can be a great way for employees to discuss and collaborate, but so many companies schedule lots of unnecessary meetings that take employees away from their work and make them feel unfocused. Make sure all meetings have three crucial components:

- Clear, necessary objectives
- Actionable follow-up items
- Clear start and end times

4.22.9   Create strong and transparent leadership

As the boss, your employees will look to you as an example of how to behave in the workplace. It is important to be transparent, approachable, and encourage open communication. Create an environment where employees feel comfortable bringing ideas or problems to your attention. Focus on being a leader who inspires and guides rather than acting bossy or authoritarian.

Building a supportive and engaging workplace environment may be challenging, but by taking small steps such as effective communication, observation, and transparency, you can understand your employees' needs and find ways to meet them.

4.23   The final words

Credit counseling and repair is a growing industry, and starting your own business in this field can be a promising venture. There are various options to consider, including

- Starting with a franchise model,
- Purchasing an existing business, or
- Building your brand from scratch.

Assess your goals, resources, and preferences to determine the best path for your credit counseling and repair business.

Summary of Chapter 4

The chapter focuses on the basics of starting a credit counseling and repair business. It begins by providing nine tips for starting a credit counseling and repair business:

- Give time to involve
- Proper planning
- Identify your target audience
- Learning attitude
- Use delegation
- Build relationships to create affiliates
- Educate your affiliates
- Plan out operational system
- Educate your clients

Furthermore, the chapter outlines the primary steps for starting a credit counseling and repair business, which include:

- Get a copy of your credit report to study
- Learn credit reporting system
- Understand your role in the process
- Understand what you are offering and be cautious with what you promise
- Develop a smart work attitude
- Make it people's business
- Promote and market your business
- Start with small

Initially, the concept of credit counseling and credit repair may seem overwhelming and confusing. In such cases, considering a credit counseling and repair franchise can be beneficial. Franchises have a proven working model and an established brand with well-established customers.

When starting a credit counseling and repair business, defining charges for your services becomes crucial. Franchises typically have a pre-defined pricing structure, but when operating independently, you need to create a price model based on market trends.

Managing sales through a sales funnel is the next step in starting your business. Understanding the sales funnel and how to utilize it effectively can help generate leads, convert them into customers, and retain them. Sales funnels are powerful marketing tools for increasing sales.

The sales funnel is made up of five stages:

- Awareness
- Consideration
- Evaluation
- Decision
- Post-Purchase

The chapter has defined how you can create a sales funnel to maximize your sales:

- Attracting new potential clients
- Converting visitors into leads
- Nurturing leads until they become customers

You also use technology to smooth your sales process. To optimize your sales funnel, you can use automation, analytics, and personalized tools. However, you should keep the following points in mind while handling sales:

- Your lead is lead until you start communication.
- Whatever you have communicated with them, note down in the remark whether interested or not or maybe need to follow up.

- You can use CRM or Excel sheets for keeping the entire sales funnel process in streamline.
- The top of your sales funnel should be full of leads, so the conversation ratio will increase.
- You can start building referrals to generate more leads at the top of your sales funnel.
- You can start meeting different loan providers, and credit card providers to get more leads.
- Educate your customers about the credit repair and credit reporting system, it will create a good impact on them about your services. Apart from educating your customers, provide great service. So, they will refer their friends and family to opt for your services.
- To get your sales like wildfire, you should use different tactics to generate new leads.

Once you have created a sales funnel according to your needs, it is time to manage your leads.

Lead management has three goals:

- To increase sales opportunities by identifying potential customers who might be interested in your business or product (this is called prospecting).
- To nurture those prospects until they are ready to buy from you (this is called qualification).
- And finally, when someone does buy from you, make sure they have an amazing experience so that they come back for more lately.

Managing leads further falls into 8 subparts:

- Gathering leads
- Qualifying leads
- Organizing leads

- Engaging leads
- Nurturing leads
- Analyzing leads
- Tracking leads
- Converting leads

Each of the subparts is well defined in the chapter so that you can use it to increase your sales. Once you are ready with your sales funnel and sales planning, you need a pro sales pitch to rock your sales and get the customers on board.

Before creating your pitch, research your prospects and their needs. As you develop your pitch, keep the following points in mind:

- Develop a crisp and narrative pitch.
- It has highlighting points about your services and how it helps customers.
- Do not overuse lots of jargon or terminologies.
- Focus on building opportunities rather than just jumping into closing the sales.
- It should be in a straight line – opening pitch followed by a presentation and completed with the close.
- Keep your pitch flexible whenever needed so there is a good opportunity to engage with prospects to build trust.

Your sales pitch should be in the following manner to create an impactful sales conversation with your prospect:

- Start by building a rapport
- Ask about their goal
- Identity their problems
- Know the decision maker and time frame
- Budget
- Soft close

If you want to grow your business, it is crucial to build trust and integrity. For this, you have to keep some points in mind while interacting with customers:

- Identify the problem
- Ask the right questions
- Discuss their goals
- Creating your marketing strategy
- Closing deal
- Be transparent

Being in the credit counseling and repair business, you should be well-versed with business credit, which includes CMR ranking and credit reports for businesses. Here are some points you should know about business credit:

- Business credit is separate from individual credit
- Banks can see delinquent accounts
- Banks check individual credit along with business credit

Unlike any other business, starting a credit counseling and repair business involves several steps:

- Business plan
- Research and analysis
- Defining business name
- Legal requirements
- Financial resources
- Business website
- Design pricing structure
- Hiring and training
- Customer service
- Data security
- Marketing strategies
- Affiliates partners

Further, the chapter provides a checklist to launch credit counseling and repair business, which is handy to refer to whenever needed.

You need to find ways to differentiate yourself from your competition. One way to do this is by building strong relationships with your customers. The chapter provides detailed information on how to effectively communicate with customers to build strong relationships.

- Communication with customers
- Developing a strategy
- Use marketing automation
- Provide value
- Collect testimonials

Maintaining transparency with customers is crucial to gaining their trust. In the credit counseling and repair business, counseling customers is essential. Developing good listening skills is important in this regard.

When dealing with a new customer, there are three basic questions to ask to determine which types of services best fit their needs:

- What made you contact me today?
- Why do you want to go ahead with credit repair?
- Are you a business owner?

After asking these questions, it is time to schedule an appointment to conduct a credit counseling session with your first customer.

- The simple free credit counseling
- Create step-by-step process
- Don't be pussy to close the deal
- Give them time to think
- Educating customers

When you provide exceptional credit counseling and repair services, it will create a positive impact on customers and leave them with a sense of satisfaction.

The benefits of providing exceptional customer service include:

- Higher customer satisfaction
- Increased customer loyalty
- Improved customer retention

However, it can be challenging to implement exceptional customer service. But with our hands-on tips, you can provide exceptional service to your customers.

- Know your service
- Maintain positive attitude
- Personalize your service
- Respond quickly
- Listen to them

Tips for Improving Customer Service:

- Listen to your customers.
- Invest in customer service training for your employees.
- Use customer service technology to improve the way you interact with customers, like chatbots and live chat software that can help you respond quickly so that they don't have to wait for a response from a human being (which can take days).
- Create a positive company culture.
- Foster a customer-centric environment, where everyone is focused on providing the best service possible. Make sure that your employees are trained in the latest techniques and tools for providing exceptional customer service, including how to handle difficult situations with empathy and grace.
- Prioritize customer service over other business goals, such as profit or growth targets. This can be done by offering

incentives for employees who go above and beyond their job descriptions (e.g., "best customer service" awards).

- Be friendly and polite when interacting with customers.
- Listen to their concerns, and address them promptly.
- Offer solutions that fit each customer's needs and budget (if applicable).

Here are some ways to be truly awesome with your credit counseling and repair business:

- Be trusted expert
- Be customer focused
- Be transparent
- Know your customers
- Money back guarantee

By following these strategies, you can provide exceptional customer service, enhancing customer satisfaction, loyalty, and retention in your credit counseling and repair business.

It is important to have well-defined marketing strategies to grow your business. Here are some marketing strategies you can consider for your business to grow:

- Social media
- Content marketing
- Print marketing
- Direct mail marketing
- Mini billboard
- Start small and slowly expand
- Networking
- Know online marketing
- Customer testimonials

In this digital age, if you want to scale your business faster than you think, you need a professional website for your business.

Here are some tips to create an effective website for your credit counseling and repair business:

- Design an engaging homepage
- Create quality content
- Make the website mobile friendly
- Keep it clean
- Make the website accessible
- Monitor the website performance
- Keep the website updated

Getting referrals from affiliates is one of the best ways to generate leads for your credit counseling and repair business. You can use the following tips to build strong relationships with your affiliates:

- It is important to help affiliates see the long-term benefits of your relationship. When your affiliates see that the business comes back around, they will be rushing to send more referrals your way.
- When you build a high level of trust with a client, you are also helping build trust between that customer and your affiliates.
- Affiliates do not want to turn down customers. Giving awesome customer service as an advisor will build trust and word of mouth, with each client becoming an ambassador for your business and your affiliate's business.

As a business owner, if you do not focus on the internal growth of your business and only prioritize external growth, you risk losing the battle for success. It is crucial to hire a capable team and effectively manage them. Here are some key points to consider:

- Set clear goals and expectations
- Create a collaborative environment
- Smothering bosses

- Encourage continuous learning
- Encourage open communication
- Monitor progress
- Implement performance reviews
- Meeting overload
- Create strong and transparent leadership

In summary, the chapter provides valuable insights into starting and managing a credit counseling and repair business, emphasizing the importance of internal growth. By hiring a strong team, setting clear goals, promoting collaboration and continuous learning, encouraging open communication, monitoring progress, conducting performance reviews, managing meetings effectively, and demonstrating strong leadership, you can position your business for success.

Chapter 05

Credit Counseling and Repair in Global

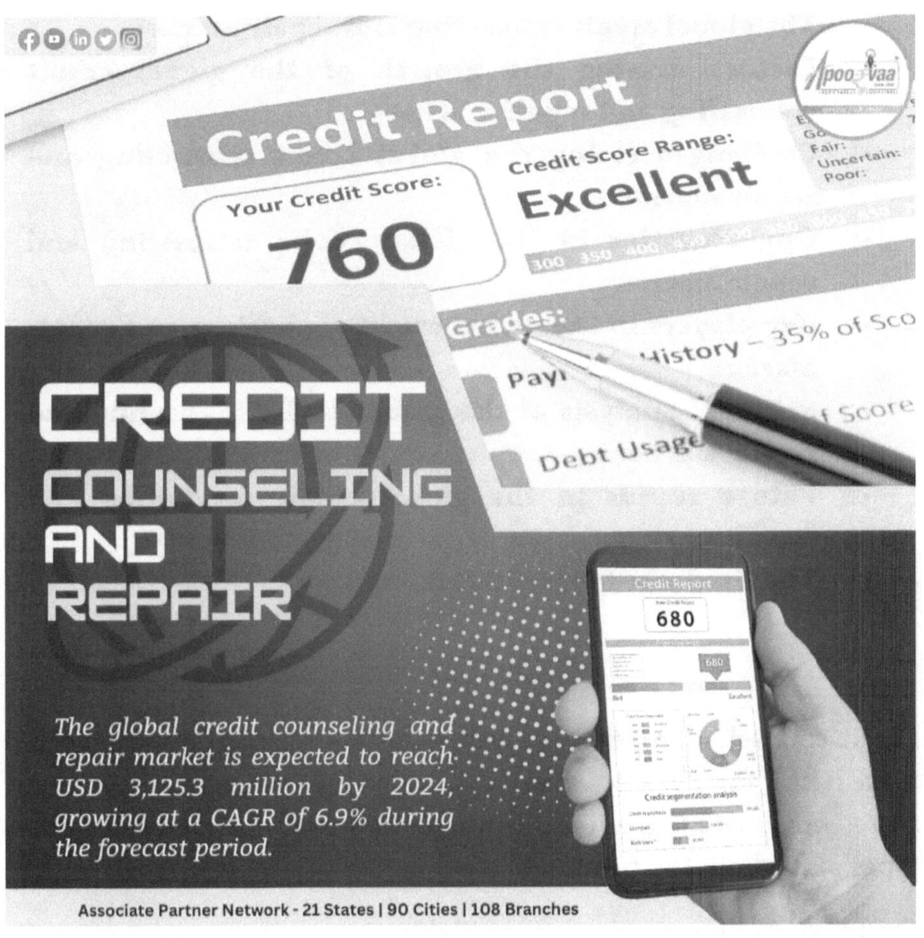

WHAT'S INCLUDED IN THIS CHAPTER

- **Credit repair process**
- **Credit repair services in global**
- **Credit counseling and repair can help you resolve common credit issues**
- **Types of credit repair in global**
- **Credit repair in other countries**
- **Credit repair laws around the world**
- **Credit counseling and repair business in global**
- **The global credit counseling and repair market**
- **Factors driving the growth of the global credit counseling and repair market**
- **Challenges facing the global credit counseling and repair market**
- **Opportunities in the global credit counseling and repair market**
- **Key players in the global credit counseling and repair market**
- **Regional analysis of the global credit counseling and repair market**
- **Future trends in the global credit counseling and repair market**
- **The final words**

Credit counseling is a process that helps you manage your debt and make better financial decisions. It can also help you repair your credit score, which will make it easier to get approved for loans and other types of credit in the future.

Credit counseling services are available at no cost through nonprofit organizations like Consumer Credit Counseling Service (CCCS) or National Foundation for Credit Counseling (NFCC) in the UK. These organizations offer free tools and resources to help you plan out your finances so that they are more manageable in the long run.

When you approach debt counseling, you may have trouble paying off debts because of an unexpected medical emergency or job loss. These organizations may also be able to help negotiate lower interest rates or reduced monthly payments with creditors on behalf of their clients and even prevent foreclosure if necessary.

5.1   Credit repair process

The credit repair process is not as simple as it may seem, but it can be done easily. The first step is to get a copy of your credit report from one of the three major credit bureaus (Equifax, Experian, and TransUnion) in the UK. However, there are other credit bureaus in the world, and many countries have their regional credit bureau, like Saudi Arabia, Singapore, Thailand, UAE, New Zealand, etc. But, these three bureaus are the major players in the global credit reporting market. Once you have this information in hand, you will want to look over it carefully to ensure that everything on the credit report is accurate. If any errors or incorrect information is listed on your credit report, those items need to be corrected before moving forward with any other steps in improving your finances.

If there are no evident errors in your reports after carefully reviewing them to ensure everything is accurate, you should consider getting in touch with a specialist who helps people raise their scores by removing negative items from their records. These negative items may include late payments or collections accounts that have been charged off by lenders after being unable to collect payment from borrowers who defaulted on loans due to a lack of funds available at the time when the due date arrived.

5.2 Credit repair services globally

Credit repair services are available to help you improve your credit score, get out of debt, and prevent future problems. Both nonprofit and for-profit businesses offer credit counseling and repair services. The specific services provided may vary depending on the organization and can include:

- A review of your credit report
- An analysis of all accounts listed on your report
- Recommendations for improving your situation based on the information provided by these reviews
- Common credit issues

5.3 Credit counseling and repair can help resolve common credit issues

5.3.1 Credit fraud

Credit fraud occurs when someone uses your identity to open new accounts or make purchases in your name.

5.3.2 Identity theft

Identity theft involves someone stealing your personal information, such as your social security number or bank account numbers, to open new credit accounts in your name. This can lead to serious financial problems and requires time and effort to clear up the fraudulent accounts once discovered.

5.3.3 Late payments

Late payments on bills, whether it's a car payment or credit card bill, can negatively impact your credit report. Instances of late payments over time can affect how lenders view your creditworthiness and may impact future loan applications.

5.3.4 Bankruptcy

Bankruptcy filings are public record and can impact your creditworthiness. Potential employers and others who review your credit history may consider bankruptcy as a factor in their decisions.

5.4 Types of credit repair in global

5.4.1 Credit counseling

A credit counselor helps you understand your financial situation and makes a plan for getting out of debt. They can also help you set up a budget, which is a way of tracking how much money comes in, goes out, and is surplus at the end of each month.

5.4.2 Debt consolidation

You may be able to consolidate all of your debts into one loan with lower interest rates or payments that are easier to manage. It means that instead of paying several different creditors every month (and possibly paying more than what is due), all of those payments go toward paying off one loan with one interest rate and payment amount per month.

5.4.3 Debt settlement

If it looks like there is no way out from under heavy debt loads without filing bankruptcy or declaring personal insolvency, debt settlement may be an option worth considering as well. However, keep in mind that this approach can have serious consequences including ruining one's credit score further down the road so make sure not only they know what they are doing but also whether or not this will work first before proceeding further into any type.

5.5 Credit repair in other countries

Credit counseling and repair services are available in other countries as well. In the United States, the National Foundation for Credit

Counseling (NFCC) offers a variety of programs designed to help people get out of debt and improve their credit scores. The NFCC also provides referrals to local counselors who can help you get started on your path toward financial stability.

In the United Kingdom, a similar organization called Step Change Debt Charity offers free advice on how to manage your money better and pay off outstanding debts more quickly. The charity also has an online tool called "Debt Remedy" where users can create customized plans based on their own circumstances, and it is 100% free.

Canada has its own version, Money Mentors Canada provides free financial education workshops across Canada through partnerships with community organizations like libraries or schools. These workshops cover topics like budgeting skills or managing debt effectively so you are prepared when problems arise down the road (like when interest rates rise). They also offer individualized coaching sessions where participants work one-on-one with trained professionals who specialize in helping people get back on track financially after experiencing hardship such as unemployment or illness/injury requiring long-term care from family members who are not able to provide support during this time period due to inability to work.

5.6   Credit repair laws around the world

United States – The Fair Credit Reporting Act (FCRA) is the main law that regulates credit reporting agencies in the U.S., and it protects consumers from inaccurate or incomplete information on their reports. You can request a free copy of your report every 12 months at AnnualCreditReport.com, but you must do so from each bureau separately. They are not all available at once. If there is something on your report that is not accurate, you have the right to dispute it with the CRA before they remove it from your file; this process could take up to 30 days unless there is an error in writing on their part or if they fail to respond within 15 days after receiving notice of dispute from you.

United Kingdom – The Financial Conduct Authority regulates consumer credit businesses such as banks and lenders who provide loans for personal use.

Canada – The Office of Consumer Affairs monitors all financial institutions including banks, credit unions, and insurance companies.

Australia – The Australian Securities & Investments Commission (ASIC) oversees ASIC licensees that include banks/financial institutions offering financial products such as loans, etc.

5.7   Credit counseling and repair business in global

Credit counseling and repair services are professional services that help individuals and families improve their financial situation. Credit counseling is a process that helps people understands how to manage money, make wise spending decisions, avoid debt, and build wealth.

Credit repair refers to the process of correcting inaccuracies on your credit report so you can obtain better loan terms or lower interest rates on existing loans.

5.8   The global credit counseling and repair market

The global credit counseling and repair market is expected to reach USD 3,125.3 million by 2024, growing at a CAGR of 6.9% during the forecast period. The market is driven by factors such as rising unemployment rates and increasing consumer spending habits, coupled with technological advancements in the banking sector.

The major players operating in this industry include Accion International Inc., American Financial Benefits Center Inc., Consumer Credit Counseling Service (CCCS), Debt Management Services Inc., and National Foundation for Credit Counseling (NFCC), among others.

5.9 Factors driving the growth of the global credit counseling and repair market

5.9.1 Rising consumer debt

According to a report by the International Monetary Fund (IMF), global debt has reached $164 trillion, an increase of $52 trillion since 2008, and represents 225% of the global GDP. The increasing level of consumer spending has led to a rise in personal loans, mortgages, credit cards, and other types of debt instruments.

5.9.2 Increasing awareness about credit counseling and repair services

Consumers are becoming more aware of the importance of managing their finances effectively to avoid bankruptcy or foreclosure in case of financial distress due to unforeseen circumstances such as job loss or illness. They are seeking help from companies offering these services at more affordable prices compared to traditional banks that charge high fees for similar services.

5.10 Challenges facing the global credit counseling and repair market

The global credit counseling and repair market is expected to reach $13.96 billion by 2027, growing at a CAGR of 5%. Some major challenges faced by this market include the high cost of services, limited access to services, and a lack of consumer awareness.

5.11 Opportunities in the global credit counseling and repair market

Opportunities in the global credit counseling and repair market include:

- Growth in online services
- Use of artificial intelligence and machine learning for credit repair services
- Expansion into new markets

5.12 Key players in the global credit counseling and repair market

- Credit Sesame
- Credit Karma
- Quizzle
- Credit.com

There are 43,507 businesses in the credit repair industry in the U.S. New York, Florida, and California have the highest number of credit repair companies. In a featured article by USA Today on "Credit Repair Services of the Year," the New Jersey-based Credit Saint was rated the highest.

5.13 Regional analysis of the global credit counseling and repair market

The global credit counseling and repair market is segmented into North America, Europe, Asia-Pacific, Latin America, the Middle East, and Africa. The North American region holds the largest share of the global market due to its high per capita income and strong economic growth rate. However, Asia-Pacific is expected to grow at a faster pace than any other region during the forecast period 2019-2027, driven by rising disposable incomes among consumers in developing countries such as India and China.

5.14 Future trends in the global credit counseling and repair market

5.14.1 Increased focus on customer experience

The credit counseling and repair market is witnessing an increased emphasis on customer experience and improving existing processes. This is driven by the competition among providers to attract and retain customers by offering better services and products. Companies are focusing on enhancing their offerings to provide a better customer experience and build long-term customer relationships.

5.14.2   Expansion of mobile services

With the widespread use of smartphones, many companies in this industry are expanding their mobile-based solutions to cater to customer needs. Offering mobile services allows for cost savings and increased efficiency as employees can work remotely, leading to higher productivity levels.

5.15   The final words

Credit counseling and repair services are projected to experience significant growth, with a compound annual growth rate (CAGR) of 8.8% during the forecast period, reaching a market value of $4.2 billion by 2023.

The North American region is expected to maintain its dominance in the global credit counseling and repair market, accounting for over 35% of the total revenue in the years 2022-2023.

The key players in this market include Experian Information Solutions Inc., TransUnion LLC., Equifax Inc., and others.

Summary of Chapter 5

The chapter focuses on the global presence of credit counseling and repair businesses. Globally, nonprofit or for-profit organizations can offer both credit counseling and repair services. The services provided include:

- A review of your credit report
- An analysis of all accounts listed on your report
- Recommendations for improving your situation based on the information provided by these reviews
- Common credit issues

Credit counseling and repair services can help resolve common credit issues such as credit fraud, identity theft, late payments, and bankruptcy. Different types of credit counseling are available globally:

- Credit counseling
- Debt consolidation
- Debt settlement

Countries have established dedicated organizations to handle credit counseling and repair services:

- In the United States, the National Foundation for Credit Counseling (NFCC) offers programs to help people get out of debt and improve their credit scores.
- In the United Kingdom, Step Change Debt Charity provides free advice on managing money and paying off debts.
- In Canada, Money Mentors Canada offers free financial education workshops and individual coaching sessions.

Various countries have specific laws governing credit reporting systems and providing consumers with the ability to dispute inaccuracies in their credit reports. The global credit counseling and repair market is expected to reach USD 3,125.3 million by 2024, with a projected growth rate of 6.9% during the forecast period.

Factors driving the growth of the global credit counseling and repair market include rising consumer debt and increasing awareness of credit counseling and repair services. However, challenges such as the high cost of services, limited access, and lack of consumer awareness exist in this market.

Opportunities in the global credit counseling and repair market include:

- Growth in online services
- Use of artificial intelligence and machine learning for credit repair services
- Expansion into new markets

Key players in the global credit counseling and repair market are:

- Credit Sesame
- Credit Karma
- Quizzle
- Credit.com

In summary, credit counseling and repair services are projected to experience a compound annual growth rate (CAGR) of 8.8% during the forecast period, reaching a market value of $4.2 billion by 2023.

Credit Counseling and Repair in India

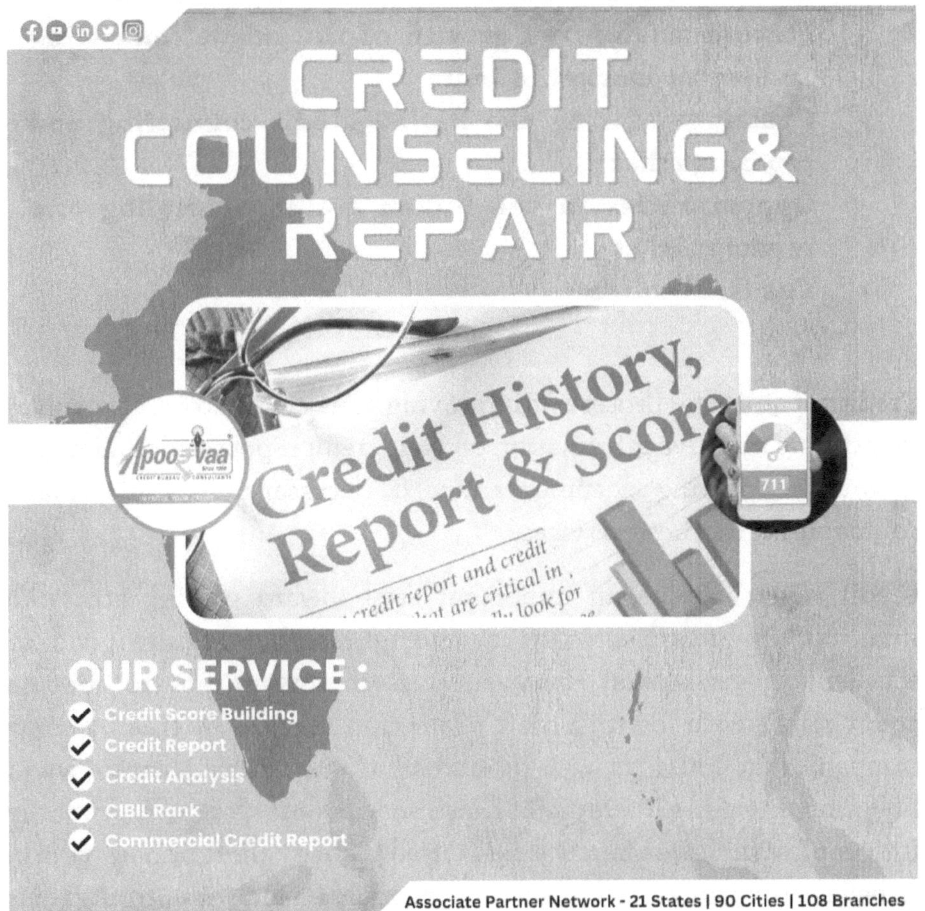

WHAT'S INCLUDED IN THIS CHAPTER

- **Credit repair process in India**
- **Credit repair services in India**
- **Common credit issues in India**
- **Credit repair laws in India**
- **Impact of credit repair**
- **Credit repair companies in India**
- **Credit counseling and repair business in India**
- **The credit counseling and repair market in India**
- **Factors driving the growth of the credit counseling and repair market in India**
- **Challenges facing the Indian credit counseling and repair market**
- **Opportunities in the Indian credit counseling and repair market**
- **The final words**

Credit repair is the process of improving your credit score. It involves identifying negative information on your credit report and challenging it with supporting documentation, if necessary. In India, many companies offer these services.

Credit repair can be an important step toward gaining access to financial products like loans or mortgages that require good or excellent credit scores. However, it is important not to confuse credit repair with identity theft protection services offered by some companies in India as well as abroad (for example, https://www.lifelocknowreviews2019info/). These services are designed primarily for people who have already experienced identity theft or have reason to believe they might be targets and generally include monitoring their accounts for suspicious activity and offering advice about how best to protect themselves against fraudsters trying to steal their personal information.

6.1   Credit repair process in India

The credit repair process in India involves several steps. The first step is to understand your credit reports, which will help you understand what information they contain and how it affects your ability to get loans and other financial products.

Next, you should dispute any errors on your report. If any mistakes could be affecting your score negatively, they need to be removed so that lenders can see the true picture of who you are as a borrower. Once these errors have been addressed, it is time for the final stage – improving your overall score by paying down debt or ensuring that all accounts are current and up-to-date with payments made on time (or early).

6.2   Credit repair services in India

Credit repair is a process of correcting and improving your credit score. It can be done by you or with the help of a professional, but the latter option is more effective and efficient. There are several types of credit repair services:

6.2.1   Credit report review

This service checks for errors in your report and helps you dispute them with the credit bureau.

6.2.2   Credit score improvement

It is possible to raise your score by making changes to your behavior or lifestyle that will improve it over time (e.g., paying bills on time).

6.2.3   Debt settlement

If you have unpaid debts, they may be settled for less than what they are worth so that they do not appear on your report anymore. However, this is not always possible because some creditors won't accept less than what they are owed.

6.3   Common credit issues in India

6.3.1   Credit fraud

This is the most common type of credit issue, where a person uses someone else's identity to obtain credit. The victim may not even know they have been a victim until they receive their credit report or statement.

6.3.2   Identity theft

A criminal steals your personal information and uses it to open new accounts in your name or make purchases with your existing accounts, resulting in negative marks on your credit report that can take years to remove from the system.

6.3.3   Late payments

If you are late paying bills on time, it will impact both your current score as well as future scores since lenders will see this behavior as risky and assume that other debts may go unpaid if given another chance at extending credit (even if those debts are not reported).

6.4   Credit repair laws in India

The Credit Information Companies (Regulation) Act of 2005 is legislation that regulates credit information companies and their activities in India. The act came into force on October 1, 2005, after being passed by both houses of Parliament. It aims to protect a consumer's right to access his/her credit information by making it mandatory for all CICs to provide free credit reports once every year if requested by them within 30 days from the date of request. This law also requires all CICs to maintain strict confidentiality of personal information collected from consumers as well as ensure that no false information is provided about any borrower or prospective borrower under its purview by any means whatsoever, including but not limited to telephone calls, text messages, emails, etc.

6.5 Impact of credit repair

6.5.1 Improve access to credit

A higher credit score can help you obtain loans, mortgages, and other forms of financing.

6.5.2 Increase credit score

Post credit repair, there is a high chance of a significant increase in your credit score.

6.5.3 Reduce interest rates

A higher credit score means you are less likely to default on your loan payments and more likely to qualify for lower interest rates on future loans or lines of credit.

6.6 Credit repair companies in India

Credit repair companies in India are available to help you with your financial problems. Credit counseling is a process that helps people who have bad credit or no credit, improve their situation by providing them with advice and assistance on how they can improve their credit scores. A credit counselor will review your finances and recommend steps for improving your situation, such as paying off debts and saving money for emergencies. However, it's important to note that the number of credit repair companies in India is limited, making it challenging to find the best option.

6.7 Credit counseling and repair business in India

Credit counseling and repair organizations offer credit counseling and repair services to help customers manage their debt. Credit counselors help people who are struggling to pay their bills, improve their credit scores, or prevent foreclosure on their homes.

Credit counselors also assist with debt management plans (DMPs), which are formal agreements between creditors and borrowers that set out payment schedules for unpaid debts. These plans may include reduced interest rates or lower monthly payments; however, they do not involve forgiveness of any part of the principal owed by the borrower.

6.8　The credit counseling and repair market in India

The credit counseling and repair market in India is still in its early stages due to limited awareness and understanding of credit management and repair concepts. However, it has significant growth potential.

The credit repair market in India is rapidly expanding due to the increasing number of individuals with poor credit scores. Specialized services, such as credit repair companies, are helping individuals improve their credit scores and gain access to better loan terms.

Credit repair services are gaining popularity in India because they offer a quick and effective solution to fix bad credit scores. These services provide personalized guidance on debt management and financial improvement. They also assist in disputing inaccurate information on credit reports and negotiating with creditors for better loan terms. As a result, more individuals are turning to these services to enhance their financial standing.

6.9　Factors driving the growth of the credit counseling and repair market in India

The growth of the credit counseling and repair market in India is driven by factors such as rising consumer debt, increasing awareness about credit counseling and repair services, and government initiatives.

The increasing number of banks offering loans has resulted in higher levels of consumer debt. The rise in income levels has led to an increase in consumption expenditure, which has further increased personal loan demand. This trend is expected to continue over the forecast period due to factors such as an improving economy, rising disposable incomes, and increased spending power among households owing to better job opportunities.

In addition, several state governments have launched financial literacy programs across India to educate people about managing their finances effectively so that they can avoid defaulting on payments or accumulating more debt than necessary.

6.10   Challenges facing the Indian credit counseling and repair market

The main challenge for the Indian credit counseling and repair market is the lack of knowledge among individuals about managing finances effectively, leading them to ruin their credit and stay away from accessing new credit. Prevailing myths and rumors around credit repair, such as the belief that there is no concept of credit repair in India or that credit repair companies are scams, further deter people from seeking credit repair services. Additionally, the habit of seeking advice from friends and family rather than experts prevents individuals from accessing credit repair services and maintaining a healthy credit life.

The importance of credit repair and keeping credit healthy is often overlooked due to a lack of financial knowledge, making credit repair a foreign concept for many individuals. Misinformation about credit counseling and repair, spread by self-proclaimed experts on platforms like YouTube, adds to the confusion and hinders people from accessing accurate information.

The attitude of refraining from checking credit reports and the desire for free or low-cost credit repair services also pose challenges in the Indian credit counseling and repair industry. These factors prevent individuals from proactively managing their credit history and seeking professional help when needed.

These challenges slow down the growth of the credit counseling and repair industry in India. However, they also present opportunities to create awareness, educate individuals about the benefits of credit repair, and dispel myths surrounding the industry.

6.11   Opportunities in the Indian credit counseling and repair market

The banking system is the backbone of a country's economy, and credit repair services will always be in demand. In India, the opportunities for credit counseling and repair are unlimited due to the country's growing population and consumer debt.

Credit reports often contain errors, making the credit counseling and repair business highly lucrative. Even during challenging economic times, it remains one of the fastest-growing industries. Additionally, in times of financial difficulty, individuals tend to accumulate more debt and struggle to maintain good credit.

In India, most public and private banks require a credit score of 750 or higher to extend credit. They also look for a healthy credit history and an error-free credit report. This makes it crucial for individuals to maintain a good credit history, credit report, and credit score. If they are unable to do so, they may need to mend their credit on their own or seek help from credit counseling and repair services.

However, due to a lack of information about the credit repair process and banking terminologies, many people seek credit repair services. In India, all credit bureaus are licensed and regulated under the Credit Information Companies (Regulation) Act, although most people are unaware of this. They are also unaware of their right to dispute erroneous credit report information. This presents an opportunity for credit counseling and repair services to grow in the Indian market.

Furthermore, credit repair is essential for individuals facing a bad credit score, poor credit history, identity theft victims, and those with inaccurate data in their credit reports. The fast-paced nature of life leaves people with less time to handle credit issues on their own, creating a high demand for credit repair services in India.

The lending and borrowing process has evolved with time. Personal judgment used to play a significant role, but now credit reports and credit scores have taken its place. In many countries, credit reports are checked for purposes such as job hiring, renting an apartment, and insurance decisions. Although India does not have the same level of credit report usage, some employers still consider credit reports when hiring candidates. This increases the need for credit repair services compared to earlier times.

Previously, TransUnion CIBIL was the only credit bureau, and banks primarily checked the CIBIL report and CIBIL score. However, there are now four credit bureaus (TransUnion CIBIL, Equifax, Experian, and CRIF High Mark) operating across the nation. Banks now check reports from all four credit bureaus, creating a demand for credit repair services as not everyone is familiar with all four bureaus.

Rectifying credit issues can be challenging for individuals as each credit bureau has its dispute-handling process and presents credit information differently in their reports. Analyzing credit reports can be difficult for people, increasing the need for credit repair services.

Overall, the Indian credit counseling and repair market presents numerous opportunities for growth and expansion.

6.12   The final words

The Indian credit counseling and repair market is experiencing significant growth and prosperity due to the country's population, lack of knowledge about credit, and increased consumer usage of credit. This business has proven to be recession-proof, even in challenging economic times.

Furthermore, with the large banking and financial industry in India, people heavily rely on loans and credit cards to meet their financial needs. This reliance creates a high demand for credit counseling and repair services.

In conclusion, the Indian credit counseling and repair market presents a lucrative opportunity for businesses operating in this industry. The ongoing need for credit repair services, coupled with the country's banking landscape, provides a favorable environment for growth and success.

Summary of Chapter 6

The chapter focuses on the Indian credit counseling and repair market and how the credit counseling and repair process works. In India, there are several types of credit repair services:

- Credit report review
- Credit score improvement
- Debt settlement

Credit fraud, identity theft, and late payments are common issues in India for which credit counseling and repair services are required. The Credit Information Companies (Regulation) Act of 2005 is legislation that regulates credit information companies and their activities in India.

Credit repair has an impact on accessing credit, increasing credit scores, and reducing interest rates. The credit counseling and repair market in India is still in a crawling stage due to ignorance towards managing credit and credit repair concepts. The growth of the credit counseling and repair market in India is driven by factors such as rising consumer debt, increasing awareness about credit counseling and repair services, and government initiatives.

The main challenge for the Indian credit counseling and repair market is that people are ruining their credit and refraining from getting any new credit due to a lack of knowledge about managing finances. Apart from the lack of knowledge, another drawback is the prevailing misinformation about credit counseling and repair that keeps people away from accessing their right to information. So-called experts on YouTube are spreading such information that cannot be trusted.

The opportunities in India for credit counseling and repair are unlimited due to its growing population and consumer debt.

In a nutshell, the opportunity is huge in the Indian credit counseling and repair market despite the challenges. The skyrocketing demand for credit repair makes this business recession-free even in the most troubling economy.

Credit Terminologies

Credit is an essential aspect of financial planning, and understanding the various terminologies associated with it is crucial. Familiarity with credit terms enables informed decision-making in managing finances, especially when it comes to loans, credit cards, and credit repair.

Lots of credit terminologies are prevailing in the banking and financial sectors related to different services and products.

Loans and credit cards have different terminologies. At the same, credit repair or rectification do have different terminologies. All of those are used in day-to-day terms or understanding of specific products or services. Apart from this, insurance and stock markets have their own related terminologies.

Credit terminology can be confusing for individuals unfamiliar with its intricacies. To facilitate comprehension, this guide has been created to provide a clearer understanding of these terms.

7.1   What is credit monitoring?

Credit monitoring is a service that keeps you informed about changes or errors in your credit report. It provides timely alerts in case of any suspicious activity, such as attempts to open fraudulent accounts using your personal information.

Credit monitoring also serves as a protective measure against identity theft by allowing users to monitor who has accessed their credit information and from where.

7.1.1   The benefits of credit monitoring

Credit monitoring helps protect your financial security. It can help you stay informed about the status of your credit and detect fraud, which is important because identity theft is on the rise.

Credit monitoring can also be used to monitor other types of accounts like insurance policies or bank accounts.

7.1.2   Credit monitoring services

There are a few different types of credit monitoring services, and each one has its own set of features. Here is what you should look for in a service:

- How often do they check your report? (the more often, the better)
- What kind of alerts do they send out (do they just notify you when there is something important to know? or do they also provide information about how to fix things?)
- Whether or not they have an app or website where you can access your reports on the go.

7.1.3   Credit monitoring cost

You may be wondering how much credit monitoring costs. Well, it depends on the service and the amount of information you want to receive. There are also ways you can save money when signing up for a credit monitoring service. For example, some companies offer discounts if you have multiple family members who want their accounts. Some may have different packages to opt for.

Once you have signed up for a service, it will begin monitoring your credit report and alert you if anything changes that might affect your credit score. You can then take action to correct any errors or disputes with the reporting agency directly through the website of the company providing your service.

7.1.4   How to get the most out of credit monitoring

You have signed up for a credit monitoring service, but what does it mean to use one? How can you get the most out of your subscription and make sure that you are not missing anything important?

Here are some tips:

Make sure that your information is updated. If there are any changes in your personal information (such as a new address or phone number), make sure to update them with each bank before they update their records with the bureaus. This way, no one will have incorrect information on file about you.

Stay up-to-date on what is happening with all four major credit bureaus: TransUnion CIBIL, Equifax, Experian, and CRIF High Mark. Look out for any suspicious activity like identity theft or fraud attempts by checking in regularly. You should also check in once every few months as a general practice. This can help prevent issues from occurring down the road, such as getting denied at checkout because someone else tried using your card first.

7.2   What is credit analysis?

Credit analysis is a process that involves collecting and analyzing information about a company or individual's financial situation to determine their ability to pay off loans. Lenders need to understand the creditworthiness of their borrowers so they can make informed decisions about whether or not to lend money and at what interest rate. Credit analysis is also used when determining the amount of collateral required as security against defaulting on loan payments.

Credit analysts work in banks, insurance companies, and other lending institutions. They may also be self-employed consultants who work with businesses or individuals seeking financing options for large purchases such as homes or cars.

Apart from this, credit analysis is a term used for analyzing credit reports for individuals and companies to understand and identify incorrect, incomplete, and inaccurate information. This analysis helps customers in credit repair or rectification.

7.2.1   Types of credit analysis

Credit analysis is used before the approval process of any loan or credit card. There are different types of credit analysis, and lenders or banks use them as per the requirement to evaluate credit applications.

7.2.1.1 Qualitative analysis

Qualitative analysis is a method of evaluating how a company's financial statements compare with other companies in its industry. It focuses on qualitative factors, such as management quality and reputation, rather than quantitative measures like sales growth or profit margins. Qualitative analysis is most useful when you're trying to decide whether a company will be able to maintain its current position in the marketplace over time.

7.2.1.2 Quantitative analysis

Quantitative analysis is the process of analyzing a company's financial statements and other quantitative data to determine its value. The data used in this type of analysis can include:

- Cash flow statements
- Balance sheets
- Income statements

7.2.1.3 Fundamental analysis

Fundamental analysis is a method of evaluating a company's stock by analyzing its financial statements and other factors that affect the company's performance. A fundamental analyst looks at a company's assets, liabilities, revenues, and expenses to determine whether it has enough money coming in to pay its bills. The goal is to determine if the stock price should be higher or lower than its current trading price based on these numbers.

Fundamental analysts often use ratios such as the price-to-earnings ratio (P/E), the price-to-book value (P/BV), and dividend yield when making their decisions about whether or not it's time for investors who own shares in this company to sell them at current market prices or hold onto them until they rise further from their current levels.

7.2.2 Components of credit analysis

Credit analysis is the process of evaluating a person's creditworthiness. It involves looking at three main components:

Credit score – A credit score is a numerical representation of an individual's creditworthiness. It is based on their credit history, payment behavior, and other factors. Lenders use credit scores to assess the risk of lending to an individual.

Credit report – A credit report is a detailed record of an individual's credit history, including their payment history, outstanding debts, and credit inquiries. It provides information about their creditworthiness and helps lenders make informed decisions.

Credit history – Credit history refers to an individual's track record of managing credit over time. It includes information on their past loans, credit card payments, and other credit-related activities. A positive credit history indicates responsible credit management, while a negative history may raise concerns for lenders.

7.2.3 When is credit analysis used?

Credit analysis is used in various scenarios related to accessing credit:

When you face challenges in obtaining new credit, it is essential to conduct a credit analysis of your entire credit report and history. This analysis helps identify possible reasons that may have led to financial distress and hindered your ability to obtain new credit. Understanding your credit report and history is crucial, even before considering large loans. Analyzing your credit report ensures the accuracy and completeness of the information listed.

When you apply for any form of credit, lenders and banks utilize credit analysis to assess your repayment potential. This analysis helps them determine the likelihood of receiving timely repayments in the form of EMIs (Equated Monthly Installments). Based on the credit analysis, lenders proceed with the credit approval and decision-making process. They determine terms, tenure, interest rates, loan amounts, credit card limits, and other relevant factors.

Credit analysis is a comprehensive term widely used in the banking and finance sector when evaluating creditworthiness and facilitating access to credit.

7.3   What is the credit decision process?

The credit decision process is the process through which a lender decides whether or not to extend credit to you. It is important because it helps lenders make smart decisions about how they lend money and how much they should charge for it.

The credit decision process is a multi-step process that lenders use to determine whether or not to extend credit to an applicant. It involves analyzing the borrower's financial situation and determining whether they are likely to repay their loans on time.

The first step in this process is gathering information about the borrower, including their income, assets, and liabilities. This information helps lenders determine whether they can afford their loan payments without falling behind on other bills like rent or utilities. If you are applying for a home loan, banks or lenders use their proprietary underwriting software to make "Credit Decisions". They use these factors to calculate your risk score based on your credit score.

The credit decision is the second process before approving a loan. Post credit analysis, banks or lenders jump into credit decision-making whether to extend a loan or not, and finally, they come to the credit approval process. Many times, credit analysis, credit decision, and credit approval are used interchangeably. But there is a slight difference in their actual definition and role.

7.3.1 Steps of the credit decision process

7.3.1.1 Gather information

Collect information about your customer, such as their credit score and income.

7.3.1.2 Analyze the information

Use this information to determine if they are a good risk for you to lend money to and what kind of interest rate you should charge them based on their creditworthiness (if any).

7.3.2 Credit decision models

The traditional credit decision model is the most common and is used by most lenders. The automated credit decision model is similar to the traditional model, but it uses software to help make decisions instead of human beings. The credit scoring model uses algorithms to determine whether or not you are likely to pay back a loan or line of credit.

7.3.3 Advantages of the credit decision process

The credit decision process offers several advantages, including:

7.3.3.1 Reduced risk of bad debt

When you approve a customer for a loan or credit card, you can be confident that they will pay their bills on time. This reduces the risk of having to write off bad debts and increases your profits and customer satisfaction.

7.3.3.2 Improved customer service

By understanding the needs of individual customers and tailoring your products and services accordingly, you can provide a better customer experience. This leads to increased customer loyalty, repeat business, and ultimately, higher sales.

7.3.4 Disadvantages of the credit decision process

The credit decision process also has some disadvantages, including:

7.3.4.1 Cost of implementation

Implementing a credit decision system can be expensive, requiring investment in advanced technology and software. This cost may pose a challenge for smaller companies with limited budgets or resource constraints.

7.3.4.2 Difficulty in setting credit limits

When using this method, it is important to establish clear guidelines for determining acceptable customer behavior to avoid the risk of providing excessive or insufficient credit. Without sufficient information on each customer's ability to repay debts, including associated interest rates, bank managers responsible for making credit decisions may rely solely on their own past experiences. This approach can lead to mistakes such as approving loans without a comprehensive understanding of the potential financial returns and initial costs involved in ensuring the ongoing financial stability of each client.

7.3.5 The future of the credit decision process

The credit decision process is a complex one, and it is constantly evolving. The future of the industry will likely see more integration between lenders and third-party providers, as well as the adoption of artificial intelligence (AI) to help make decisions more quickly and efficiently.

AI has already been used in other industries like healthcare, but there are still some barriers to its widespread use in finance. For example, concerns about the reliability of AI-generated data when making decisions about people's finances or healthcare needs could lead to discrimination if not handled properly by companies using AI for their products or services.

The credit decision process is a critical part of the loan process. It is important to understand how it works and why it is important to have a good process in place for all employees.

The first step in the credit decision process is determining whether or not an applicant should be approved for financing based on their credit score, income, and other factors. If they are approved, you can move on to the next step: determining what type of loan they qualify for based on their income level and other factors like debt-to-income ratio (DTI). Once you have made these decisions about whether or not they should get financing and what kind of loan they qualify for, comes the final step, which is negotiating terms with your customer so that both parties are happy with how things turned out!

7.4   What is the credit approval process?

A credit approval process is the procedure that a bank or lender follows to approve or decline a credit application. It includes steps such as verifying income, employment history, and credit history.

7.4.1   Types of credit approval processes

There are two main types of credit approval processes: manual and automated.

7.4.1.1   Manual credit approval process

This type of process is used when there are only a few applications for loans or credit cards received at a time, which means that the lender can go through each application individually. The lender will review each applicant's information and decide whether or not to approve them for the loan or credit card based on their financial situation and other factors such as past payment history with other creditors, etc. If approved, they will send out an offer letter stating what type of loan/card was given along with its terms (interest rate).

7.4.1.2   Automated credit approval process

The automated credit approval process is becoming an increasingly popular way to make credit decisions. This technology uses artificial intelligence (AI) to analyze data and identify patterns that can help lenders make better decisions. By using automated processes, lenders can reduce the amount of time and effort required to review applications and make a decision on whether or not to approve a loan. Additionally, this technology can also help lenders identify potential fraudulent activity before it becomes an issue. An automated credit approval process is quickly becoming the preferred method for many financial institutions as it provides a more efficient and accurate way of making credit decisions.

7.4.2 Components of the credit approval process

A credit approval process is a complex and time-consuming process. It involves several components that are essential for determining your eligibility for a loan or credit card. The following are some of the components of this process:

7.4.2.1 Credit report

This contains information about your previous financial history, such as whether you have paid off any loans on time or defaulted on them, how many times you have applied for credit in the past year, and so on.

7.4.2.2 Credit score

A credit score is an evaluation of your ability to repay future debts based on information in your credit report. It is calculated by looking at factors like how much money is owed compared with how much income is earned, how long someone has been employed (and if they have been fired), and whether there were any late payments made in previous months/years. Lenders use credit scores to assess the risk associated with lending money to an individual and determine the terms and conditions of the loan.

7.4.3 Methods used in the credit approval process

The credit approval process is a process that helps evaluate the financial strength and creditworthiness of a company or individual. It involves analyzing historical data, such as financial statements, to assess whether a borrower can repay their debts.

There are different methods used in the credit approval process. These methods include:

7.4.3.1   Financial ratio analysis

This method uses ratios calculated from past financial statements to predict future performance. For example, if your business has been profitable for the last five years but your debt-to-equity ratio has increased each year (meaning more money was used for financing), this may indicate trouble ahead for your company's profitability.

7.4.3.2   Cash flow analysis

This method analyzes how much cash comes into and out of an organization over time by looking at its balance sheet and income statement (also known as profit and loss statement). If there is not enough incoming cash flow relative to outgoing expenses or if there are large swings between these numbers, it could indicate problems with liquidity or solvency issues that could impact repayment ability down the road.

7.4.4   Data sources used in the credit approval process

The data sources used in the credit approval process include credit reports, financial statements, bank statements, and tax returns. These documents are crucial for verifying your financial status and helping lenders make informed decisions about lending money.

7.4.5   Credit approval tools

Credit approval tools are software applications that automate credit scoring and risk management processes. Credit scoring software analyzes a borrower's credit report to determine their likelihood of repaying the loan. Credit risk modeling software uses historical loan data to predict future defaults, and credit analysis software assists in making financing decisions based on applicant information, such as income statements.

7.4.6   Impact of the credit approval process

The credit approval process plays a crucial role in granting credit to individuals or businesses. By analyzing a borrower's financial history, creditworthiness, and repayment ability, the process helps protect all parties involved from risks while maximizing profits for lenders. It has a significant impact on the lending process as it ensures responsible lending practices and helps maintain the stability of the financial system.

7.4.7   Benefits of the credit approval process

The credit approval process offers several benefits:

7.4.7.1   Access to credit

The credit approval process allows individuals to access credit, such as credit cards or loans, even if they have limited or no credit history. This provides opportunities for people to obtain the funds they need for various purposes, including starting businesses or purchasing homes.

7.4.7.2   Lower interest rates

Having a good credit history enables borrowers to qualify for loans at lower interest rates. Lenders consider borrowers with good financial habits to be less risky, resulting in more favorable terms and conditions for loans.

7.4.7.3   Increased efficiency/Improved risk management

By conducting a thorough credit approval process, companies can gather accurate information about the financial situations of potential borrowers. This enables them to make informed decisions based on factors like past performance rather than relying solely on intuition. This improved risk management leads to more efficient allocation of funds and reduces the likelihood of financial losses.

7.4.8   The future of the credit approval process

The future of the credit approval process is expected to be more automated, transparent, and efficient.

As technology continues to advance and become more affordable, businesses will find it easier to automate their processes. This automation can help reduce costs and increase efficiency by eliminating human errors.

Automation will also facilitate the sharing of information between companies, allowing for better decisions regarding who should receive financing or credit cards based on their risk profiles. Additionally, it will enable companies to offer better rates since fewer manual steps will be involved in processing applications, compared to traditional methods such as paper-based forms or phone calls between agents at different banks or lenders, which often takes days.

The credit approval process is a valuable tool for financial institutions and businesses, ensuring that both consumers and providers of services or products on credit terms are offered fair terms and conditions.

In conclusion, the credit approval process offers numerous benefits to both parties involved in transactions where money is exchanged.

7.5   What is a credit analyst?

In banking and finance, a credit analyst is a professional who analyzes the creditworthiness of customers. The role of a credit analyst is to assist banks and lenders in making informed decisions about whether or not to lend money to customers based on their past performance and future prospects.

Credit analysts employ statistical analysis techniques such as regression analysis and time series analysis to assess a company's ability to repay its loans. They also examine factors such as cash flow statements, balance sheets, and income statements to project a business's future earnings and determine its ability to meet loan obligations.

Credit analysts typically hold a bachelor's degree in finance or accounting and possess experience working with financial statements and other financial data.

Credit analysts must possess the ability to swiftly analyze large volumes of data in order to make sound judgments regarding whether an individual should be approved for financing.

In the context of credit repair, credit counseling, or credit rectification, a credit analyst is responsible for analyzing the credit reports, credit scores, and credit histories of customers to identify incorrect, inaccurate, incomplete, and unverified information within their credit reports. The role of a credit analyst is to help individuals or companies understand their credit reports and identify factors that may have adversely impacted their credit scores or rankings.

Furthermore, credit analysts provide personalized recommendations and solutions to rectify credit issues, enabling individuals or companies to improve their credit health, qualify for credit, and enhance their overall financial strength.

7.5.1   Skills of a credit analyst

7.5.1.1   Analytical skills

Analytical skills are an essential aspect of being a credit analyst. They involve the ability to identify patterns, analyze data, and make informed decisions based on the findings. A proficient credit analyst can gather information from various sources, assess it in the context of previous experiences, and arrive at well-supported conclusions.

7.5.1.2   Financial modeling skills

Credit analysts utilize financial models to assess customers' repayment capabilities under different scenarios. These skills enable them to predict future cash flows and determine the availability of funds for loan repayment purposes, considering variables like changes in interest rates.

7.5.1.3   Communication skills

Effective communication skills are crucial for credit analysts. In credit repair, it is important to communicate findings from credit reports to customers. While in loan credit analysis, direct communication with customers may not be required, strong communication skills are still valuable in collaborating with colleagues and conveying complex analyses to stakeholders.

7.5.1.4 Domain knowledge

Credit analysts must possess expert knowledge within their specific domain to conduct thorough evaluations and provide accurate recommendations. Understanding the requirements and practices of the industry in which they operate ensures reliable and well-informed analyses.

7.5.1.5 Attention to detail

Attention to detail is a critical skill for credit analysts as they handle sensitive and significant information. It ensures accuracy in analyzing data, identifying discrepancies, and making precise recommendations.

7.5.1.6 Investigative skills

Credit analysts often engage in investigative tasks, gathering information, and verifying the veracity of client responses. Managing large amounts of information and conducting thorough investigations are vital aspects of their role.

7.5.1.7 Problem-solving

Credit analysts frequently assist clients in achieving their objectives, requiring strong problem-solving skills. This entails applying analytical abilities, resourcefulness, industry knowledge, and a proactive approach to finding effective solutions.

7.5.2 Types of credit analysts

There are several types of credit analysts, each with its own focus:

7.5.2.1 Credit repair analyst

Credit repair analysts specialize in helping individuals and businesses improve their credit scores. They offer services such as reviewing past credit reports, negotiating with creditors, and creating customized debt repayment plans. By understanding the intricacies of the credit system, credit repair analysts provide tailored advice that assists clients in achieving their financial goals. They also stay updated on relevant laws and regulations to ensure their clients are protected from unfair practices.

7.5.2.2 Corporate credit analyst

Corporate credit analysts work within the corporate sector, analyzing the financial health and stability of companies. They assess factors such as cash flow, profitability, and risk to determine the creditworthiness of corporations. Their analysis helps guide decisions related to lending, investment, and business partnerships.

7.5.2.3 Consumer credit analyst

Consumer credit analysts focus on studying the credit history of individual consumers. They assess an individual's ability to repay debts based on factors such as credit scores, payment history, and outstanding debts. Consumer credit analysts often work with banks or other lenders to determine whether a borrower is suitable for credit approval and what terms and conditions should be set.

7.5.2.4 Commercial credit analyst

Commercial credit analysts specialize in assessing the creditworthiness of businesses. They analyze financial statements, cash flow, industry trends, and other factors to evaluate the credit risk associated with lending to a particular company. Their analysis helps financial institutions and investors make informed decisions about providing loans or extending credit to commercial entities.

7.5.2.5 Investment banking analysts

Investment banking analysts work in the financial sector, specifically in investment banking. They analyze financial data and market trends to provide insights and recommendations for investment decisions.

Investment banking analysts typically work for large banks, hedge funds, or private equity firms, assisting with research, financial modeling, due diligence, and deal closings.

7.5.2.6   Treasury analysts

Treasury analysts are responsible for managing an organization's financial resources and investments. They analyze financial data, forecast cash flow, and make decisions about how to allocate funds to maximize profitability. They also ensure that the company complies with all relevant laws and regulations. Treasury analysts play a key role in helping organizations reach their financial goals.

7.5.2.7   Equity research analysts

Equity research analysts are financial professionals who specialize in researching and analyzing publicly traded companies. They use their expertise to provide insights on stocks, bonds, and other securities to help investors make informed decisions. Equity research analysts also provide reports on the performance of stocks and other securities, which can be used by investors to make better investment decisions.

7.5.2.8   Financial planning and analysis (FP&A) analysts

Financial planning and analysis (FP&A) analysts are responsible for providing financial guidance and analysis to companies. They help organizations make informed decisions about their budgets, investments, and other financial matters. They use their understanding of accounting principles, financial statements, and financial models to analyze data, identify trends, and develop reports that can be used by senior management to make decisions.

7.5.2.9   Risk analysts

Risk analysts are professionals who assess the risk of a certain situation or event. They use their expertise to identify, analyze, and mitigate risks associated with different activities. They evaluate possible outcomes and make recommendations to reduce potential losses. Risk analysts also provide advice on how to manage risks in the future. Their work is essential for businesses as it helps them make informed decisions and protect their investments.

7.5.2.10 Rating analysts

Rating analysts play a crucial role in the financial industry by providing investors with accurate and timely ratings of companies, bonds, and other financial instruments. They use sophisticated analytical techniques to evaluate the risk associated with these investments and provide meaningful insights that help investors make informed decisions. Rating analysts also work closely with portfolio managers to ensure they are making sound investment decisions. With their deep understanding of the financial markets, rating analysts are an invaluable asset in assessing the potential return on investment for any given security.

7.5.2.11 Budget analysts

A budget analyst is an important role in any organization, responsible for managing the financial resources of the company. Budget analysts make sure that the organization's funds are used efficiently and effectively to achieve its goals. They analyze financial data, create and monitor budgets, develop strategies to control costs, and provide advice on how to best allocate resources. Budget analysts also work closely with other departments to ensure that their financial decisions are aligned with the organization's objectives. With their expertise in finance and accounting, budget analysts can play a critical role in helping organizations maximize their profits while minimizing their risks.

7.5.3 The future of credit analysts

The future of credit analysts is bright. The profession is expected to grow by 10% over the next decade, which is faster than average for all occupations. As companies rely more heavily on data analysis and artificial intelligence (AI), the need for human input will increase as well.

Credit analysts are also likely to see an increase in demand because of their skill set. They are trained to understand financial statements and can spot trends that may affect a company's ability to pay back its debts or meet its other obligations. This makes them uniquely qualified to help companies plan for the future while minimizing risk. If you're interested in pursuing a career as a credit analyst, now might be the best time to do so.

Credit analysts play a crucial role in financial decision-making. Their ability to analyze data, assess risk, and provide informed recommendations is highly valuable in today's complex business landscape. With the continued advancement of technology and the increasing importance of data-driven insights, credit analysts will continue to be in demand.

7.6 What is the difference between credit counselors, credit analysts, and credit repair consultants?

Credit Counselors, Credit Analysts, and Credit Repair Consultants are professionals who help people with their finances. They can provide a range of services including debt counseling and financial advice.

Credit Counselors work in organizations that offer financial services to people who need them. These organizations may be credit repair or rectification organizations or credit counseling organizations.

While credit counselors, credit analysts, and credit repair consultants all work in the realm of finance and credit, their specific roles and focus areas differ. Credit counselors provide guidance and support to individuals facing financial difficulties, credit analysts assess creditworthiness and evaluate risk, and credit repair consultants help individuals or businesses improve their credit scores and resolve credit-related issues.

7.6.1 Credit counselors

Credit counselors are individuals who assist in managing credit and financial issues specific to the industry. If you are facing debt issues, you may seek debt counseling, while credit repair counseling can help with credit issues.

Credit counselors have various responsibilities, all with the aim of aiding consumers struggling with their finances. They work with you to develop a plan to address negative items on your credit report and may offer advice on managing your credit score effectively.

The benefits of credit counseling include:

- Assisting individuals in finding solutions for their financial problems by providing them with the necessary tools and resources to manage debt effectively.
- Helping individuals become more aware of their spending habits to avoid future issues and saving their time by helping clients understand what options are available before making any decisions regarding their finances.

7.6.2   Credit analysts

Credit analysts are professionals responsible for assessing the creditworthiness of individuals and businesses. Their expertise lies in determining whether borrowers are likely to repay their loans on time and the appropriate interest rates to be applied.

Credit analysts can be employed by commercial banks that offer loans directly to consumers or businesses. They can also work for non-bank lenders, such as peer-to-peer lending platforms, that provide financing options for individuals or small businesses.

Credit analysts also work for credit reporting organizations to assist individuals in understanding their credit reports and addressing any queries or concerns related to their credit history. As we have previously discussed, there are different types of credit analysts who specialize in various areas and perform different roles based on their expertise and industry focus. They work on analyzing creditworthiness, assessing risk, and providing recommendations based on their findings.

7.6.3 Credit repair consultants

A credit repair consultant is someone who assists individuals in improving their bad credit. They provide guidance and support in addressing both the financial and emotional aspects of managing debt.

Credit repair consultants offer advice on how to enhance your financial situation. However, it is important to note that they do not provide any guarantees or promises regarding the outcome of their services or a guaranteed improvement in your credit score.

7.7 The final words

We trust that this chapter has provided valuable information regarding credit terminologies, particularly those related to credit repair. However, it is important to note that the specific terms and keywords used in credit reports for individuals and companies are not covered in this chapter, as they have been previously included in our earlier book "The Indian Credit Reporting System."

We hope that the knowledge gained from this chapter will be beneficial in understanding the credit repair process and navigating the world of credit effectively.

Summary of Chapter 7

Credit is a significant part of financial planning, and it is important to understand the various terminologies associated with it. Credit terminology can be confusing for some people who are not familiar with how it works, so we have created this guide to help you understand these terms better. Hence, the chapter focuses on defining those credit terminologies.

Credit monitoring is a service that keeps you up-to-date on your credit report. It can alert you to any changes or errors in your credit report so that if something happens and someone tries to open an account in your name, you will know about it right away.

Credit analysis is a process that involves collecting and analyzing information about a company or an individual's financial situation to determine their ability to pay off loans.

There are different types of credit analysis, and lenders or banks use credit analysis as per the requirement to evaluate credit applications.

- Qualitative analysis
- Quantitative analysis
- Fundamental analysis

Credit analysis involves looking at three main components:

- Credit score
- Credit report
- Credit history

Credit analysis is a term used to analyze the credit report before the loan approval process. The credit decision process is the process through which a lender decides whether or not to extend credit to you. Credit decisions have two steps – gathering the information and analyzing the information.

Advantages of the credit decision process include:

- Reduced risk of bad debt
- Improved customer service

Disadvantages of the credit decision process include:

- Cost of implementation
- Difficulty in setting credit limits

The future of the industry will likely see more integration between lenders and third-party providers, as well as the adoption of artificial intelligence (AI) to help make decisions more quickly and efficiently.

A credit approval process is the procedure that a bank or lender follows to approve or decline a credit application. It includes steps such as the verification of income, employment history, and credit history.

There are two main types of credit approval processes: manual and automated.

- Manual credit approval process
- Automated credit approval process

The following are some of the components of the credit approval process:

- Credit report
- Credit score

Different methods are used in the credit approval process, including:

- Financial ratio analysis
- Cash flow analysis

The credit approval process has several benefits:

- Access to credit
- Lower interest rates
- Increased efficiency/Improved risk management

In banking and finance, a credit analyst is a professional who analyzes the creditworthiness of customers. In credit repair, credit counseling, or credit rectification, a credit analyst is a professional who analyzes the credit report, credit score, and credit history of customers to identify incorrect, inaccurate, incomplete, and unverified information listed on the credit report of individuals or companies.

The credit analyst requires the following skills to conduct fruitful credit counseling sessions:

- Analytical skills
- Financial modeling skills
- Communication skills
- Knowledge of domain
- Attention to details
- Investigative skills
- Problem-solving

There are many types of credit analysts, each with its focus:

- Credit repair analyst
- Corporate credit analyst
- Consumer credit analyst
- Commercial credit analyst
- Investment banking analysts
- Treasury analysts
- Equity research analysts

Financial planning and analysis (FP&A) analysts

- Risk analysts
- Rating analysts
- Budget analyst

The future of credit analysts is bright. The profession is expected to grow by 10% over the next decade, which is faster than the average for all occupations.

Furthermore, the chapter differentiates between credit counselors, credit analysts, and credit repair consultants.

In a nutshell, if you possess the necessary skills to be a good credit analyst, there are significant career opportunities available, and you can also help people overcome their financial crises.

FIT Rank

FIT Rank model uses machine learning algorithms to predict the probability of a borrower defaulting on its loan repayment in the next 12 months. FIT Rank risk differentiates on a scale of 1 to 10, FIT-1 being the least risky borrower and FIT-10 being the riskiest.

The trend of digitization in credit industry

The changing dynamics of the lending industry makes it pertinent to understand the nuances of credit behavior with the use of alternative data and not relying upon credit information alone. With $1/3^{rd}$ of the demand for credit coming from the New to Credit (NTC) borrower profiles, it is extremely relevant & crucial to use alternative data analytics to assess more MSME profiles.

This is the first time TransUnion CIBIL in collaboration with OPL, have created a credit default predictor model leveraging financial, income and trade data which has been made possible due to the increasing digitization efforts in the credit industry.

FIT Rank – for more confident, sharper, faster MSME lending decisions

TransUnion CIBIL, in its endeavor to help the lending industry take better informed decisions and remove information asymmetry, has partnered with Online PSB Loans Limited (OPL) to provide an objective risk assessment tool using alternative data sources – Financial, Income & Trade data-based Rank – FIT Rank.

FIT Rank makes use of:

- Banking information through bank statements
- Financial & Income Information from Income Tax Returns
- Trade data through GST Returns

The new age FIT Rank that will redefine risk assessment

- With the implementation of FIT Rank, banks and financial institutions will be able to assess profiles of many more MSMEs with sharper risk differentiation and can drive incremental credit growth for India's MSME sector by having access to better means of assessing risk.
- Combined with CIBIL MSME Rank (CMR), FIT Rank enhances the risk differentiation capability as well as assesses more MSMEs.
- FIT Rank's efficacy as a strong default predictor is empirically proven as it is able to differentiate the good performing borrowers from the non-performing ones.
- The New to Credit (NTC) base that was earlier unranked on the CIBIL MSME Rank (CMR) model due to lack of credit footprint will now be assessed based on either or all of the following alternative data – bank statement, IT returns, GST returns.
- FIT Rank will help drive more adoption of digital lending processes thereby improving efficiency and reducing the time taken for loan decisions.

Features of Fit Rank

FIT Rank for Acquisition – Pre-screen and provide financial assistance to many more MSME profiles, thus driving incremental credit and revenue growth for lenders.

FIT Rank for Risk Appraisal – Information from multiple sources provide an objective and improved risk differentiation enabling sharpened credit underwriting for MSME loans.

360-degree MSME view with FIT Rank & CMR – FIT Rank combined with CIBIL MSME Rank (CMR) provides more detailed view on the MSMEs credit profile by combining the credit (loan) behavioral aspects with financial, trade and income characteristics.

Frequently Asked Questions

1. What is a credit reporting agency, and how do they work?

Currently, there are four credit reporting agencies or credit information companies in India: TransUnion CIBIL, Equifax, Experian, and CRIF High Mark. Creditors or lenders, such as banks, small finance banks, NBFCs (Non-Banking Financial Companies), and credit card companies, report consumer payment information to these credit reporting agencies. These agencies act as repositories of information. When creditors or lenders consider lending money to consumers or approving credit cards, they refer to the credit bureau information. Essentially, a credit reporting agency or credit bureau is a databank that collects, stores, and maintains information regarding a consumer's payment history. Creditors or lenders receive this information in the form of a credit report, which also contains personal information, employment information, account information related to creditors or lenders, public records, and inquiry information. A credit score is a numeric expression based on the information contained in the credit report.

2. How does someone get erroneous information removed from their credit report?

It is crucial that all information on a credit report is accurate, as negative information can remain on your credit report for a longer period and negatively impact your credit score. If you find an inaccurate or erroneous item listed on your credit report, you can contact the four credit bureaus individually, as well as the creditor itself, and raise a dispute to have it removed. If the negative information is legitimate, you should directly contact the creditors or lenders and work with them to resolve the dispute. However, if you are unable to resolve the issue with the creditors, it is advisable to hire credit rectification services and seek their assistance in resolving the negative information.

3. What is the process for getting incorrect information removed from a credit report?

The process for removing incorrect information begins by obtaining your credit report and identifying the incorrect information. Next, contact your creditors directly and attempt to resolve the dispute. If that doesn't work, you can dispute the information on your credit report directly with the credit bureau. For quick and hassle-free results, it is recommended to contact credit rectification services and seek counseling from them, as they are experts in this domain. Remember that each credit bureau may have slightly different information, so it is necessary to review your information from all four credit bureaus.

4. Can anyone access my credit report?

Any consumer can access their own credit report. When a consumer applies for credit, such as a loan or a credit card, lenders or creditors can also access their credit report. Employers and other companies or individuals can gain access to your credit report, but only with your prior consent.

5. How does the credit score relate to the credit report?

The credit score is a meaningful representation of the credit report as it summarizes all the aspects included in the report, such as payment history, length of credit history, and types of accounts. It is calculated through a complex formula based on all the information, positive or negative, in the credit report. Positive information boosts the credit score, while negative information brings it down. The credit score is a helpful tool for both creditors and consumers.

6. If you are shopping for a great home loan deal or a car loan, does it hurt your credit score to have multiple lenders access your credit report during this shopping process?

No, having multiple lenders access your credit report within a short period, typically 30 days, for a home loan or car loan will be grouped together and counted as just one inquiry by the credit bureaus. This grouping will not have a negative impact on your credit score.

7. What are some of the biggest misconceptions consumers have for their credit reports and credit score?

One common misconception is that checking your own credit report will lower your credit score, which is untrue. There are two types of inquiries. A "hard inquiry" occurs when creditors or lenders check your credit score, and this can impact your credit score. However, a "soft inquiry" occurs when you check your own credit report, and this does not affect your credit score.

Another misconception is that closing unused or old accounts will increase your credit score. In reality, having a long and positive credit history boosts your credit score. Closing old or unused accounts that contain positive information can actually hurt your score, so it is better to keep those accounts active rather than closing them.

A third misconception is that paying off all debt for old collection accounts or old accounts will automatically remove the negative information from your credit report and improve your credit score. While paying off old debt helps by reflecting a zero balance on your credit report, the fact is that the negative information remains on your credit report unless the creditors or credit bureau choose to remove it after it has been paid off. You can request the removal of negative information from your credit report by contacting the creditors or credit bureau.

8. Are there any other common mistakes you see people make?

Yes, one common mistake is that people poorly manage their credit and then try to avoid or escape from creditors rather than discussing or negotiating with them. Another mistake is when individuals become guarantors without fully understanding the consequences. If the person for whom they became guarantors' defaults on a loan, it will reflect in their credit report and impact their credit score. Additionally, many people fail to regularly check their credit report.

9. Why having a credit score has become so important in today's society?

Having a credit score is important because when you apply for a loan or credit card, lenders or creditors will typically check your credit score first. In India, a credit score of over 750 is generally required to benefit from the best credit deals. Different types of lenders evaluate credit scores differently, but virtually all lending decisions today are made based on credit scores. This allows creditors to make fast yet accurate decisions, often automating their decision-making process to a large extent.

10. If someone needs help with credit repair or credit counseling, how can they find a reputable company to work with and avoid getting scammed?

In India, many people still struggle with removing negative information from their credit reports. While it is possible to directly contact creditors and credit bureaus, the process can be tedious and time-consuming. Alternatively, you can seek assistance from credit repair or credit counseling services. When choosing a company to work with, consider it as an investment and ensure you learn about the company and the services offered. Understand what is being offered, the associated costs, and how you will benefit from their services to avoid scams.

11. What is the difference between a credit reporting agency and a credit reporting company?

Within the industry, the term "credit reporting agency" is no longer used. In India, we use the term "credit bureau" or "credit information company" instead of "credit reporting agencies" or "credit reporting company."

12. How long does negative information stay on someone's credit report?

The duration of negative information on a credit report varies depending on its nature. A credit report is designed to reflect not just your current credit and financial standing, but also your history over a period of time.

13. What can someone do when negative information appears on their report?

When negative information appears on your credit report, the best course of action is to contact the creditors and pay off any pending debts, if applicable. The information will still remain on your credit report, but it will carry less weight if it is paid off. If the negative information is an error, you can easily correct it within 30 days by contacting the creditor or the four credit bureaus directly, or by seeking assistance from a Credit Rectification Company.

14. If someone has a lot of negative information on their credit report, what should they do to start improving their situation?

To start improving the situation, the first step is to obtain a copy of your credit report and credit score so that you have a clear understanding of your current standing. Review both the positive and negative information on your credit report to gain better insights into your situation and understand how that data influences your credit score. As a consumer, you have control over your revolving credit, including your credit cards. You can manage the balance on each credit card, make timely payments, and ensure a good credit history. These factors are considered when calculating your credit score, so it is important to have a positive impact on your credit report. It is also beneficial to maintain unused accounts in good standing, even if they are not actively used for extended periods of time.

15. What is a common mistake consumers make when managing their credit?

A common mistake consumers make is not realizing that every time a creditor checks their credit report, it impacts their credit score. It is not advisable to apply for several credits within a short period of time, as it negatively affects your credit score and may make you appear as a high-risk prospect. However, there are exceptions, such as receiving a "pre-approved" credit card offer in the mail, which does not impact your credit score as you did not actively apply. Additionally, in the case of car loans and home loans, all inquiries are grouped and counted as one inquiry.

16. How long does inquiry information remain listed on a credit report and how much of a negative impact does it have?

Hard inquiries remain on credit reports for a longer period. However, when it comes to score calculation, typically the number and types of inquiries over the previous 12-month period are considered. The impact of inquiries on the credit score varies depending on the overall credit profile and the individual's specific circumstances.

17. What can someone do to improve their credit score?

The most important step is to always pay bills on time. The later payments you have beyond 30 days, the more negative impact it has on your credit score. Even if you have an otherwise good credit history, one or two late payments appearing on your credit report can cause a drop in your credit score. Rebuilding or recovering your credit score may take some time.

Understanding the importance of your credit report and the information it provides is key to managing your credit effectively and becoming a more creditworthy consumer.

18. What is credit repair?

Credit repair involves the process of cleaning up your credit report by removing negative and inaccurate items in order to improve your credit score.

19. What does credit repair do?

Credit repair gives you the opportunity to dispute and correct inaccurate negative items on your credit reports that could be negatively affecting your credit scores. By removing or correcting these items, credit repair helps boost your credit scores.

20. Can credit report disputes lower credit scores?

The impact of credit report disputes on credit scores depends on the individual case. There is some confusion regarding whether credit report disputes have an impact on credit scores or not. The changes in credit scores, whether they increase, decrease, or remain the same, depend on the nature of the disputed information and how it is resolved.

21. Does disputing credit report errors hurt your credit score?

No, when it comes to disputing personal identification information such as name, date of birth, address, or contact details, requesting an update or removal of such information will not result in any changes to your credit scores. However, if a dispute is related to the account section or certain types of data in your credit report, the outcome could cause fluctuations in your credit score.

22. How much time credit repair takes?

Credit repair is not an overnight process. It typically takes at least 30-45 working days, but the timeframe may vary depending on the credit institution and credit bureau involved.

23. When do I need help from a credit repair company?

If you have numerous disputes to make or if you find the disputes to be complex and challenging to handle on your own, it may be beneficial to seek assistance from a professional credit repair service.

24. Why should I go for credit repair?

There are several reasons why you might consider credit repair:

- There is a chance one out of four credit reports has an error
- Chance to boost credit score if you repair your credit
- Refinance becomes easy
- Negotiation power for credit card interest rate
- Easy to get new finance
- Be home loan eligible
- Take advantage of offers on a car loan
- Say byes to collection action
- Save you from risky alternative finance options

25. What do you see when seeking help from a credit repair organization?

When looking for a credit repair organization, ensure they have a professional and knowledgeable team with expertise in the credit repair domain. They should also be familiar with RBI guidelines and The Credit Companies Regulation Act, 2005.

26. Can I do my credit repair?

Yes, you can handle credit repair on your own. However, you should have a good understanding of the credit report process, credit analysis, credit bureau dispute handling, and other related aspects. It also requires time, patience, and a thorough understanding of the process.

27. How much does that charge to use a credit repair company?

Hiring credit repair services typically comes with charges that may vary depending on the nature of your credit issues and the specific services provided. The cost will depend on the extent of the problem, but paying for professional services can be a worthwhile decision as it saves you from the lengthy credit repair process.

28. What are the common credit report errors?

Your credit report contains a lot of information, both positive and negative. Here are some common credit report errors:

- Credit bureaus may confuse you with your name, address, date of birth, or pan card or may lack some of your credit information. Here you can come across maybe your name is misspelled.
- If you can be a victim of identity theft or mixed accounts or duplicate accounts may appear in your credit report.
- Your account information is incorrect such as wrong account balance, closed account showing as open or wrong account number, and so on.
- The payment status of accounts may be incorrect.
- The account reflected in your credit report may have a chance that you did not open it.
- You can even find out the account listed more than once i.e. duplicate account.

29. When should I check my credit report ideally?

It is recommended to check your credit report every 3-4 months ideally. If you are planning a significant purchase like a home, car, or business, or if you are considering refinancing, it is advisable to review your credit reports from all credit bureaus well in advance.

30. What is identity theft?

Identity theft is the fraudulent act of obtaining someone else's personal or financial information to use their identity for fraudulent purposes, such as making unauthorized transactions or purchases.

31. How does a collection agency work?

A collection agency is engaged by creditors to collect bad debts. They operate based on instructions from the creditors and cannot sue you without the authorization of the creditor. Their role is to carry out the collection efforts on behalf of the creditor.

32. When does collection become legal action?

If collection efforts by the collection agency are unsuccessful, the creditor may consider taking legal action against you. In other scenarios, if you fail to respond or cooperate, legal action may be initiated against you. Legal actions are reflected in your credit report as a "suit filed" status, which has a negative impact on your credit history.

33. Why did your credit history get damaged?

There are several reasons that can lead to damage to your credit history:

- Your money management skills are so poor that it always leads to financial crises.
- You have never focused on saving money.
- You have spent too much on your credit card.
- You are an impulsive buyer.
- You have a shortfall of money.

34. What benefits can you get out of credit counseling?

If your credit report is filled with negative items that are hindering your ability to get a loan, credit counseling can provide several benefits. It can:

- Help you understand the credit report and its problem in a better way.
- Help you to retain a good credit score with strategic planning.
- Help you make repayment plans with creditors.

- Help you with some knowledge on how to deal with collection agents.
- Help you to manage credit so that you can keep future credit problems at bay.
- Help you to improve your credit score.
- Help you to rectify your credit report issues by being an intermediator with banks and credit bureaus.
- Help you save your time on credit repair and credit rebuilding process.
- Help you provide personalized solutions based on your credit-related issues.

35. Is credit repair legal?

Yes, credit repair is legal. The Credit Information Companies (Regulation) Act defines the customer's right to dispute and gives the authority to edit, delete, and modify information with the involvement of banks.

36. How does credit repair work?

Credit repair involves rectifying your credit report either by yourself or through a third-party service provider you have hired. The goal is to remove erroneous, incomplete, and inaccurate information from your credit reports. Credit repair companies charge professional fees for their services.

37. How can I make money through credit repair?

You can make money by charging for the services you provide to customers. You can set fees based on different types of inquiries or offer package options for credit repair work.

38. How much money can I make?

The amount of money you can make in the credit counseling and repair business depends on your individual capacity and how well you plan and execute your services. With passion, dedication, and hard work, you have the potential to earn a good income every month.

39. How do I increase my credit scores?

To increase your credit scores, it's important to ensure that your credit report is free from any errors that could lower your score. However, it's important to note that improving your credit score is not an overnight process. Credit scores are influenced by various factors and require consistent effort over time.

40. How do I get more customers?

To attract more customers, you need to work hard and smart. Utilize online presence, offline marketing strategies, referrals, and affiliate business opportunities to expand your customer base.

41. Who orders credit reports?

Both you and your customers can order credit reports from different credit bureaus. In India, the four credit bureaus are TransUnion CIBIL, Equifax, Experian, and CRIF High Mark.

42. Can I order the credit reports for the customer?

Yes, if your customers give you the authority to order credit reports on their behalf, you can do so.

43. Does my customer's credit score suffer a hit if he orders his credit report?

Does my customer's credit score suffer a hit if they order their credit report?

No, when a customer or you, as a credit counseling and repair company, order a credit report, it is considered a soft inquiry that does not impact their credit score.

44. What are the laws for starting a credit repair business?

In India, there are no specific laws governing the establishment of a credit repair business. However, you should ensure that you have the required licenses to operate your business in compliance with the laws of your state. Additionally, it is important to have a thorough understanding of how credit bureaus operate under the Credit Information Companies (Regulation) Act.

45. What if my customer undermines my work by applying for credit and keeping high balances?

Provide exceptional service to your customers and educate them about the consequences of applying for credit and maintaining high balances. Chapter four provides a detailed answer to this question.

Summary of The Indian Credit Reporting System

Chapter 1

This chapter focuses on how credit bureaus came into the picture. Before implementing the credit reporting system in India, the Indian government and the Reserve Bank of India identified the need for a credit reporting system.

With the aim of providing necessary legislative support to the credit information business, the Credit Information Companies (Regulations) Bill, 2004 was proposed to regulate Credit Information Companies and facilitate efficient distribution of credit. The Bill contains provisions for:

a. Prohibition of commencing or carrying on the business of credit information without obtaining a certificate of registration from the Reserve Bank of India;

b. Procedure for making an application for the grant of a certificate of registration, grant of a certificate of registration, cancellation of a certificate of registration, and appeal against the rejection of an application or cancellation of a certificate of registration;

c. Requirement of minimum capital;

d. Management of credit information companies;

e. Empowering the Reserve Bank of India to determine policies related to the functioning of credit information companies, issue directions to credit information companies and other players in the credit information business;

f. Functions of credit information companies;

g. Collection and furnishing of credit information by credit information companies;

h. Powers and duties of auditors;

i. Membership of credit institutions in credit information companies;

j. Information privacy principles;

k. Alterations of credit information files and credit reports;

l. Regulation of unauthorized access to credit information;

m. Offences and penalties;

n. Obligations of fidelity and secrecy;

o. Resolution of disputes between credit institutions and credit information companies or between credit institutions and their borrowers;

p. Exemptions from the proposed legislation for credit information companies or credit institutions;

q. Amendments to specified enactments in the Schedule to the Bill to allow disclosure of credit information under the proposed legislation.

A Credit Information Bureau (India) Ltd, formed and registered under the Companies Act, 1956, was established in January 2000 to effectively handle the credit reporting system. The Credit Information Companies (Regulations) Act was passed by both Houses of Parliament in 2005.

Furthermore, the chapter provides an overview of the Credit Information Companies (CIC) Act and its definition in terms of the credit reporting system. It also outlines the functions that credit information companies are required to perform. Credit information companies, credit bureaus, credit institutions, and specified users must adhere to privacy principles outlined in the CIC Act regarding the collection, processing, collating, recording, preservation, secrecy, sharing, and usage of credit information.

The act also specifies the course of action that credit institutions must follow when it comes to the disclosure of disputed data.

Chapter 2

This chapter focuses on defining the credit bureau in detail and highlighting its importance in the economy. It also takes you through the historical chronicles of the credit bureau.

A Credit Bureau, also known as a Credit Information Company (CIC), is a central repository that collects, collates, and maintains credit and loan-related information of individuals and commercial institutions. By law, each lending institution is required to be a member of at least one credit bureau and report credit information to it periodically.

The earlier scenario and the modern scenario are vastly different. In the past, when businesses or sole merchants dealt with new clients, they had to rely on personal information and relationships to extend credit. There was no credit history available, especially for migrants, making the entire process somewhat uncertain and prone to inaccuracies.

The first solution to this problem emerged in the 1860s when local merchants decided to maintain a list of individuals with a bad credit risk or a risky profile and share it with other merchants. This marked the birth of the first non-official credit bureau.

In 1899, the first official credit bureau was founded by two brothers, Cator and Guy Woolford. It was named "Retail Credit Company" and is now known as Equifax Inc. In India, CIBIL (Credit Information Bureau (India) Limited) was founded in the year 2000, almost 101 years after the pioneering efforts of the Woolford brothers.

In India, credit bureaus are licensed and regulated by the Reserve Bank of India (RBI) under the Credit Information Companies Regulations Act 2005. Currently, India has four credit bureaus that are licensed and regulated by the law:

1. TransUnion CIBIL

2. Experian

3. Equifax

4. CRIF High Mark

The chapter further provides an overview of how credit bureaus work:

- Member banks, credit card companies, and other financial institutions send financial data of registered individuals as well as commercial institutions to the Credit Bureau periodically.
- The Credit Bureau uses this financial information to create a credit report.
- When applying for a loan or credit card, lending banks or credit card companies contact the credit bureau to assess the applicant's credit history and repayment ability.

Credit reporting systems exist in every country to support their financial systems. The World Bank has played a significant role in supporting the development of credit reporting systems worldwide for several decades. The World Bank's General Principles for Credit Reporting (2011) reviews best practices and provides policy recommendations for the development of credit reporting systems.

Globally, Equifax was the first credit bureau, previously known as Retail Credit Company, and the first credit score was launched by Fair, Isaac and Company, known as the FICO Score.

Credit bureaus are vital components of any country's economy, as their systems help mitigate various market failures worldwide. The availability of high-quality information can reduce problems related to adverse selection and asymmetric information.

The chapter concludes by dispelling myths related to credit bureaus and providing factual information.

Chapter 3

This chapter focuses on the basics of credit, its historical roots, the evolution of the lending system, and its current and future implications.

The term "credit" has been in existence for a long time, but the way it is dealt with has evolved. In simple terms, credit provides buyers with the opportunity to purchase items with the promise of repayment. The repayment can be made in partial amounts, monthly installments, or as a lump sum, depending on the agreement between the buyer and the seller.

The word "credit" has various meanings:

- Praise, approval, or honor
- To do something that brings pride or receives praise
- To give praise to someone responsible for one's well-being
- Used to indicate a person deserving praise for something they have done
- A method of paying for goods or services at a later time, usually with interest added to the original amount

In earlier times, lending and borrowing relied on personal approaches, which introduced the possibility of biased decisions. Around 3000 years ago in ancient Greece and Rome, the lending system originated, and pawnbrokers began lending money by collecting collateral from borrowers to reduce lenders' risk. At that stage, the system primarily involved the exchange of goods.

The modern lending system, involving banks and lending institutions, emerged in the 1950s with the advancement of technology. Governments also took an interest in developing and regulating this system through laws and governing bodies. In India, the Reserve Bank of India (RBI) regulates banks and financial institutions.

The digital era of banking, which began in the 21st century, revolutionized the lending process with the introduction of online banking and mobile banking. Various financial software emerged to streamline manual work, saving time and energy and making the process easier and faster. The rise of fintech has further transformed the lending system and given rise to many peer-to-peer lending platforms.

Some key milestones in financial history include:

- The first loan system was implemented in 1754 BCE in Mesopotamia, along with the first interest rate system.
- The first bill of exchange had its roots in India in 321 BCE during the Maurya dynasty.
- Payday loans were used in 400 BCE in ancient Greece.
- Lending was outlawed from 1400 AD until the 18th century.
- Frank McNamara made history when he paid a restaurant bill with a cardboard card in 1950, which eventually led to the creation of the Diners Club Card.
- Quicken Loans was introduced in 1985 when computer and electronic data revolutionized the lending process.

There are primarily two types of credit:

1. **Secured Credit** – This type of credit requires borrowers to pledge collateral, such as property or assets, to secure the loan. Examples include mortgage loans, auto loans, commercial loans, gold loans, car loans, and home loans.
2. **Unsecured Credit** – This type of credit does not require collateral. Instead, it is based solely on the borrower's good credit history. Examples include credit cards, personal loans, and student loans.

The chapter provides an overview of the risk assessment process through an example and delves into credit underwriting at credit institutions:

- The underwriting process directly evaluates your finances and past credit decisions.
- The person who is involved in the underwriting process is called an underwriter and the underwriter is responsible for deciding whether to accept or reject the application for credit.
- An underwriter makes sure that you do not take any credit which you cannot afford and also ensures that you have submitted all your paperwork.

In managing risk for credit institutions, underwriters:

- Look at your credit history carefully means the underwriter pulls out your credit report and checks your score. Furthermore he/she, also analyzes your credit report to check any negative marking such as late payment, overuse of credit, bankruptcy etc.
- Order Appraisal means underwriter will order the appraisal to ensure that the amount that the lender offers for the home, matches up with the home's actual value. (In case of home loan or mortgage loan)
- The underwriter will cross check your income and employment, by asking for your income proof and employment situation.
- Look at Debt–to–Income Ratio means underwriters examine your income and debt percentage to assess your capacity to return. Your DTI is a percentage that tells lenders how much money you spend versus how much income you bring in.
- An underwriter examines your debts and compares them to your income, to verify you have more than enough cash flow to cover your monthly mortgage payments, taxes and insurance.
- Besides DTI, the underwriter shall also assess your savings account to confirm if there are enough savings to supplement your income, or to use it as a down payment at a closing.

From a risk assessment perspective, underwriters evaluate credit applications based on the 5 Cs of Credit:

5 Cs stand for Capacity, Character, Collateral, Condition and Capital.

Capacity – Capacity measures the capacity or capability of the individual/ business to repay the loan amount in time. It is the first step for any credit application to get reviewed positively. Furthermore, the underwriter examines Credit Capacity, Current Income and Stability of income (Salaried Segment and Self–Employed Segment).

- Credit capacity means how much credit you are able to handle. It is actually a mathematical calculation based on income and expenses of an individual. This is measured at 2 levels.
- To check the credit capacity, the underwriter takes Debt–to–Income ratio in consideration. From the documents of an individual the capacity of repayment is ascertained by the borrower.
- Continuous or regular income flow is necessary to prove your credit capacity. In the current volatile market, there is a high chance that your income flow is affected.

To check on stability of income, underwriter further verifies the other factors as well such as:

- Salaried Segment
- Self–employed Segment

Character – Character is the most important factor in evaluation of creditworthiness. It refers to the willingness or intention of repaying. The assessment of character of applicants is the most important step for any underwriter in the credit evaluation process.

Underwriter could determine Credit Character based on the following four methods:

1. Face–to–Face Meeting with borrower to assess the character
2. Internal Database check
3. Benchmarking the applicant (based on past lending experience) against performance of peer group/age group/geography and other factors
4. Assessment of all factors related to his/her previous borrowing records with other lending institution

Collateral – Collateral means a pledge of some asset by borrowers to lending institutions. A credit secured with collateral is called a secured credit and carries lower risk than the one without collateral is called an unsecured credit. Once the credit capacity and character are evaluated then a loan application is reviewed in the light of collateral.

Various kinds of collateral are used by lending institutions. Following are the list of collaterals accepted by lenders for different types of loans.

- Real Estate (home loan, loan against property)
- Gold (loan against gold)
- Vehicle (auto loan)
- Stock/Bonds/Mutual Funds (loan against share)
- Insurance Policy (loan against policy)

Condition – Condition refers to specific conditions such as interest rate or principal amount etc. The underwriter assesses the risk based on borrowers' plans to use money.

Capacity – Capital refers to overall assessment under the name of the borrower. It represents one's investment, savings and other assets like land, jewelry etc.

Chapter 4

This chapter focuses on the basics of the credit reporting system, its historical development, and its importance. It highlights how credit reporting was managed in earlier times and the significance of the credit reporting system.

In the past, credit reporting was not integrated into financial systems. Throughout the 5000-year history of debt, credit reporting was a personal practice. However, credit reporting as we know it today began to emerge around the 1700s. The first recorded group that shared credit information about consumers was the "Society of Guardians for the Protection of Trade Against Swindlers and Sharpers," founded in London in 1776. This society provided reports to its members on the credit history of individual customers, which often included both credit information and gossip.

Initially, manual credit reporting processes were time-consuming, prone to errors, and subjective. This began to change with the introduction of the statistical tool called the credit score in the 1950s.

The modern credit reporting industry was born in the 1970s with the advancement of technology and the advent of data collection through advanced computing. In 1971, the Fair Credit Reporting Act was passed in the US to ensure the accuracy, fairness, and privacy of information in the files of consumer reporting agencies.

In India, it took longer than in the US for credit reporting to develop. The Credit Information Companies (Regulation) Act, 2005 was introduced to regulate and provide guidelines for credit bureau work, which started in 1999.

In the 21st century, digitalization has become a necessity, and credit reporting has also evolved with technology. People are now more aware of the growing need for credit reporting, and data has become faster, more accurate, and easier to access.

Credit reporting plays a vital role in a country's financial infrastructure. When financial resources are easily, efficiently, and reliably accessible, financial services become more available to a wider population.

Access to finance is crucial for economic growth and job creation. A well-functioning financial system offers various products, such as savings, credit, and risk management, to individuals and businesses.

The credit reporting system facilitates the lending process by providing lenders with objective information that enables them to reduce risk and transaction costs. It also helps expand access to credit for creditworthy borrowers.

The key stakeholders in the credit reporting system include

- Credit reporting service providers or credit bureaus
- Data providers
- Data subjects
- Users

The system relies on technology, rules, procedures, and standards to ensure the smooth and relevant flow of information for making credit decisions.

Research has shown that a comprehensive credit reporting system produces more accurate scores in scoring models, leading to better predictions and improved ability for lenders to differentiate between low-risk and high-risk borrowers.

The 5 General Principles of Credit Reporting Systems are:

1. Data Quality

   a. Accuracy and Quality
   b. Timeliness
   c. Timeliness
   d. Sufficiency (including positive)
   e. Data Retention

2. Data Security, Reliability and Effectiveness

   a. Security Measures
   b. Reliability of Data
   c. Efficiency of Data

3. Legal and Regulatory Frameworks

   a. Clarity and Predictability
   b. Non-Discrimination
   c. Proportionality
   d. Consumer Rights and Data Protection
   e. Dispute Resolution

4. Governance Arrangements to deal with Operational, Legal and Reputational Risk

   a. Transparency
   b. Effectiveness
   c. Fair Access

5. Globalization and Access to Credit across Borders

   a. Pre-Conditions
   b. Requirement

The chapter also provides detailed information on how to measure the effectiveness of credit reporting service providers. A good performance measurement system includes multiple dimensions of performance, including financial, operational, and behavioral characteristics. The major dimensions include:

- Quality
- Quantity
- Timeliness of products and services delivered, financial
- Performance
- Customer satisfaction

Chapter 5

This chapter focuses on the basics of credit history and its importance when it comes to obtaining credit, such as loans or credit cards. Credit history plays a significant role in determining whether lenders will approve your credit application or not.

Credit history refers to a record of a borrower's repayment habits towards their debts, including credit cards and loans

It measures their responsibility in repaying their debts. This information is documented in a credit report, which includes details about the number and types of credit accounts, the duration of each account, outstanding balances, credit utilization, payment history, and recent credit inquiries.

Credit history is a crucial factor in assessing the creditworthiness of borrowers when it comes to repaying debts. Lenders rely on credit history to determine various aspects, such as the annual percentage rate (APR), grace period, and other factors when offering loans or credit cards.

The chapter further describes different types of credit history, including good credit history, bad credit history, and no credit history.

Some people have good credit history or some have bad credit history. Different things happen based on your credit history.

When you have good credit history, your chances to getting loan or credit are high.

I have Good Credit History because

- I pay my bills on time.
- I do not have big loan.
- I maintain low credit utilization.

That means:

- I have more loan choices.
- It is easier to get credit cards.
- I pay lower interest rates.
- I pay less for loans and credit cards.

Conversely, bad credit history has a negative impact on your credit score, resulting in unfavorable remarks in your credit report.

I have Bad Credit History because

- I pay my bills late.
- I owe a lot of money.

That means:

- I have fewer loan choices.
- It is harder to get credit cards.

- I pay higher interest rates.
- I pay more for loans and credit cards.

In addition to good and bad credit history, the chapter introduces the concept of no credit history, which is also taken into consideration when approving loans or credit cards.

I have No Credit History because

- I never borrowed money from a bank.
- I never had credit card.

That means:

- I have no bank loan choices.
- It is very hard to get credit cards.
- I pay high interest rates.
- Loans and credit cards are hard to get and cost a lot.

The chapter concludes with an example illustrating how good credit history, bad credit history, and no credit history impact your credit eligibility.

Chapter 6

The chapter focuses on the credit report, its definition, the information it contains, what it includes and excludes, and the types of credit reports.

Credit history is recorded in the credit report, and based on that, a credit score is generated. The credit report is an essential factor for credit applications. However, many people do not take it as seriously as they do their health reports. Checking your credit report regularly (at least every three to six months) can help prevent identity theft and keep you informed about the status of your credit report.

A credit report is a summary of information about all your current and past credit accounts. These accounts include credit cards, mortgages, student loan repayments, and any other loans reported to credit bureaus. Your credit report provides a historical record of how and when you pay your bills, the amount of debt you have taken on, and the length of time you have been managing credit accounts.

Most individuals have more than one credit report. Four major credit reporting bureaus keep track of credit reports for over 200 million Indians. These bureaus are TransUnion CIBIL, Experian, Equifax, and CRIF High Mark.

A Credit Report has two primary objectives:

- To capture and collate all details pertaining to an individual's credit accounts.
- To generate a score based on the account details.

The information stored in your credit file at each bureau is essentially the same, but each bureau organizes the data differently, and each bureau formats its credit report in its own unique way. A typical credit bureau report consists of four sections:

- Credit Score
- Personal Details
- Account Details
- Inquiries

Credit report is classified in 2 types.

1. Individual Credit Report
2. Company Credit Report

The chapter further provides detailed explanations of different types of credit reports offered by major credit reporting bureaus:

TransUnion CIBIL Individual Credit Report: This report is provided by TransUnion CIBIL and contains comprehensive information about an individual's credit history, including credit accounts, repayment history, credit inquiries, and public records. It is widely used by lenders in India to assess an individual's creditworthiness.

Equifax Individual Credit Report: Equifax provides an individual credit report that includes similar information as other bureaus, such as credit accounts, payment history, inquiries, and public records. Equifax is a global credit reporting agency and its credit reports are used by lenders and businesses worldwide.

Experian Individual Credit Report: Experian offers individual credit reports that provide a detailed overview of a person's credit history, including credit accounts, payment patterns, public records, and credit inquiries. Experian is another major credit reporting agency with a global presence.

CRIF High Mark Individual Credit Report: CRIF High Mark provides individual credit reports that encompass information about an individual's credit accounts, repayment history, public records, and inquiries. It is one of the leading credit bureaus in India and its reports are widely used by lenders and financial institutions.

In addition to individual credit reports, the chapter also covers commercial credit reports provided by these bureaus. Commercial credit reports focus on the creditworthiness of businesses and provide insights into their financial stability, payment history, and risk assessment.

Understanding these different credit reports is important for individuals and businesses to monitor their credit health, identify areas of improvement, and make informed financial decisions.

The chapter also explains the process of how credit reports are compiled:

- The details in a credit report primarily come from lenders, creditors, and collection agencies. These entities regularly report information about individuals' credit activities to one, two, or all four of the credit reporting agencies or bureaus. It is mandatory for Credit Institutions (banks) to be a member of at least one credit bureau as per The Credit Information Companies (Regulation) Act, 2005.

- Once the credit bureaus receive data from these lending institutions, they update the individual's credit report and credit score accordingly.

The chapter emphasizes the importance of credit reports, as they serve as the primary source of information for creditors and lenders to assess an individual's credit history. When applying for a loan or credit card, the credit report is typically the first thing that creditors or lenders check to evaluate an individual's creditworthiness.

The chapter also cautions against neglecting to check your credit report, as this can leave you vulnerable to credit fraud. It emphasizes the potential consequences of not monitoring your credit report, such as temporary damage to your credit and the need for significant time and effort to restore or correct it.

Furthermore, the chapter highlights two types of inquiries that can appear on a credit report:

Hard Inquiry – A Hard Inquiry occurs when a lender with whom you have applied for credit, reviews your credit report as part of their decision-making process. This type of inquiry appears on your credit report and can influence your credit scores.

Soft Inquiry – A Soft Inquiry occurs when you check your own credit report or when a lender or credit card company checks your credit to pre approve you for an offer. Soft inquiries do not impact credit scores.

It is important you should understand your credit report and it will help you in many ways

Let's understand why you need to check and understand your credit report:

- Peace of mind
- Maximize credit health
- Understanding your financial and economic responsibility

Apart from understanding credit report, you must check your credit report on regular intervals, it has the following benefits:

- It is an important step in rebuilding and maintaining good credit score
- It is an important part of managing your personal finance
- It is the first step in correcting any information you feel is inaccurate, that helps you to maintain error-free and accurate record
- Know your financial standing
- Stay in control of your loan or credit card
- Help you know whether you deserve a better car or loan
- To avoid rejection of a loan application
- To seek better jobs
- To guard against identity theft

Additionally, the chapter has provided some commonly found errors like the ones listed below will lower your chances of getting a loan or credit card.

- In correct information
- Closed accounts listed as open
- Unfamiliar accounts
- Duplicates accounts
- Inaccurate payment history

Negative Flags in your report is a proof of some past mistakes which can ruin your future plan. There are a total seven negative flags:

- Current Balance (Old due)
- Overdue
- Settlement
- Post (WO) Settlement
- Written-Off
- Willful Default
- Suit Filed

Furthermore, the chapter also gives the details on who can view your credit report and what is included and excluded in your credit report.

Inclusion

- Personal Information (Name, Address and Contact Details etc.)
- Account Information (Lender's Name, Account Number, Type, and Amount etc.)
- Enquiry Information (New Inquiry for Loan or Credit Card)

Exclusion

- No Credit Banking Information
- Beliefs and Affiliations
- Criminal Record

The chapter also dispels some myths related to credit reports at the end.

Chapter 7

The chapter focuses on in detail information about credit score, how it became part of banking and finance industry, importance of good credit score, what to do to get good credit score and so on.

In earlier times, lenders generally had a more open and social approach to get information about borrowers, and to figure out how creditworthy they were. But it was casual approach based on bias and judgmental mindset. But now the credit score is measure to judge creditworthiness and repayment capacity of borrower. Bill Fair, an engineer and Earl Isaac, a mathematician in 1950s has launched a credit score system. However, initially it was failed but with constant effort and with the use of technology and computer, it is evolved and now it is recognized as FICO Score.

A credit score is a 3-digit numerical expression, typically Between 300 to 900 based on a level analysis of a person's credit files, to represent the creditworthiness of an individual. A credit score is primarily based on a credit report, which consists of information typically sourced from credit bureaus.

In India Credit Score is referred as a "CIBIL SCORE", no matter which bureau is in charge of developing that score. We can say that "CIBIL SCORE" is synonymous with Credit Score. However, credit scores of any bureaus are valid to measure risk associated with creditworthiness of an individual; it is not as if one bureau is more reliable or preferable.

Maintaining a good credit score is important as it is a powerful tool when it comes to loan approval or credit card approval.

The chapter has provided credit score range to easily understand where you stand when it comes to loan eligibility.

Higher credit score represents that you have mindfully utilized your available credit and have not missed out on any payments hence, you will always be considered as the first priority by the lenders. But vice versa, lower credit score describes you as credit risky and it maybe likely that you get rejected for loan or credit card; or in case if you get approved then you would be charged a higher rate than usual, or be given an amount smaller than what you applied for.

Further, the chapter has detail understanding on how credit score is calculated. "Credit Scoring" is statistical system creditors use to determine whether to give you credit or not, they determine your creditworthiness in terms of your repayment habits, and then decide whether to give you loan, and if yes, how much should they charge you for it.

Let's see how Individual credit score is calculated based on that parameter.

- Payment History (35%)
- Amount Owned (30%)
- Credit History (15%)

- Types of Credit (10%)
- New Credit (10%)

Small businesses also have the same parameter like individuals to calculate credit score but it is little more elaborated with the following elements:

- Company information (including number of employees, sales, ownership, and subsidiaries)
- Historical business data
- Business registration details
- Government activity summary
- Business operational data
- Industry classification and data
- Public filings (liens, judgments, and UCC filings)
- Payment history and collections
- Number of accounts reporting and details

The chapter has answer of why credit scoring is beneficial. Let's see some benefits of scoring models:

- Accurate decision making
- Efficiency in work
- Standardized and objective decision making
- Easy to understand for all

Credit score has important role to play when it comes to your financial life. The credit score is first thing any lender check while assessing your loan or credit card application. Credit score is very important if your want to get some benefits from lenders in terms of loan amount, tenure, interest rates.

Let's see what all lucrative gains you shall get if you have a good credit score:

- High chance of loan or credit card approval
- Lower rate of interest

- Higher credit card limits
- Loan approvals
- Adds value to a visa application
- For the future

The chapter has given some reasons which make your credit score fall down and make you credit unhealthy. Whatever mistakes you do with your financials, will be directly reflected on your credit report which shall further result in a low credit score.

Let's check upon the reasons that shall result in a lower credit score.

- Your payment was more than 30 days late
- You have a high balance on one or more credit cards
- You have outstanding or overdue debts
- You made multiple enquiries for credit
- Your credit card was closed or cancelled
- Your bankruptcy fell off your credit report
- Identity theft or a mixed credit file is dragging you down
- Paying only minimum amount due for credit card
- Errors in your credit report
- Not having a credit mix
- Length of credit history
- Your unpaid account was sent to collection

The chapter has given details information on each of the above points for better understanding. Further, the chapter explains the best ways you can use to boost your credit score.

- Pay your bill on time
- Keep your credit card balance low
- Build a credit history and do not close unused credit card
- Apply and open new credit line, if it is needed
- Dispute the inaccuracies
- Avoid excess inquiries
- Avoid multiple credits

- Avoid bankruptcy
- Negotiate with your creditors
- Get a copy of your credit report and review it periodically

Apart from above best ways to boost your credit score, the chapter also glance on the good habits that people with 750+ credit score follow. Let's see here what habits of people make them to achieve 750+ credit score and make them in the top priority list of creditors when it comes to sanctioning loans or credit cards.

- They know their score
- They set up auto pay
- Low credit card limit uses
- They pay balance in full
- They know when to apply for credit

Some common mistakes, tiny things one does, have a huge toll on their credit score in the long run. Today it might feel that it is just a small thing but it has a deeper effect in future. Let's discover common credit score mistakes which should be avoided:

- Asking for credit limit increase
- Failing to check your credit report
- Overspending for the rewards
- Withdrawing cash from credit card
- Not using credit at all

Further, the chapter focuses on how credit score is significant when it comes to loan. Loans are a vital part of our finances and social well-being as they help us manage our finances; however it is important to know that creditors check your credit score and report, to evaluate your loan application.

Only those applications, who have qualified the minimum credit score criteria, will go to the underwriter for further process.

We can find the concept of loan and interest rate in Manu Smriti, Kautilya's Arthashastra and even Chanakya has narrated on this.

Furthermore, the chapter has defined which factors that do not affect credit score. Whether to consider those factors or not is up to one's own preference.

- Your Salary
- Where You Live
- The Rent you Pay
- Where You Work
- Your Bank Balance
- Utility Bill Payments
- Your Insurance Premiums
- Your Debit Card Use
- Your Spouse's Credit Score
- Checking Your Credit Score

The chapter has also covered new TransUnion CIBIL Score 2.0 which is built on more recent and richer history data, takes changing consumer profiles in account and is more accurate and effective predictor of risk.

Depending on the risk index, there is meaning to each index. This helps lenders to identify first time borrowers into high, medium and low risk.

Beside this, it is also:

- More accurate
- Gives better understanding of borrowers' creditability
- Less cases of defaulters
- Lenders can make better decision

This new updated score helps lenders make quality decisions throughout the customer's credit life cycle.

Credit score is meant for individual customer. But when it comes to business or company, CIBIL Rank will come in picture as it is risk predictor for business or company.

The CIBIL rank summarizes your Company Credit Report in the form of one number.

Just as individuals are given a CIBIL Score ranging from 300 to 900, Companies are assigned CIBIL Rank ranging from 1 to 10 where 1 is best and 10 is worst. However, a CIBIL Rank between 4 and 1 is considered good by most financial institutions. Most importantly, CIBIL Rank is an indication of a Company's creditworthiness.

A CIBIL Commercial Credit Report is a record of your company's credit history. The past payment behavior of a company is a strong indication of its future behavior. It is therefore important to understand that the Commercial Credit Report is heavily relied on by loan providers to evaluate and approve loan applications.

A typical Commercial Credit Report comprises the following information:

- Background Information
- CIBIL Rank
- Financial Information
- Financial History

The chapter has also covered what factors influence a Commercial Credit Report:

- Length of Credit History
- Credit Utilization Ratio
- Repayment History
- Outstanding Debts
- Size and Life of the company
- Industry

The major parameters that are used to calculate the CIBIL Rank are:

a. Past Re-Payment Behavior
b. Credit Utilization

CIBIL MSME Rank (CMR) is a credit risk rank for MSMEs that predicts the probability of an MSME becoming NPA in the next 12 months.

Further, the chapter has also defined CIBIL Rank model from CMR 1 to 10. Further, there are some points to consider if you want to enhance CIBIL Rank. Below are some points that can help you enhance the overall ranking of your company:

- The loan taken by you should be in the name of your company. However, make sure that you don't Default any payment.
- Pay EMIs of your credit card's outstanding debt on time.
- Stay cautious of every transaction going from your or the company's card so that the mistakes, if arising, could be rectified on time.
- Don't exhaust your Credit Limit and take a loan only when you can pay back.
- Taking long-term debts and paying on time can reflect positively on your rank.

Before concluding the chapter, it has also defined difference between CIBIL Rank and CIBIL Score to handle the confusion. At last, the chapter has broken some myths surrounding credit score.

Chapter 8

The chapter focuses on understanding your credit report and how to identify errors that can have long-term negative effects on your credit health. It is necessary to request your credit report from each credit bureau separately. In case of any errors or disputes, you need to work with the respective credit bureau to resolve them.

The process of obtaining credit reports may seem confusing because you have to maintain four different credit reports in India. Currently, banks refer to any two out of the four reports to make lending decisions. After obtaining your credit report, the next step is to review it. While reviewing your credit reports, carefully examine each credit line. The information reported on each credit report can be positive, negative, or inaccurate. If the information is positive, there is no need to worry as it will boost your credit score or maintain it in good condition. However, if you find any errors, negative items, or discrepancies, you may need to take further action.

While reviewing your credit reports, carefully examine each credit line. Determine if the information reported is positive, negative, or inaccurate. Positive information will help boost or maintain your credit score, so there's no need to worry. However, if you find any errors, negative items, or other discrepancies, you will need to take action.

The chapter also covers identity theft, including how fraudsters obtain your data, warning signs of identity theft, and steps to take if you become a victim. Discovering that you are a victim of identity theft or another type of credit score malfunction can be extremely stressful. It can also be costly, as it lowers your creditworthiness. Identity theft occurs when someone steals your personal information to fraudulently establish credit in your name and make unauthorized charges.

Several ways are commonly employed to produce this information:

- Obtaining discarded bills or statements
- Gaining possession of lost or stolen wallet
- Stealing your mail
- Acquiring a copy of your credit report
- Through fraudulent and deceptive internet scam

Let's get into the warning signs which should not be ignored from the early stage itself:

- Unfamiliar activity on your credit report
- Charges for account you know nothing
- Missing or unfamiliar bills
- You receive call from debt collectors

If you discover that you are victim of identity theft or some type of credit-related fraud, here are some steps to follow:

- Notify your creditors and bank immediately to discuss this issue. In case if you had a credit card lost or stolen or you find out potentially fraudulent charges on your statement, report that immediately to the bank or credit card issuer.
- Immediately contact the local police department and file a report and obtain its copy.
- Do not throw away or destroy any paperwork related to credit fraud or identity theft.
- Change your password and PIN on all Debit card, Credit card, Internet banking and Mobile banking.
- File a complaint on National Cyber Crime Reporting Portal (https://cybercrime.gov.in/).
- Hire a professional Credit Counseling Organization or Credit Counselor to assist you in this matter to resolve it.

Not all errors are worth disputing so the chapter has given information on what credit report errors are not worth disputing and what credit report are worth disputing.

Minor errors like a misspelled former employer or an outdated phone number — don't affect anyone's assessment of creditworthiness and aren't worth disputing.

The most concerning errors are those that could hurt your scores or the ones that suggest identity theft. Those include:

- Wrong account status (such as a payment mistakenly reported late when you paid on time).
- Negative information that's too old to be reported; most derogatory marks on your credit must be removed after seven years.
- An ex-spouse incorrectly listed on a loan or credit card.
- Wrong account numbers or accounts that aren't yours.

- Inaccurate credit limits or loan balances.
- Accounts you don't recognize.
- Addresses where you've never lived.

When you find errors in your credit report, what next you should do. The answer lies itself in the chapter for correcting errors.

You can use three ways to correct errors on your credit report:

1. Contact creditors or lenders directly via written communication/ mail/directly visiting them in the branch office.
2. Initiate a dispute with the appropriate credit bureau, based on which of your credit reports include errors in it.

Above two ways are a little time consuming because this needs lots of communication and other tiny details to work on, so here is a third way.

3. Hire a professional credit counseling service which will work on your behalf and they are experts in this domain so you need not worry but remember for this service they will charge you their professional fee, but it is worth paying if you do not want to take the headache of going here and there.

Further, the chapter has given details on how to contact and negotiate with your creditors as they are the one who provide data to credit bureau of their borrowers. Keep it in mind that when you negotiate with creditors, your ultimate objective is to convince them to list the account as "Paid" or "Account Closed" with each of the credit bureaus.

Let's find out some tips which will help you negotiate with creditors or collection agency:

- If you make a request for something and they are denying it or not responding to you then ask to speak with the supervisor.
- Do not agree to pay anything which you cannot afford while negotiating. Before proceeding for negotiation, keep in mind

about your financial situation and also communicate the same with creditors. Work within your confinements.

- During the negotiation process, figure out what the creditor is willing to accept and what is their bottom line. Also check with you finances how much can you stretch. It is not unreasonable to look for debt settlement or lump sum payment or through a payment plan for what you owed.
- Do not be influenced by the person you are negotiating with, even if they make threats about lawsuit.
- Always remember that successful negotiation requires several rounds of discussion, offers and counter offers, hence it is a time-consuming process and could take days or even weeks.
- If you can afford to settle your account in one go i.e., lump sum, and then you have more negotiating leverage.
- Keep it in mind that the person who is negotiating with you is a trained professional, so it is obvious that during the process he/she may use legal terminology or in writing. It is a common tactic to confuse or intimidate you, so it is better that you listen carefully and make sure you understand exactly what you are committing to. In case of any query or question which you are not able to understand, consult a credit counselor.
- Make sure whatever you ultimately agree to should be in writing, signed and dated by both the parties.

As a part of negotiation, some of the things you can ask for include:

- A lower interest rate.
- Waiver in late fees, penalties or legal fees.
- Loan to be extended or restructured, allowing you to skip one or more payments with no penalty.
- A payment plan for your current credit with no added interest or fees added in the future.
- A settlement that would include a significantly lower balance due.

- Favor the removal of negative information from the credit report.

At last, the chapter ends with a warning or caution to keep away from misconception and wrong information about your credit report and credit score as only right information and right use of that information will help you boost your credit score.

Chapter 9

The chapter focuses on credit management and future planning in your financial life. It is crucial to have a solid plan for your financial needs in the future.

First and foremost, it is important to understand your current credit situation. To do this, you should practice good money management and regularly analyze your credit. Only you know if you have money in the bank, a steady income, and whether you can cover your monthly bills.

The information on your credit report reflects your credit management habits, such as the amount you owe, your history of on-time payments, and your creditors.

The first step towards proper credit management is to thoroughly evaluate your current situation. It is also important to develop a habit of regularly evaluating and analyzing your credit utilization in your everyday life. To gain a better understanding of your credit, consider finding answers to the following questions:

- Are you paying too much interest on your home loan?
- Can you qualify for a better deal based on your current credit score?
- Are you using your credit cards in the best way possible to ensure you are not overpaying interest or damaging your credit score?
- Are you maintaining a good reputation by paying all of your bills of time?

Additionally, the chapter has covered things that can hurt your credit score and it is necessary that you can also know about it and work on it:

- Being delinquent on one or more accounts.
- The length of your credit history is short.
- You have too many ongoing accounts for credit cards or loans.
- The amount you owe on accounts is too high.
- The time since one or more late payments is too short.
- The total amount owed on credit cards is too high.
- You have too few accounts shows up as "Paid" or "Account Closed".
- You have too many accounts with balance.
- You have too many new accounts opened in the last 12 months.
- You have no credit history at all.
- You have one or more accounts that have been handed in for collection to a collection agency.
- You have too many 30–, 60–, 90–, or 120– days past due (DPD).
- Your account payment history is new and the new creditors have not yet enough information about you and your payment habit.
- You do not maintain a proper credit mix.
- Not allowing enough time to pass since your most recent account was opened.

Further, the chapter emphasizes the importance of managing your current financial habits. To ensure future financial stability, it is crucial to be mindful of your present financial choices. High credit card balances, excessive utilization of credit cards, and late payments can have a negative impact on your credit score.

Relying heavily on credit cards, especially if you have multiple cards with balances exceeding 50% of their limits, can be risky. It is advisable to maintain a separate record of your finances, including loans and credit card expenses. This allows you to track where your money is going and understand the costs associated with credit card usage, such as interest fees and penalties. By incorporating this information into your personal or family budget, you can gain a comprehensive view of your financial situation.

Seeking the assistance of a finance planner and considering your current savings, investments, and income can further support your future goals. By creating a plan based on these insights, you can better manage your finances and work towards achieving your short, medium, and long-term objectives.

The chapter also provides insights on reducing the costs associated with credit, as credit is not a freebie that comes without fees. Here, fees refer to interest rates and processing charges associated with credit cards or loans. It is advisable to research the market for the best possible deals before applying for any new credit card or loan. This will help you save on costs related to interest rates and other charges.

It is necessary to consider the costs associated with any form of credit, whether it's a loan or a credit card, before making any decisions. While it may seem tempting at first, it can lead to bitterness and overwhelming debt if not managed properly.

Before making significant purchases like a car or a home, it is important to carefully consider all aspects of finance, loans, and future commitments. The chapter emphasizes the significance of credit reports and scores when applying for a home loan, as it involves a large expense and a long-term commitment. Your credit reports, credit scores, affordability, down payment capabilities, long-term goals, and personal preferences all determine what you can qualify for.

Before searching for home loan deals, it is advisable to evaluate your current financial standing and check your credit score with all four bureaus. The recommended approach is to find a reliable home loan professional or lender who can assist you throughout the loan process and documentation. They can also help you find the best possible interest rate and home loan deal.

The chapter provides a cautionary note to not wait until the last minute, as the home loan process can be time-consuming. It is crucial to have the best credit score and credit report possible when applying for a home loan, as your credit score directly impacts the interest rate and loan deal you qualify for.

Additionally, the chapter covers some information on applying for low-fee and low-interest credit cards, as they are widely used for cashless transactions. It advises careful shopping and comparison of offers, interest rates, and charges, particularly for individuals with average or below-average credit.

For those with excellent credit scores, the benefit of zero percent interest rates for a year and no annual fees can be enjoyed. However, it is essential to thoroughly read all documents and service terms and conditions, ensuring a clear understanding of all fees, charges, and penalty clauses.

If you have plans to purchase your own home or car in the future or are seeking a credit card, it becomes necessary to have a "Good" or "Excellent" credit score. This highlights the importance of starting on the right foot in the present to shape your future.

Chapter 10

The chapter focuses on the basics of credit rectification companies and how they can assist individuals in need of professional help. These companies, also known as credit counseling companies, provide guidance and support in understanding credit reports and scores.

To begin, let's clarify what credit rectification companies are. They are companies that offer credit counseling services to help individuals with various credit-related issues.

A credit rectification company consists of a team of experts who specialize in determining the most suitable methods for managing your credit. They can provide assistance with money debt management, debt consolidation, and budgeting. These professionals possess domain knowledge and expertise in the field, enabling them to offer valuable guidance and support.

Credit Rectification Company works as an intermediary between you and your creditors to resolve your credit related issues. They also have role of –

- Answer questions about various options for relief.
- Assisting you in identifying the right solutions for your needs.
- Helping you eliminate your existing credit card balances.
- Eliminating the hassle of collection calls. Once you enroll, you can pick up the phone and tell them you are working with Credit Rectification Company. Collectors must then go through them.
- Providing you resources to build financial literacy.
- Teaching you how to budget and manage credit effectively.
- Helping you establish long–term financial stability.

One of the most common problems people face is not knowing the appropriate steps to take when they find themselves in serious debt, regardless of the underlying reasons. Often, individuals fail to realize the severity of the problem until it has escalated, and they may even choose to ignore it, which only exacerbates the situation. Seeking help from credit rectification services can be beneficial in such cases.

A credit counseling session typically takes place over the phone. During the session, the counselor will gather information about your financial situation. This includes details about your income, expenses, debts, and any other relevant financial obligations. The purpose of this information-gathering process is to gain a comprehensive understanding of your financial standing and challenges.

To start the process, the Credit Analyst will ask for some basic information about your financial situation. This includes:

- Current debts, including secured loans like your mortgage or auto loan
- Current balances on your credit cards, as well as the APR on each account
- Other obligations, such as payday loans and unpaid EMIs

Next, the credit analyst will retrieve your credit report from one or all four credit bureaus for analysis. After thoroughly examining your credit report, the analyst will identify problem areas and discuss them with you. They will then provide recommendations on how to address these issues, offering the best possible solutions.

If you agree to proceed with the rectification work after being informed of the professional fees involved, the credit rectification company will initiate the necessary steps. They will communicate with your creditors, aiming to achieve three primary goals:

- Make sure your creditor is agreeing to accept the payment you make
- Reduce charges, penalties and legal charges, if any
- Negotiate with interest rate and principal amount

If you find yourself in serious debt or facing significant credit problems, it is important not to hesitate in seeking help from a credit rectification company. Doing so can help you address and rectify your issues before they spiral out of control.

Seeking professional assistance with your financial problems can be an incredibly valuable investment. Following the advice and guidance provided by the credit rectification company can lead you towards resolving your financial challenges.

Additionally, the chapter aims to dispel some myths associated with credit rectification companies.

Chapter 11

The chapter aims to address frequently asked questions and provide expert knowledge on credit-related topics. It offers expert advice and credit-related information that many consumers may be unaware of.

While reading the chapter, you will come across various layers of credit information. It is ultimately up to you how you choose to utilize this information and apply it to your own financial situation.

Summary of Improove Your Credit Health

Chapter 1

The chapter is more focused on credit repair and the need to credit repair. Furthermore, the chapter is headed to provide you with more insight into whether credit repair has an impact on your credit report or not.

This also includes how credit repair works and how credit repair service works to provide you with the glance of both to understand the basics and when you require repair, you would know the process, its time frame, and whether you want to go by your own or hire a credit repair professional.

This further includes the easier and simpler process you can do for yourself such as,

- Do not let your bad credit score keep you away from getting credit.
- Make arrangements to pay your bills when you are on break.
- Be tech-savvy.
- Pay your bills as soon as you get them.
- Spare a time and day to pay your repayment.
- Record your financial obligations on a calendar.

This chapter also focuses on the emotion attached to money and how you can overcome the negative emotions and practice some basic habits which can help you to manage a good credit score such as,

- Be patient and take a break.
- Avoid making excuses.
- Reward yourself without affecting your credit.
- Work on your emotional response to debt and money.
- Be practical with your debt and control your emotions.
- Seek help if you need it.

You never know which leads to a credit score drop a bit or huge but when you have certain habits in day-to-day life; you can have a good to excellent credit score. Some of your actions can affect your credit scores like repossession, foreclosure, and settlement. Before considering these actions, always check their pros and cons.

Being a student when you have an education loan is a good start to your credit life journey. However, a single wrong step can ruin your start of good credit history whereas if you have taken good care in repayment then the outcome is excellent in a form of good and neat-o-clean credit history.

The tips listed in this chapter can make the college years a credit booster instead of a credit disaster when you have an education loan.

There are some reasons why you need to consider going for credit repair such as,

- Out of four credit reports, there is a chance one has an error.
- Chance to boost credit score if you repair your credit.
- Refinance becomes easy.
- Negotiation power for credit card interest rate.
- Easy to get new finance.
- Be home loan eligible.
- Take advantage of offers on a car loan.
- Say bye to collection action.
- Save you from risky alternative finance options.

While dealing with a professional credit repair service, you should check some basics so that the process becomes easy and not nerve-wracking. Look out for credit repair companies but be aware of credit repair scams.

There are certain indications that you may need credit counseling or credit repair including:

- You are not getting a new loan or credit card.
- You avoid phone or emails or knocking on doors because you are being harassed by collection agencies.
- You find that your credit report contains an item that you do not know or is incorrect.
- You have no idea how you will repay your bills and loans. You do not know where to start.

When you are looking for an ideal credit repair company, you would have certain questions in your mind. This chapter has as many answers to your questions to resolve your doubts.

It is wise that before heading to credit repair, you check the options based on your financial situation to get maximum output.

Chapter 2

This chapter focuses on the rectification of credit report errors as your credit repair is 90% repairing or rectifying the credit report errors. The chapter provides you with glance at the most common types of credit report errors and what you need to check when you have your credit report in your hand.

Some best things you can keep in mind are:

- Correct errors and make sure your report is error-free.
- Check your report has positive information.
- Avoid unrealistic credit report suggestions.
- Pay your credit card bills on time.
- Pay your EMIs without a miss.
- Keep and maintain limited credit cards and other credit accounts.

- Keep credit limit below requirement.
- Apply for new credit only if you require it.

Further, the chapter lists out the common credit report errors which need to be rectified and how you should review your credit report, and what to look at in each section. The chapter has elaborate information on disputing incorrect and inaccurate information from your credit report and how it will work.

It is important to dispute inaccurate and incomplete information but at the same time, it is also important that your credit report have positive information and positive account histories.

Besides, creditors also want to see stability in your credit report. You may check the details to add like:

- Your current employment
- Your previous employment
- Your current residence
- Your previous residence
- Your telephone numbers
- Your date of birth
- Your KYC details

It is good practice that you check your credit report either from one bureau or all bureaus regularly which can help you to safeguard from identity theft and if you have any major purchase plan then it is good that beforehand you check your credit report to find the accurate information.

The chapter has a detailed explanation to safeguard your identity so that you would not have to face the problem later. You should be alert as there are some ways which can lead to stealing your identity such as,

- Stealing your wallet.
- A former known person can gather your information out of personal grudges and may use it to attempt an act of revenge.

- Snatching pre-approved credit card or loan offers form from trash or recycle bin.
- Ordering unauthorized credit reports posing potential employer.
- Illegal tapping of a computer by a dishonest employee at a business you have provided information.
- Looking over your shoulder at phones and ATMs to gather PINs.
- Breaking computer systems.
- Using telemarketing schemes.
- Using personal information, you have shared on the internet.
- Using information, you have shared on the app and providing some access to your mobile.

You need to take care of your KYC and other identities so that they cannot be in the hands of a fraudster. The chapter has given some action to take if you find that you are an identity theft victim.

Going forward the chapter has provided some strategies for credit repair which can help you in boosting or maintain your credit score.

- Keep your finance organized.
- Do frequent self-credit-check to track your process and set short-term goals.
- Double-check your details.
- Don't think a small difference in credit score or loan interest rate is fine.
- If you want to go for credit repair, keep some points handy to avoid any last moment rush or mistake.
- Auto set your EMIs or bills.

Chapter 3

It is heartbreaking when you have to face collection agencies and many of you do not know how to deal with them. But this chapter has everything that you are looking for while dealing with collection agencies.

You need to understand how a collection agency works and know your rights when you are approached by collection agents or collection agencies.

Under the Recovery of Debts and Bankruptcy Act, 1993, there are certain rights a customer can use. Unlike in foreign countries, in India, there is nothing like debt verification. However, you can ask for certain details such as,

- The amount of the debt.
- The name of creditors for whom the current debt is currently owned.
- The copy of a sanctioned letter of your debt.
- Their authentic and valid ID address proof.
- The authority to collect the debt from you by the creditor.

There are debt collection standards in India to which banks and collections need to adhere.

1. Customer deserves to be treated with dignity

    - Communication with you
    - Harassment or abuse

2. False or misleading representation
3. Customer's privacy
4. Unfair practices

The chapter has covered certain points that you need to keep in mind when you are approached by a collection agent.

You can use strategies listed here while negotiating with them such as,

- Offering a lump-sum settlement.
- Offering to make payments.
- Stopping collection agent to contact you.
- Negotiating with a collection agency.

Keep in mind that when the collection agency and bank failed to collect the debt, they will consider taking legal action against you. In other scenarios when you do not show up or do not answer, then perhaps they think of legal action against you which reflects as suit-filed in your credit report and ruins your entire credit history and credit.

Chapter 4

When you are done with credit repair, the next process is to rebuild credit from scratch. Initially, the process seems difficult but not impossible. This chapter is going to explain the entire credit rebuilding process which you can take into consideration.

A few inexpensive ways you can consider while you are into the credit rebuilding process are:

- Secured credit card
- Secured bank loan
- Becomes authorized user
- Use a co-signer to get a credit

Before checking any option to rebuild, you always need to list out its pros and cons. When you are sure that you can take this option ahead, then only you have to work on that option. Else search for other options.

Furthermore, you have to work on minimizing the negative impact of true information in your credit report by following:

- Using written statements
- Settling the dues fully
- Resolve past dues

When you have a good credit history, you need to maintain and work on the good habits which can give you great sense to maintain it so that there is no repetition of having bad credit history again.

You also need to check why your credit history got damaged because when you know the reasons, you can know possible solutions to handle that.

When you cannot take up the credit rebuilding on your own, it is wise you should consider getting credit rebuilding help

- Credit Counseling Organization
- Credit Monitoring Organization
- Protecting your good credit
- Change the role of money in your life
- How to be smarter with money
- Avoiding financial problems in future
- Minimizing the damage while facing money problem
- Contact your creditors or banks

Chapter 5

Credit repair is not only helping individuals but also helping banks and the economy in many ways. The chapter focuses on credit repair organization and its detailed overview.

One can have a good career in credit repair by having it as a business. The chapter is giving you details on the scope of the credit repair business in India and how you can take it forward.

- A credit repair business:
- Is recession-free.
- Better prosper in a tough economy.
- Provides an opportunity to serve the nation and society.
- Creates passive income.
- Is a great supplement to your existing business and clients.

In earlier times, the credit reporting system was very different and there was hardly any scope for credit repair but in the current situation, every bank would like to have a credit healthy profile for their borrowers and the need for credit repair is tremendous.

So, when you are looking to have a credit repair business, you need to know some basics which can help you to understand credit repair and also need to work on the skill to deal with clients. The most important factor to handle the credit repair business is to educate clients on credit repair. Creating awareness is the best way to indulge in the credit repair business.

Further, you need to understand how to tackle the credit repair business, and know about the Credit Information Companies (Regulation) Act, 2005. The book further has the details on this act and its amendments.

Unique Business Opportunity in a form of Credit Repair with No Recession & Competition

If you have a poor credit score or a poorly maintained credit history, you would not be allowed a credit.

Do you have a question in mind then what to do? Is there a Credit Repair in India? Is there any law related to it? Is it worth seeking help for Credit Repair? The Answer for all is yes and positive. Though you can do Credit Repair by yourself, seeking help from Credit Repair Company will provide you a way better benefit as Credit Repair involves lots of process, lots of paperwork, knowledge, time and patience to get a positive result.

There are some myths surrounding Credit Repair due to unawareness about it such as there is no concept like credit repair in India, those who do this are fraud, Credit Repair Companies are a scam, It is better to do credit fix by yourself etc. but these are just myths without any sense.

Credit Repair is a process of fixing poor credit standing that may have deteriorated for a variety of reasons. Consumer's credit scores are based on a number of factors, including whether they pay bills on time or not as missing payments can hurt their credit score and, in turn, make it more difficult for them to obtain other credit such as home loans or car loans etc. In India, all banks have different terms and condition for offering loan and credit card but the common thing every financial institution is looking for a neat-o-clean Credit History and error free Credit Report with 750+ Credit Score, and they rely heavily on this to make lending decision hence, it is absolutely necessary that you maintain it and when you fail in the above conditions, start mending it and take a help of Credit Repair Service. Credit Repair is not just only to help individuals to improve Credit Score but also to help the economy of the country as the economy relies on the responsible behavior of citizens in maintaining credit liability. The more debt every citizen holds, the more it can damage the economy of the country as well.

Apoorvaa Foundation is the pioneer in this unique concept of Credit Repair in India thus, giving a new financial line in banking and finance field. Credit Repair experts are knowledgeable about laws that banks and credit bureaus follow. They understand how the Credit Information Companies (Regulation) Act, 2005 work. They can use law in a better way by understanding the actual problem and help you with legal solutions. Apoorvaa is also a pioneer of Credit Awareness Seminar with an aim to help society and banks to know the depth of Credit Report and Credit Bureaus which mean more and more people will be financially educated to handle their own credit. Mr. Apurva Bhagat, a Founder and President of Apoorvaa Foundation, himself conducting the Credit Awareness Seminars and extending his skill of Credit Analysis to people who need to work on their credit issue.

"Our motive behind Credit Repair is to build credit healthy nation and with this, we are moving ahead to extend our services in PAN India Level and to fulfill this at present we have 108 branches in 90 cities of 21 states," said Apurva Bhagat, Founder and President of Apoorvaa Foundation.

Credit Repair is also important when it comes to dealing or negotiating with banks or collection agencies as not everybody is professional to tackle the situation but the company who deals with Credit Repairs; they have professionals with the skills and knowledge to handle customers, banks and collection agencies. Furthermore, the Credit Repair is needed for those who are facing a bad credit score, poor credit history, victim of identity theft and inaccurate data loaded in the credit report. You must know that the recent ongoing pandemic has taken a toll on everyone's financial situation. At the same time it has also affected credit score. The current scenario is different from earlier times, as in earlier times personal judgment was part of checking creditworthiness while today it is thoroughly based on Credit Report and Credit History. Now-a-days the job hiring process also involves credit report scrutiny to judge the creditworthiness of candidates.

The agony is that people are not aware about the importance of Credit Repair and at the same time the business opportunity is also untouched here in this field. The door for Credit Repair Business is open to all, due to skyrocketing credit requirements in day to day life to maintain the need for individual and business expansion for entrepreneurs, we can say it is recession free and no more competition to handle and expand it. Moreover, you can have ease of involvement in this with minimum investment and high return if you pursue it with due diligence and perseverance.

Apoorvaa – Credit Repair Lawyer of India is on a mission to create credit awareness, make people credit healthy and help the bank to reduce their NPA

To walk an extra mile, Apoorvaa – Credit Repair Lawyer of India has made 2022 stupendous year with launch of two books, "The Indian Credit Reporting System" and "Improove Your Credit Health."

The main objective behind launch of The Indian Credit Reporting System and Improove Your Credit Health is to provide accurate and genuine information to all those looking to mend their credit, want to analyze credit reports and improve their credit score. Because the refraining attitude towards credit report analysis and periodical checking leads to incorrect data, inaccurate data or identity theft popping out from one's credit report and ignoring all these not only keep one away from taking credit cards or loans but also toll on one's reputation.

These books are concise in comprehensible language aiming to provide hand-on knowledge on basics of credit, credit reporting system, credit score, credit report, credit analysis, dealing with credit repair, credit rebuilding and credit repair business in depth.

"People can access every tiny detail of credit repair. Thus, we have launched two books, The Indian Credit Reporting System and Improove Your Credit Health. Our motive is always to support customers, banks, and society because financial health is significant not only for people, but also for the economy of the country. With every new step, we ensure to tackle credit repair issues in a more advanced way", said Apurva Bhagat – Founder & President Apoorvaa – Credit Repair Lawyer of India.

When anyone is surrounded by misconceptions and myths, one can no longer access the right information and always stay in dilemma. Being in Credit Repair for more than 15 years, Apoorvaa Foundation – Credit Repair Lawyer of India knows better how people and financial professionals are lack of awareness or required knowledge on credit repair.

Downfall of one's credit score and negative issues in credit reports fuelled by many reasons. Process of fixing and tackling all these issues/ reasons is called a credit repair. The reasons could be anything from late repayment to missing payment, but these can hurt your credit score and make it difficult for you to get a new credit.

Over time, the Apoorvaa has become more adept at earning customers' faith in its brand. Trusted by its customers, it has expanded throughout the country in India. Customers' willingness to use the Apoorvaa as a reference for credit repair demonstrates established credibility of the organization. The Apoorvaa's forward thinking has left an indelible impression on customers since it helps people and businesses establishing good credit.

An advocate of knowledge sharing, Apoorvaa – Credit Repair Lawyer of India has started creating awareness in the form of Credit Awareness Seminars for the general public and bankers since its inception. To educate and empower people in financial education, Mr. Apurva Bhagat – Founder & President Apoorvaa – Credit Repair Lawyer of India has conducted more than 600 seminars. Due to the 2020 pandemic, they have switched to webinar and continued their mission to empower people. But this year, the credit awareness seminar restarted.

Additionally, they have launched a banker's helpline to address queries of bankers.

There are several ways in which the organization's efforts have benefited society, including resolving NPA problems at financial institutions, improving consumers' credit standing, and helping MSME to extend their financial requirements by tackling their CIBIL Rank issues. Divya Bhaskar newspaper has recognized these efforts. They have started featuring their articles to provide credit repair knowledge.

Apoorvaa – Credit Repair Lawyer of India, a novel service provider, is accelerating day-by-day to fulfill its mission to build a credit healthy nation with tireless efforts and hard work. To applaud these efforts, Blindwink has selected the entire team for India Excellence Awards 2022 under stewardship of Mr. Apurva Bhagat. The award ceremony was organized on 06th November 2022 at Taj Bangalore.

Awards are reinforcing tools to anyone or any company for motivation that have a direct impact on enhanced performance, productivity and commitment to keep going with their phenomenal work. It is an ode to keep going in 2023 for the entire team of Apoorvaa. Before closing 2022, Apoorvaa – Credit Repair Lawyer of India has one more breakthrough to nominate for National Legal Excellence Award 2022. It will be organized in 2023 by Assocham. The awards and nominations demonstrate that the Apoorvaa – Credit Repair Lawyer of India has earned the confidence of its target market and established a strong presence in the eyes of credit repair customers.

With a vision to provide credit repair services in PAN India, Apoorvaa – Credit Repair Lawyer of India made its presence in 108 branches in 90 cities of 21 states. Mr. Apurva Bhagat has a clear vision on growth projection in the market. With his vast experience in finance, taxation, project financing and retail sector, he believes that credit score and credit rank have a significant role while applying for any form of credit. He further added that lack of awareness makes credit journeys more difficult, but he ensured that his team works on every possible measure to spread credit repair awareness.

Unlocking Business Success: The Dual Role of CIBIL Rank for Entrepreneurs and CA Credit Repair Opportunities

Apoorvaa – Credit Repair Lawyer of India, recently sponsored and participated in the Anant National Conference organized by the Bhilwara Branch of CIRC of ICAI. The platform saw thought-provoking discussions on various topics indirectly associated with the Indian economy and MSMEs as CA. Aniket Talati – ICAI President, and Mr Satish Marathe – RBI Director, both expressed their aspirations to benefit the MSMEs and society.

During the event, CA. Aniket Talati – ICAI President launched a book titled "The Indian Credit Reporting System" and Mr. Satish Marathe – RBI Director launched a book titled "Improove Your Credit Health", both authored by Advocate Apurva Bhagat.

Furthermore, Mr Satish Marathe – RBI Director, has added that once your Credit Score and CIBIL Rank are affected, you may not be eligible to access credit. He appreciatively acknowledged Apoorvaa – Credit Repair Lawyer, for helping people and MSMEs to be credit healthy and contributing to the economy.

2023 is a breakthrough year for Apoorvaa – Credit Repair Lawyer of India as they have extended their horizon by associating with CA Fraternity and started Credit Awareness Seminar with ICAI branches. These seminars will add value to them on how credit bureaus work and the extensive impact they can have on individuals and businesses in India, considering CAs are directly associated with MSMEs.

CIBIL Rank plays a vital role for MSMEs because as a business owner, the constant goal is to expand the business, and financial resources play a crucial role in that expansion. Whether seeking government loans or bank loans, the key factor is the CIBIL Rank, a vital indicator of creditworthiness. The Company Credit Report (CCR) holds essential information such as past loans, credit obligations, credit utilization ratio, and credit history inquiries.

The CIBIL Rank is a single number derived from the CCR, ranging from 1 to 10, with 1 being the best rank achievable. Regardless of the business type (proprietorship, partnership, Pvt Ltd, or LLP), checking the company credit report at least once a year is essential, whether in need of a loan or not.

Several factors influence the Company Credit Report and CIBIL Rank, including the length of credit history, credit utilization ratio, repayment history, outstanding debts, and the company's size and age. The major parameters considered are past repayment behavior and credit utilization, both of which significantly impact the CIBIL Rank.

Delinquencies, such as old current balances, outstanding balances, wrong reported loans or overdraft statuses, duplicate entries, and closed accounts still shown as open, can negatively affect the CIBIL Rank to go between 7 to 10, making it challenging to secure loans. Correcting these issues requires strategic efforts but may take time, so it is best not to delay the process until the need for a loan arises.

Although the CIBIL Rank is now available for companies with current credit exposure of up to Rs. 50 crores, its non-availability is not detrimental. Nevertheless, maintaining a strong CIBIL Rank and company credit report is essential for faster and hassle-free access to loans. A favorable rank inspires confidence in banks and lenders, leading to quicker and more affordable credit options. Additionally, a good CIBIL Rank improves chances of negotiating favorable interest rates, benefiting business owners in various ways.

Advocate Apurva Bhagat, Founder and President Apoorvaa – Credit Repair Lawyer of India, firmly says that CIBIL Rank and Commercial Credit Report is a 360° business analysis of any company to understand its creditworthiness. With his decade of experience in finance, taxation, retail loan, and project finance, he emphasizes understanding commercial credit reports and CIBIL Rank for MSMEs.

Apoorvaa – Credit Repair Lawyer of India, a novel service provider in credit rectification, focuses on the financial health of MSMEs by tackling their CIBIL Rank issues. Currently Apoorvaa – Credit Repair Lawyer of India is assisting Individuals and MSMEs in becoming credit-savvy and subsequently credit healthy and wealthy.

On the inaugural ceremony speech of Anant National Conference at Bhilwara, CA. Anitket Talati – ICAI President focused on new developments for CA Fraternity and expanding the horizons of their practices.

"The credit repair business is a new practice area for CA Fraternity, serving the purpose of CA. Aniket Talati to expand the horizon of practicing as CAs are directly associated with MSMEs. They will help MSMEs to boost their financial horizon, and assist banks in reducing their NPA. Additionally, the credit repair business helps them to support social-economy causes." said Advocate Apurva Bhagat Founder and President Apoorvaa – Credit Repair Lawyer of India, at Anant National Conference at Bhilwara.

"Apoorvaa – Credit Repair Lawyer of India plays a significant role in contributing to the economy as they works towards strengthening MSMEs through their rectification", said Mr. Satish Marathe – RBI Director, while discussing the topic of MSMEs, Future of Indian Economy at Bhilwara.

Media Coverage Links

Sr. No.	Newspaper/ Magazine	Links
1	**ANI 2023**	https://www.aninews.in/news/business/business/ unlocking-businesssuccess-the-dual-role-of-cibil-rank-for-entrepreneurs-and-ca-credit-repairopportuniti es20230810161042/#:~:text=CIBIL%20Rank%20p-lays%20a%20vital,a%20vital%20indicator%20of%20 creditworthiness
2	**Zee5 2023**	https://www.zee5.com/articles/unlocking-business-success-the-dual-role-ofcibil-rank-for-entrepreneurs-and-ca-credit-repair-opportunities
3	**Business Standard 2023**	https://www.business-standard.com/content/press-releases-ani/unlockingbusiness-success-the-dual-role-of-cibil-rank-for-entrepreneurs-and-ca-creditrepair-opportunities-123081000541_1.html
4	**The Print 2023**	https://theprint.in/ani-press-releases/ unlocking-business-success-the-dualrole-of-cibil-rank-for-entrepreneurs-and-ca-credit-repairopportunities/1708948/
5	**Daily Hunt 2023**	https://m.dailyhunt.in/news/india/english/ ani67917250816496966-epaperanieng/unlocking +business+success+the+dual+role+of+cibil+rank+f or+entrepreneurs+and+ca+credit+repair+opportu nities-newsidn526838524?listname=newspaperLa-nding&index=24&topicIndex=4&mode=

Sr. No.	Newspaper/ Magazine	Links
6	Latestly 2023	https://www.latestly.com/agency-news/business-news-unlocking-businesssuccess-the-dual-role-of-cibil-rank-for-entrepreneurs-and-ca-credit-repairopportunities-5330962.html
7	Lokmat Times 2023	https://www.lokmattimes.com/business/unlocking-business-success-the-dualrole-of-cibil-rank-for-entrepreneurs-and-ca-credit-repair/
8	Herald Globe 2023	https://www.heraldglobe.com/news/273927529/unlocking-business-successthe-dual-role-of-cibil-rank-for-entrepreneurs-and-ca-credit-repairopportunities
9	South East Asia Post 2023	https://www.southeastasiapost.com/news/273927529/unlocking-businesssuccess-the-dual-role-of-cibil-rank-for-entrepreneurs-and-ca-credit-repairopportunities
10	Kualalumpur News 2023	https://www.kualalumpurnews.net/news/273927529/unlocking-businesssuccess-the-dual-role-of-cibil-rank-for-entrepreneurs-and-ca-credit-repairopportunities
11	Bangladesh Sun 2023	https://www.bangladeshsun.com/news/273927529/unlocking-businesssuccess-the-dual-role-of-cibil-rank-for-entrepreneurs-and-ca-credit-repairopportunities
12	Kolkata News 2023	https://www.kolkatanews.net/news/273927529/unlocking-business-successthe-dual-role-of-cibil-rank-for-entrepreneurs-and-ca-credit-repairopportunities
13	Bangkok News 2023	https://www.bangkoknews.net/news/273927529/unlocking-business-successthe-dual-role-of-cibil-rank-for-entrepreneurs-and-ca-credit-repairopportunities
14	New Delhi News 2023	https://www.newdelhinews.net/news/273927529/unlocking-businesssuccess-the-dual-role-of-cibil-rank-for-entrepreneurs-and-ca-credit-repairopportunities
15	Mumbai News 2023	https://www.mumbainews.net/news/273927529/unlocking-business-successthe-dual-role-of-cibil-rank-for-entrepreneurs-and-ca-credit-repairopportunities
16	Big News Network 2023	https://www.bignewsnetwork.com/news/273927529/unlocking-businesssuccess-the-dual-role-of-cibil-rank-for-entrepreneurs-and-ca-credit-repairopportunities

Sr. No.	Newspaper/ Magazine	Links
17	**Brunei News 2023**	https://www.bruneinews.net/news/273927529/ unlocking-business-successthe-dual-role-of-cibil-rank-for-entrepreneurs-and-ca-credit-repairopportunities
18	**Srilanka Source 2023**	https://www.srilankasource.com/news/273927529/ unlocking-businesssuccess-the-dual-role-of-cibil-rank-for-entrepreneurs-and-ca-credit-repairopportunities
19	**Nepal National 2023**	https://www.nepalnational.com/news/273927529/ unlocking-businesssuccess-the-dual-role-of-cibil-rank-for-entrepreneurs-and-ca-credit-repairopportunities
20	**Indias News 2023**	https://www.indiasnews.net/news/273927529/ unlocking-business-successthe-dual-role-of-cibil-rank-for-entrepreneurs-and-ca-credit-repairopportunities
21	**Cambodian Times 2023**	https://www.cambodiantimes.com/news/273927529/ unlocking-businesssuccess-the-dual-role-of-cibil-rank-for-entrepreneurs-and-ca-credit-repairopportunities
22	**Indonesia News 2023**	https://www.indonesianews.net/news/273927529/ unlocking-businesssuccess-the-dual-role-of-cibil-rank-for-entrepreneurs-and-ca-credit-repairopportunities
23	**Malaysia News 2023**	https://www.malaysianews.net/news/273927529/ unlocking-business-successthe-dual-role-of-cibil-rank-for-entrepreneurs-and-ca-credit-repairopportunities
24	**The Cambodia News 2023**	https://www.thecambodianews.net/news/273927529/ unlocking-businesssuccess-the-dual-role-of-cibil-rank-for-entrepreneurs-and-ca-credit-repairopportunities
25	**Nepal News 2023**	https://www.nepalnews.net/news/273927529/ unlocking-business-successthe-dual-role-of-cibil-rank-for-entrepreneurs-and-ca-credit-repairopportunities
26	**Srilankan News 2023**	https://www.srilankannews.net/news/273927529/ unlocking-businesssuccess-the-dual-role-of-cibil-rank-for-entrepreneurs-and-ca-credit-repairopportunities
27	**Pakistan News 2023**	https://www.pakistannews.net/news/273927529/ unlocking-business-successthe-dual-role-of-cibil-rank-for-entrepreneurs-and-ca-credit-repairopportunities

Sr. No.	Newspaper/ Magazine	Links
28	**Loas News 2023**	https://www.laosnews.net/news/273927529/unlocking-business-success-thedual-role-of-cibil-rank-for-entrepreneurs-and-ca-credit-repair-opportunities
29	**Indian News Network 2023**	https://www.indiannewsnetwork.net/news/unlocking-business-success-thedual-role-of-cibil-rank-for-entrepreneurs-and-ca-cr
30	**West Bengal Khabar 2023**	https://www.WestBengalKhabar.in/news/unlocking-business-success-thedual-role-of-cibil-rank-for-entrepreneurs-and-ca-credit-repairopportuniti es20230810161034/
31	**Vanakkam Tamil Nadu 2023**	https://www.VanakkamTamilnadu.com/news/unlocking-business-success-thedual-role-of-cibil-rank-for-entrepreneurs-and-ca-credit-repairopportuniti es20230810161034/
32	**UP Today 2023**	https://www.UPtoday.news/news/unlocking-business-success-the-dual-roleof-cibil-rank-for-entrepreneurs-and-ca-credit-repairopportunities20230810161034/
33	**Telangana Journal 2023**	https://www.Telanganajournal.in/news/unlocking-business-success-the-dualrole-of-cibil-rank-for-entrepreneurs-and-ca-credit-repairopportuniti es20230810161034/
34	**South India News 2023**	https://www.SouthIndiaNews.in/news/unlocking-business-success-the-dualrole-of-cibil-rank-for-entrepreneurs-and-ca-credit-repairopportuniti es20230810161034/
35	**Punjab Live 2023**	https://www.PunjabLive.news/news/unlocking-business-success-the-dualrole-of-cibil-rank-for-entrepreneurs-and-ca-credit-repairopportunities20230810161034/
36	**Odisha Post 2023**	https://www.OdishaPost.news/news/unlocking-business-success-the-dualrole-of-cibil-rank-for-entrepreneurs-and-ca-credit-repairopportuniti es20230810161034/

Sr. No.	Newspaper/ Magazine	Links
37	**North East Times 2023**	https://www.NorthEastTimes.in/news/unlocking-business-success-the-dualrole-of-cibil-rank-for-entrepreneurs-and-ca-credit-repairopportunities20230810161034/
38	**Maharashtra Samachar 2023**	https://www.MaharashtraSamachar.com/news/unlocking-business-successthe-dual-role-of-cibil-rank-for-entrepreneurs-and-ca-credit-repairopportunities20230810161034/
39	**Madhya Pradesh Chronicle 2023**	https://www.MadhyaPradeshChronicle.com/news/unlocking-businesssuccess-the-dual-role-of-cibil-rank-for-entrepreneurs-and-ca-credit-repairopportunities20230810161034/
40	**Kashmir News Line 2023**	https://www.KashmirNewsline.in/news/unlocking-business-success-the-dualrole-of-cibil-rank-for-entrepreneurs-and-ca-credit-repairopportunities20230810161034/
41	**Kashmir Breaking News 2022**	https://www.KashmirBreakingNews.com/news/unlocking-business-successthe-dual-role-of-cibil-rank-for-entrepreneurs-and-ca-credit-repairopportunities20230810161034/
42	**Karnataka Live 2022**	https://www.KarnatakaLive.in/news/unlocking-business-success-the-dualrole-of-cibil-rank-for-entrepreneurs-and-ca-credit-repairopportunities20230810161034/
43	**Jharkhand Times 2022**	https://www.JharkhandTimes.in/news/unlocking-business-success-the-dualrole-of-cibil-rank-for-entrepreneurs-and-ca-credit-repairopportunities20230810161034/
44	**Indian Economic Observer 2023**	https://www.IndianEconomicObserver.com/news/unlocking-business-successthe-dual-role-of-cibil-rank-for-entrepreneurs-and-ca-credit-repairopportunities20230810161034/

Sr. No.	Newspaper/ Magazine	Links
45	**Himachal Patrika 2023**	https://www.HimachalPatrika.com/news/unlocking-business-success-thedual-role-of-cibil-rank-for-entrepreneurs-and-ca-credit-repairopportunities20230810161034/
46	**Haryana Today 2023**	https://www.HaryanaToday.in/news/unlocking-business-success-the-dualrole-of-cibil-rank-for-entrepreneurs-and-ca-credit-repairopportunities20230810161034/
47	**Gujarat Varta 2023**	https://www.GujaratVarta.com/news/unlocking-business-success-the-dualrole-of-cibil-rank-for-entrepreneurs-and-ca-credit-repairopportunities20230810161034/
48	**Gujarat Samachar 2023**	https://www.GujaratSamachar.news/news/unlocking-business-success-thedual-role-of-cibil-rank-for-entrepreneurs-and-ca-credit-repairopportunities20230810161034/
49	**Delhi Live News 2023**	https://www.DelhiLiveNews.in/news/unlocking-business-success-the-dualrole-of-cibil-rank-for-entrepreneurs-and-ca-credit-repairopportunities20230810161034/
50	**Chhattisgarh Today 2023**	https://www.ChhattisgarhToday.in/news/unlocking-business-success-thedual-role-of-cibil-rank-for-entrepreneurs-and-ca-credit-repairopportunities20230810161034/
51	**Bihar Times 2023**	https://www.BiharTimes.news/news/unlocking-business-success-the-dualrole-of-cibil-rank-for-entrepreneurs-and-ca-credit-repairopportunities20230810161034/
52	**Bihar 24x7 2023**	https://www.Bihar24x7.com/news/unlocking-business-success-the-dual-roleof-cibil-rank-for-entrepreneurs-and-ca-credit-repairopportunities20230810161034/

Sr. No.	Newspaper/ Magazine	Links
53	**Andhra Pradesh Mirror 2023**	https://www.AndhraPradeshMirror.com/news/ unlocking-business-successthe-dual-role-of-cibil-rank-for-entrepreneurs-and-ca-credit-repairopportuniti es20230810161034/
54	**World News Network 2023**	https://www.worldnewsnetwork.net/news/unlocking-business-success-thedual-role-of-cibil-rank-for-entrepreneurs-and-ca-credit-repairopportuniti es20230810161034/
55	**ANI 2022**	https://www.aninews.in/news/business/business/ apoorvaa-credit-repair-lawyer-of-india-is-on-a-mission-to-create-credit-awareness-make-people-credit-healthy-amp-help-banks-reduce-their-npa20221-228183632/
56	**Zee5 2022**	https://www.zee5.com/articles/apoorvaa-credit-repair-lawyer-of-india-is-on-a-mission-to-create-credit-awareness-make-people-credit-healthy-help-banks-reduce-their-npa
57	**Business Standard 2022**	https://www.business-standard.com/content/ press-releases-ani/apoorvaa-credit-repair-lawyer-of-india-is-on-a-mission-to-create-credit-awareness-make-people-credit-healthy-help-banks-reduce-their-npa-122122801006_1.html
58	**The Print 2022**	https://theprint.in/ani-press-releases/apoorvaa-credit-repair-lawyer-of-india-is-on-a-mission-to-create-credit-awareness-make-people-credit-healthy-help-banks-reduce-their-npa/1286717/
59	**Daily Hunt 2022**	https://m.dailyhunt.in/news/india/english/ani679172 50816496966-epaper-anieng/apoorvaa+credit+repair+lawyer+of+india+is+on+a+mission+to+create+credit+awareness+make+people+credit+healthy+help+banks+reduce+their+npa-newsid-n456558452?listname= newspaperLanding&topic=business&index=1&topic Index=4&mode=pwa&action=click

Sr. No.	Newspaper/ Magazine	Links
60	Latestly 2022	https://www.latestly.com/agency-news/business-news-apoorvaa-credit-repair-lawyer-of-india-is-on-a-mission-to-create-credit-awareness-make-people-credit-healthy-help-banks-reduce-their-npa-4644179.html
61	Economic Times 2022	https://www.economictimes.com/blindwink-announces-the-winners-of-india-excellence-awards-2022/articleshow/95609616.cms
62	Times of India 2022	https://www.timesofindia.com/blindwink-announces-the-winners-of-india-excellence-awards-2022/articleshow/95609614.cms
63	Mumbai Mirror 2022	https://mumbaimirror.indiatimes.com/blindwink-announces-the-winners-of-india-excellence-awards-2022/articleshow/95572998.cms
64	Bangalore Mirror 2022	https://bangaloremirror.indiatimes.com/blindwink-announces-the-winners-of-india-excellence-awards-2022/articleshow/95620028.cms
65	Correct Success 2022	https://correctsuccess.com/how-to-repaircredit/apoorvaa-credit-repair-lawyer-of-india-is-on-amission-to-create-credit-awareness-make-people-credithealthy-help-banks-reduce-their-npa/
66	Mantras 2022	https://mantras.tv/2022/12/28/apoorvaa-credit-repairlawyer-of-india-is-on-a-mission-to-create-creditawareness-make-people-credit-healthy-help-banksreduce-their-npa/
67	News Now 2022	https://www.newsnow.co.uk/h/?search=Credit+Repair+Lawyer+of+India+is+on+a+mission+to+create+credit+awareness%2C+make+people+credit+healthy+%26+help+banks+reduce+their+NPA&lang=en
68	Jio News 2022	https://jionews.com/home/article/5/2180673344/Apoorvaa-Credit-Repair-Lawyer-of-India-is-on-a-mission-tocreate-credit-awareness-make-people-credit-healthyhelp-banks-reduce-their-NPA

Sr. No.	Newspaper/ Magazine	Links
69	**Herald Globe 2022**	https://www.heraldglobe.com/news/273280452/ apoorvaa---credit-repair-lawyer-of-india-is-on-a-mission-tocreate-credit-awareness-make-people-credit-healthy--help-banks-reduce-their-npa
70	**South East Asia Post 2022**	https://www.southeastasiapost.com/news/273280452/ apoorvaa---credit-repair-lawyer-of-india-is-on-a-missionto-create-credit-awareness-make-people-credit-healthy--help-banks-reduce-their-npa
71	**Kualalumpur News 2022**	https://www.kualalumpurnews.net/news/273280452/ apoorvaa---credit-repair-lawyer-of-india-is-on-a-missionto-create-credit-awareness-make-people-credit-healthy--help-banks-reduce-their-npa
72	**Bangladesh Sun 2022**	https://www.bangladeshsun.com/news/273280452/ apoorvaa---credit-repair-lawyer-of-india-is-on-a-mission-tocreate-credit-awareness-make-people-credit-healthy--help-banks-reduce-their-npa
73	**Kolkata News 2022**	https://www.kolkatanews.net/news/273280452/ apoorvaa---credit-repair-lawyer-of-india-is-on-a-mission-tocreate-credit-awareness-make-people-credit-healthy--help-banks-reduce-their-npa
74	**Bangkok News 2022**	https://www.bangkoknews.net/news/273280452/ apoorvaa---credit-repair-lawyer-of-india-is-on-a-mission-tocreate-credit-awareness-make-people-credit-healthy--help-banks-reduce-their-npa
75	**New Delhi News 2022**	https://www.newdelhinews.net/news/273280452/ apoorvaa---credit-repair-lawyer-of-india-is-on-a-mission-tocreate-credit-awareness-make-people-credit-healthy--help-banks-reduce-their-npa
76	**Mumbai News 2022**	https://www.mumbainews.net/news/273280452/ apoorvaa---credit-repair-lawyer-of-india-is-on-a-mission-tocreate-credit-awareness-make-people-credit-healthy--help-banks-reduce-their-npa

Sr. No.	Newspaper/ Magazine	Links
77	**Big News Network 2022**	https://www.bignewsnetwork.com/news/273280452/ apoorvaa---credit-repair-lawyer-of-india-is-on-a-missionto-create-credit-awareness-make-people-credit-healthy--help-banks-reduce-their-npa
78	**Brunei News 2022**	https://www.bruneinews.net/news/273280452/ apoorvaa---credit-repair-lawyer-of-india-is-on-a-mission-tocreate-credit-awareness-make-people-credit-healthy--help-banks-reduce-their-npa
79	**Srilanka Source 2022**	https://www.srilankasource.com/news/273280452/ apoorvaa---credit-repair-lawyer-of-india-is-on-a-mission-tocreate-credit-awareness-make-people-credit-healthy--help-banks-reduce-their-npa
80	**Nepal National 2022**	https://www.nepalnational.com/news/273280452/ apoorvaa---credit-repair-lawyer-of-india-is-on-a-mission-tocreate-credit-awareness-make-people-credit-healthy--help-banks-reduce-their-npa
81	**Indias News 2022**	https://www.indiasnews.net/news/273280452/ apoorvaa---credit-repair-lawyer-of-india-is-on-a-mission-tocreate-credit-awareness-make-people-credit-healthy--help-banks-reduce-their-npa
82	**Cambodian Times 2022**	https://www.cambodiantimes.com/news/273280452/ apoorvaa---credit-repair-lawyer-of-india-is-on-a-missionto-create-credit-awareness-make-people-credit-healthy--help-banks-reduce-their-npa
83	**Indonesia News 2022**	https://www.indonesianews.net/news/273280452/ apoorvaa---credit-repair-lawyer-of-india-is-on-a-mission-tocreate-credit-awareness-make-people-credit-healthy--help-banks-reduce-their-npa
84	**Malaysia News 2022**	https://www.malaysianews.net/news/273280452/ apoorvaa---credit-repair-lawyer-of-india-is-on-a-mission-tocreate-credit-awareness-make-people-credit-healthy--help-banks-reduce-their-npa

Sr. No.	Newspaper/ Magazine	Links
85	**The Cambodia News 2022**	https://www.thecambodianews.net/news/273280452/apoorvaa---credit-repair-lawyer-of-india-is-on-a-missionto-create-credit-awareness-make-people-credit-healthy--help-banks-reduce-their-npa
86	**Nepal News 2022**	https://www.nepalnews.net/news/273280452/apoorvaa---credit-repair-lawyer-of-india-is-on-a-mission-tocreate-credit-awareness-make-people-credit-healthy--help-banks-reduce-their-npa
87	**Srilankan News 2022**	https://www.srilankannews.net/news/273280452/apoorvaa---credit-repair-lawyer-of-india-is-on-a-mission-tocreate-credit-awareness-make-people-credit-healthy--help-banks-reduce-their-npa
88	**Pakistan News 2022**	https://www.pakistannews.net/news/273280452/apoorvaa---credit-repair-lawyer-of-india-is-on-a-mission-tocreate-credit-awareness-make-people-credit-healthy--help-banks-reduce-their-npa
89	**Loas News 2022**	https://www.laosnews.net/news/273280452/apoorvaa---credit-repair-lawyer-of-india-is-on-a-mission-to-createcreditawareness-make-people-credit-healthy--helpbanks-reduce-their-npa
90	**Indian News Network 2022**	https://www.indiannewsnetwork.net/news/apoorvaacreditrepair-lawyer-of-india-is-on-a-mission-to-createcredit-awarenessmake-people-credit-healthy-helpbanks-reduce-their-npa20221228183626/
91	**West Bengal Khabar 2022**	https://www.WestBengalKhabar.in/news/apoorvaacredit-repair-lawyer-of-india-is-on-a-mission-to-createcredit-awareness-make-people-credit-healthy-helpbanks-reduce-theirnpa20221228183626/
92	**Vanakkam Tamil Nadu 2022**	https://www.VanakkamTamilnadu.com/news/apoorvaa-credit-repair-lawyer-of-india-is-on-a-mission-to-createcredit-awareness-make-people-credit-healthy-helpbanks-reduce-their-npa20221228183626/

Sr. No.	Newspaper/ Magazine	Links
93	**UP Today 2022**	https://www.UPtoday.news/news/apoorvaa-creditrepair-lawyer-of-india-is-on-a-mission-to-create-creditawareness-make-people-credit-healthy-help-banksreduce-their-npa20221228183626/
94	**Telangana Journal 2022**	https://www.Telanganajournal.in/news/apoorvaacredit-repair-lawyer-of-india-is-on-a-mission-to-createcredit-awareness-make-people-credit-healthy-helpbanks-reduce-theirnpa20221228183626/
95	**South India News 2022**	https://www.SouthIndiaNews.in/news/apoorvaacreditrepairlawyer-of-india-is-on-a-mission-to-create-creditawareness-make-people-credit-healthy-help-banksreduce-theirnpa20221228183626/
96	**Punjab Live 2022**	https://www.PunjabLive.news/news/apoorvaa-creditrepair-lawyer-of-india-is-on-a-mission-to-create-creditawareness-make-people-credit-healthy-help-banksreducetheirnpa20221228183626/
97	**Odisha Post 2022**	https://www.OdishaPost.news/news/apoorvaa-creditrepair-lawyer-of-india-is-on-a-mission-to-create-creditawareness-make-people-credit-healthy-help-banksreduce-theirnpa20221228183626/
98	**North East Times 2022**	https://www.NorthEastTimes.in/news/apoorvaa-creditrepair-lawyer-of-india-is-on-a-mission-to-create-creditawareness-make-people-credit-healthy-help-banksreduce-their-npa20221228183626/
99	**Maharashtra Samachar 2022**	https://www.MaharashtraSamachar.com/news/apoorvaa-credit-repair-lawyer-of-india-is-on-a-mission-tocreate-creditawareness-make-people-credit-healthyhelp-banks-reduce-their-npa20221228183626/
100	**Madhya Pradesh Chronicle 2022**	https://www.MadhyaPradeshChronicle.com/news/apoorvaa-credit-repair-lawyer-of-india-is-on-a-mission-tocreate-credit-awareness-make-people-credit-healthyhelp-banks-reduce-their-npa20221228183626/

Sr. No.	Newspaper/ Magazine	Links
101	**Kashmir News Line 2022**	https://www.KashmirNewsline.in/news/apoorvaacredit-repair-lawyer-of-india-is-on-a-mission-to-createcredit-awareness-make-people-credit-healthy-helpbanks-reduce-their-npa20221228183626/
102	**Kashmir Breaking News 2022**	https://www.KashmirBreakingNews.com/news/apoorvaa-credit-repair-lawyer-of-india-is-on-a-mission-tocreate-credit-awareness-make-people-credit-healthyhelp-banks-reduce-their-npa20221228183626/
103	**Karnataka Live 2022**	https://www.KarnatakaLive.in/news/apoorvaa-creditrepair-lawyer-of-india-is-on-a-mission-to-create-creditawareness-make-people-credit-healthy-help-banksreduce-their-npa20221228183626/
104	**Jharkhand Times 2022**	https://www.JharkhandTimes.in/news/apoorvaa-creditrepair-lawyer-of-india-is-on-a-mission-to-create-creditawareness-make-people-credit-healthy-help-banksreduce-their-npa20221228183626/
105	**Indian Economic Observer 2022**	https://www.IndianEconomicObserver.com/news/apoorvaa-credit-repair-lawyer-of-india-is-on-a-mission-tocreate-credit-awareness-make-people-credit-healthyhelp-banks-reduce-their-npa20221228183626/
106	**Himachal Patrika 2022**	https://www.HimachalPatrika.com/news/apoorvaacredit-repair-lawyer-of-india-is-on-a-mission-to-createcredit-awareness-make-people-credit-healthy-helpbanks-reduce-theirnpa20221228183626/
107	**Haryana Today 2022**	https://www.HaryanaToday.in/news/apoorvaa-creditrepair-lawyer-of-india-is-on-a-mission-to-create-creditawareness-make-people-credit-healthy-help-banksreduce-their-npa20221228183626/
108	**Gujarat Varta 2022**	https://www.GujaratVarta.com/news/apoorvaa-creditrepair-lawyer-of-india-is-on-a-mission-to-create-creditawareness-make-people-credit-healthy-help-banksreduce-their-npa20221228183626/

Sr. No.	Newspaper/ Magazine	Links
109	Gujarat Samachar 2022	https://www.GujaratSamachar.news/news/apoorvaacredit-repair-lawyer-of-india-is-on-a-mission-to-createcredit-awareness-make-people-credit-healthy-helpbanks-reduce-their-npa20221228183626/
110	Delhi Live News 2022	https://www.DelhiLiveNews.in/news/apoorvaa-creditrepair-lawyer-of-india-is-on-a-mission-to-create-creditawareness-make-people-credit-healthy-help-banksreduce-their-npa20221228183626/
111	Chhattisgarh Today 2022	https://www.ChhattisgarhToday.in/news/apoorvaacredit-repair-lawyer-of-india-is-on-a-mission-to-createcredit-awareness-make-people-credit-healthy-helpbanks-reduce-their-npa20221228183626/
112	Bihar Times 2022	https://www.BiharTimes.news/news/apoorvaa-creditrepair-lawyer-of-india-is-on-a-mission-to-create-creditawareness-make-people-credit-healthy-help-banksreduce-their-npa20221228183626/
113	Bihar 24x7 2022	https://www.Bihar24x7.com/news/apoorvaa-creditrepair-lawyer-of-india-is-on-a-mission-to-create-creditawareness-make-people-credit-healthy-help-banksreduce-their-npa20221228183626/
114	Andhra Pradesh Mirror 2022	https://www.AndhraPradeshMirror.com/news/apoorvaa-credit-repair-lawyer-of-india-is-on-a-mission-tocreate-creditawareness-make-people-credit-healthyhelp-banks-reduce-their-npa20221228183626/
115	World News Network 2022	https://www.worldnewsnetwork.net/news/apoorvaacredit-repair-lawyer-of-india-is-on-a-mission-to-createcredit-awareness-make-people-credit-healthy-helpbanks-reduce-their-npa20221228183626/
116	Australia Morning Tribune 2022	https://www.australiamorningtribune.com/news/apoorvaa-credit-repair-lawyer-of-india-is-on-a-mission-tocreate-credit-awareness-make-people-credit-healthyhelp-banks-reduce-their-npa20221228183626/

Sr. No.	Newspaper/ Magazine	Links
117	**Birminghamall News Network 2022**	https://www.birminghamallnewsnetwork.com/news/apoorvaa-credit-repair-lawyer-of-india-is-on-a-mission-tocreate-credit-awareness-make-people-credit-healthyhelp-banks-reduce-their-npa20221228183626/
118	**British Columbia Times 2022**	https://www.britishcolumbiatimes.com/news/apoorvaa-credit-repair-lawyer-of-india-is-on-a-mission-to-createcredit-awareness-make-people-credit-healthy-helpbanks-reduce-their-npa20221228183626/
119	**British News Network 2022**	https://www.britishnewsnetwork.com/news/apoorvaacredit-repair-lawyer-of-india-is-on-a-mission-to-createcredit-awareness-make-people-credit-healthy-helpbanks-reduce-their-npa20221228183626/
120	**Buffalo Despatch 2022**	https://www.buffalodespatch.com/news/apoorvaacredit-repair-lawyer-of-india-is-on-a-mission-to-createcredit-awareness-make-people-credit-healthy-helpbanks-reduce-theirnpa20221228183626/
121	**Capitol Hill Reporter 2022**	https://www.capitolhillreporter.com/news/apoorvaacredit-repair-lawyer-of-india-is-on-a-mission-to-createcredit-awareness-make-people-credit-healthy-helpbanks-reduce-their-npa20221228183626/
122	**Dubai City Reporter 2022**	https://www.dubaicityreporter.com/news/apoorvaacredit-repair-lawyer-of-india-is-on-a-mission-to-createcredit-awareness-make-people-credit-healthy-helpbanks-reduce-their-npa20221228183626/
123	**East Coast American News 2022**	https://www.eastcoastamericannews.com/news/apoorvaa-credit-repair-lawyer-of-india-is-on-a-mission-tocreate-credit-awareness-make-people-credit-healthyhelp-banks-reduce-their-npa20221228183626/
124	**England News Portal 2022**	https://www.englandnewsportal.com/news/apoorvaacredit-repair-lawyer-of-india-is-on-a-mission-to-createcredit-awareness-make-people-credit-healthy-helpbanks-reduce-their-npa20221228183626/

Sr. No.	Newspaper/ Magazine	Links
125	**European Sun Times 2022**	https://www.europeansuntimes.com/news/ apoorvaacredit-repair-lawyer-of-india-is-on-a-mission- to-createcredit-awareness-make-people-credit-healthy- helpbanks-reduce-their-npa20221228183626/
126	**Florida Breaking News 2022**	https://www.floridabreakingnews.com/news/ apoorvaacredit-repair-lawyer-of-india-is-on-a-mission- to-createcreditawareness-make-people-credit-healthy- helpbanks-reduce-theirnpa20221228183626/
127	**France Network Times 2022**	https://www.francenetworktimes.com/news/ apoorvaacredit-repair-lawyer-of-india-is-on-a-mission- to-createcredit-awareness-make-people-credit-healthy- helpbanks-reduce-their-npa20221228183626/
128	**Japan Times Today 2022**	https://www.japantimestoday.com/news/ apoorvaacredit-repair-lawyer-of-india-is-on-a-mission- to-createcredit-awareness-make-people-credit-healthy- helpbanks-reduce-theirnpa20221228183626/
129	**London Channel News 2022**	https://www.londonchannelnews.com/news/ apoorvaacredit-repair-lawyer-of-india-is-on-a-mission- to-createcredit-awareness-make-people-credit-healthy- helpbanks-reduce-their-npa20221228183626/
130	**Los Angeles Evening Despatch 2022**	https://www.losangeleseveningdespatch.com/ news/apoorvaa-credit-repair-lawyer-of-india-is- on-a-mission-tocreate-credit-awareness-make- people-credit-healthyhelp-banks-reduce-their- npa20221228183626/
131	**Maldives Star Plus 2022**	https://www.maldivesstarplus.com/news/ apoorvaacredit-repair-lawyer-of-india-is-on-a-mission- to-createcredit-awareness-make-people-credit-healthy- helpbanks-reduce-their-npa20221228183626/
132	**Miami News Herald 2022**	https://www.miaminewsherald.com/news/ apoorvaacredit-repair-lawyer-of-india-is-on-a-mission- to-createcredit-awareness-make-people-credit-healthy- helpbanks-reduce-their-npa20221228183626/

Sr. No.	Newspaper/ Magazine	Links
133	**Mountain View Sentinel 2022**	https://www.mountainviewsentinel.com/news/apoorvaa-credit-repair-lawyer-of-india-is-on-a-mission-tocreate-credit-awareness-make-people-credit-healthyhelp-banks-reduce-their-npa20221228183626/
134	**Newyork Despatch 2022**	https://www.newyorkdespatch.com/news/apoorvaacredit-repair-lawyer-of-india-is-on-a-mission-to-createcredit-awareness-make-people-credit-healthy-helpbanks-reduce-their-npa20221228183626/
135	**Richmond Evening News 2022**	https://www.richmondeveningnews.com/news/apoorvaa-credit-repair-lawyer-of-india-is-on-a-mission-tocreate-credit-awareness-make-people-credit-healthyhelp-banks-reduce-their-npa20221228183626/
136	**South China herald 2022**	https://www.southchinaherald.news/news/apoorvaacredit-repair-lawyer-of-india-is-on-a-mission-to-createcredit-awareness-make-people-credit-healthy-helpbanks-reduce-their-npa20221228183626/
137	**Srilanka Island News 2022**	https://www.srilankaislandnews.com/news/apoorvaacredit-repair-lawyer-of-india-is-on-a-mission-to-createcredit-awareness-make-people-credit-healthy-helpbanks-reduce-their-npa20221228183626/
138	**Sydney Evening Post 2022**	https://www.sydneyeveningpost.com/news/apoorvaacredit-repair-lawyer-of-india-is-on-a-mission-to-createcredit-awareness-make-people-credit-healthy-helpbanks-reduce-their-npa20221228183626/
139	**Toronto Sun Times 2022**	https://www.torontosuntimes.com/news/apoorvaacredit-repair-lawyer-of-india-is-on-a-mission-to-createcredit-awareness-make-people-credit-healthy-helpbanks-reduce-their-npa20221228183626/
140	**US World Today 2022**	https://www.usworldtoday.com/news/apoorvaacreditrepair-lawyer-of-india-is-on-a-mission-to-createcreditawareness-make-people-credit-healthy-helpbanksreduce-their-npa20221228183626/

Sr. No.	Newspaper/ Magazine	Links
141	**Washington DC Despatch 2022**	https://www.washingtondcdespatch.com/news/apoorvaa-credit-repair-lawyer-of-india-is-on-a-mission-tocreate-credit-awareness-make-people-credit-healthyhelp-banks-reduce-their-npa20221228183626/
142	**Whitehouse News Times 2022**	https://www.whitehousenewstime.com/news/apoorvaa-credit-repair-lawyer-of-india-is-on-a-mission-to-createcredit-awareness-make-people-credit-healthy-helpbanks-reduce-their-npa20221228183626/
142	**ANI 2021**	https://www.aninews.in/news/business/business/unique-business-opportunity-in-a-form-of-credit-repair-with-no-recession-amp-competition20210608131844/
143	**Business Standard 2021**	https://www.business-standard.com/content/press-releases-ani/unique-businessopportunity-in-a-form-of-credit-repair-with-no-recession-competition-121060800606_1.html
144	**The Print 2021**	https://theprint.in/ani-press-releases/unique-businessopportunity-in-a-form-of-credit-repair-with-no-recession-competition/673909/
145	**Zee5 2021**	https://www.zee5.com/zee5news/unique-business-opportunity-in-a-form-of-credit-repair-with-no-recessioncompetition
146	**English Lokmat 2021**	https://english.lokmat.com/business/unique-businessopportunity-in-a-form-of-credit-repair-with-no-recession-competition/
147	**Yahoo 2021**	https://in.finance.yahoo.com/news/unique-business-opportunity-form-credit-075342731.html
148	**Just Dial 2021**	https://www.justdial.com/JdSocial/news/Latest-generic/Unique-business-opportunity-in-a-form-of-credit-repair-with-no-recession-competition/1623139030496000?dl=1
149	**Mantras 2021**	https://mantras.tv/2021/06/08/unique-business-opportunity-ina-form-of-credit-repair-with-no-recession-competition/

Sr. No.	Newspaper/ Magazine	Links
150	India News 2021	https://in.shafaqna.com/EN/AL/3559909
151	Rajasthan Ki Khabar 2021	https://www.rajasthankikhabar.com/news/unique-businessopportunity-in-a-form-of-credit-repair-with-norecession-competition20210608131841/
152	Odisha Post 2021	https://www.odishapost.news/news/uniquebusinessopportunity-in-a-form-of-credit-repair-with-no-recessioncompetition20210608131841/
153	West Bengal Khabar 2021	https://www.westbengalkhabar.in/news/unique-business-opportunity-in-a-form-of-credit-repair-with-no-recessioncompetition20210608131841/
154	Bihar 24x7 2021	https://www.bihar24x7.com/news/unique-business-opportunityin-a-form-of-credit-repair-with-no-recession competition20210608131841/
155	Web India 123 2021	https://news.webindia123.com/news/Articles/Business/2021068/3768344.html
156	South China Herald 2021	https://www.southchinaherald.news/news/unique-businessopportunity-in-a-formof-credit-repair-with-no-recessioncompetition20210608131841/
157	Richmond Evening News 2021	https://www.richmondeveningnews.com/news/uniquebusiness-opportunity-in-a-form-of-credit-repair-with-no-recession-competition20210608131841/
158	Mountain View Sentinel 2021	https://www.mountainviewsentinel.com/news/uniquebusiness-opportunity-in-a-form-of-credit-repair-with-no-recession-competition20210608131841/
159	Birmingham All News Network 2021	https://www.birminghamallnewsnetwork.com/news/uniquebusiness-opportunity-in-a-form-of-credit-repairwith-no-recession-competition20210608131841/
160	Australia Morning Tribune 2021	https://www.australiamorningtribune.com/news/uniquebusiness-opportunity-ina-form-of-credit-repair-with-no-recession-competition20210608131841/

Sr. No.	Newspaper/ Magazine	Links
161	Middle East Times 2021	https://www.middleeasttimes.news/news/unique-businessopportunity-in-a-formof-credit-repair-with-no-recessioncompetition20210608131841/
162	Maldives Star Plus 2021	https://www.maldivesstarplus.com/news/unique-businessopportunity-in-a-formof-credit-repair-with-no-recessioncompetition20210608131841/
163	Los Angeles Evening Despatch 2021	https://www.losangeleseveningdespatch.com/news/uniquebusiness-opportunity-in-a-form-of-credit-repair-with-no-recessioncompetition20210608131841/
164	London Channel News 2021	https://www.londonchannelnews.com/news/unique-businessopportunity-in-a-form-of-credit-repair-with-norecession-competition20210608131841/
165	France Network Times 2021	https://www.francenetworktimes.com/news/unique-businessopportunity-in-a-form-of-credit-repair-with-norecession-competition20210608131841/
166	Florida Breaking News 2021	https://www.floridabreakingnews.com/news/unique-businessopportunity-in-a-form-of-credit-repair-with-norecession-competition20210608131841/
167	Federal Despatch 2021	https://www.federaldespatch.com/news/uniquebusinessopportunity-in-a-form-of-credit-repair-with-no-recession-competition20210608131841/
168	European Sun Times 2021	https://www.europeansuntimes.com/news/unique-businessopportunity-in-a-form-of-credit-repair-with-norecession-competition20210608131841/
169	Japan Times Today 2021	https://www.japantimestoday.com/news/unique-businessopportunity-in-a-form-of-credit-repair-with-norecession-competition20210608131841/
170	East Coast American News 2021	https://www.eastcoastamericannews.com/news/uniquebusiness-opportunity-in-a-form-of-credit-repair-withno-recession-competition20210608131841/
171	East Asia All News Portal 2021	https://www.eastasiaallnewsportal.com/news/unique-businessopportunity-in-aform-of-credit-repair-withno-recessioncompetition20210608131841/

Sr. No.	Newspaper/ Magazine	Links
172	Punjab Live 2021	https://www.punjablive.news/news/uniquebusinessopportunity-in-a-form-of-credit-repair-with-no-recession-competition20210608131841/
173	Capitol Hill Reporter 2021	https://www.capitolhillreporter.com/news/unique-businessopportunity-in-a-form-of-credit-repair-with-norecession-competition20210608131841/
174	Buffalo Despatch 2021	https://www.buffalodespatch.com/news/unique-businessopportunity-in-a-form-of-credit-repair-with-norecession-competition20210608131841/
175	British News Network 2021	https://www.britishnewsnetwork.com/news/unique-businessopportunity-in-a-form-of-credit-repair-with-no-recession-competition20210608131841/
176	British Columbia Times 2021	https://www.britishcolumbiatimes.com/news/unique-businessopportunity-in-a-form-of-credit-repair-with-no-recession-competition20210608131841/
177	Wisconsin Journal 2021	https://www.wisconsinjournal.news/news/unique-business-opportunity-in-a-formof-credit-repair-with-no-recession-competition20210608131841/
178	Westminster Times 2021	https://www.westminstertimes.news/news/unique-business-opportunity-in-a-form-of-credit-repair-with-norecession-competition20210608131841/
179	California Star 2021	https://www.californiastar.news/news/unique-business-opportunity-in-a-form-ofcredit-repair-with-no-recession-competition20210608131841/
180	Wall Street Sentinel 2021	https://www.wallstreetsentinel.news/news/unique-business-opportunity-in-a-form-of-credit-repair-with-no-recessioncompetition20210608131841/
181	Vancouver Herald 2021	https://www.vancouverherald.news/news/unique-business-opportunity-in-a-formof-credit-repair-with-no-recessioncompetition20210608131841/
182	Miami News Herald 2021	https://www.miaminewsherald.com/news/unique-business-opportunity-in-a-formof-credit-repair-with-no-recessioncompetition20210608131841/

Sr. No.	Newspaper/ Magazine	Links
183	Sri Lanka Island News 2021	https://www.srilankaislandnews.com/news/unique-businessopportunity-in-a-form-of-credit-repair-with-norecession-competition20210608131841/
184	Toronto Sun Times 2021	https://www.torontosuntimes.com/news/unique-businessopportunity-in-a-form-of-credit-repair-with-norecession-competition20210608131841/
185	UAE Times 2021	https://www.uaetimes.news/news/unique-business-opportunity-in-a-form-of-credit-repair-withnorecessioncompetition20210608131841/
186	USA Report 2021	https://www.usareport.news/news/unique-businessopportunity-in-a-form-of-credit-repair-withnorecessioncompetition20210608131841/
187	US World Today 2021	https://www.usworldtoday.com/news/unique-business-opportunity-in-a-form-of-credit-repair-with-no-recession-competition20210608131841/
188	Maharashtra Samachar 2021	https://www.maharashtrasamachar.com/news/unique-business-opportunity-in-aform-of-credit-repair-withno-recessioncompetition20210608131841/
189	India News Network 2021	https://www.indiannewsnetwork.net/news/unique-business-opportunity-in-a-form-of-credit-repair-with-norecession-competition20210608131841/
190	Vanakkam Tamil Nadu 2021	https://www.vanakkamtamilnadu.com/news/unique-business-opportunity-in-a-form-of-credit-repair-with-no-recession-competition20210608131841/
191	South India News 2021	https://www.southindianews.in/news/unique-business-opportunity-in-a-form-ofcredit-repair-with-no-recession-competition20210608131841/
192	Dubai City Report 2021	https://www.dubaicityreporter.com/news/unique-business-opportunity-in-a-formof-credit-repair-with-no-recession-competition20210608131841/

Sr. No.	Newspaper/ Magazine	Links
192	**Prime Insights 2022**	https://primeinsights.in/apoorvaa-foundation/ https://www.facebook.com/Primeinsightsmagazine/ posts/pfbid02KNHmetgBMco1Q8SMYD1vxSDspGv Jtque9WQPfYyAG9dfnkm8t3BDmRSB3GLp4xAil https://twitter.com/Prime_Insights1/status/1596 077574886920192
193	**Global Business Line 2021**	https://www.businessline.global/apoorvaa-foundation-is-driving-the-financial-sector-to-a-new-dimension/ startup/
194	**Brandz magazine 2020**	https://brandzmagazine.com/?p=1287
195	**Success Magazine 2020**	https://successmagazine.in/helping-smes-to-get-fund-their-business/
196	**Unified Brainz 2020**	https://youtu.be/EF48f5DnAOk

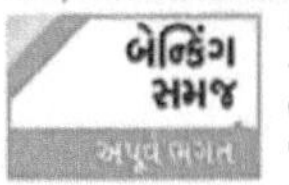 **અમદાવાદ** 25-07-2022

શું તમે લોન લીધી છે ? ક્યારેય EMI લેટ ભર્યો અથવા તો નથી ભર્યો તો સિબિલ સ્કોર ખરાબ

શા કારણોથી CIBIL સ્કોર વધતો નથી?

તમારામાંથી ઘણા લોકો ને CIBIL સ્કોર્સ કઈ રીતે સુધારવો એનો ખ્યાલ જ હશે પરંતુ મૂળભૂત/પાયાના સ્તર ની પ્રક્રિયા ઘણાને ખબર નથી તેથી તેમને ઇચ્છિત પરિણામો મળતા નથી. CIBIL સ્કોર સુધારવા માટે વિચારતા પેહલા શું ધ્યાન માં લેવું જોઈએ? જ્યારે CIBIL સ્કોર ઓછો થવાનું પર્યાપ્ત કારણ ખ્યાલ આવી જાય અને એને સુધારવાનું કાર્ય કરવામાં આવે, ત્યારે CIBIL સ્કોર વધે એવી

બેન્કિંગ સમજ
અપૂર્વ ભગત

શક્યતાઓ વધુ પ્રબળ બની જાય છે. વ્યક્તિએ હંમેશા ધ્યાનમાં રાખવું જોઈએ કે ઘણા પરિબળો CIBIL સ્કોર ને અસર કરે છે, જ્યારે તે પરિબળો તમારા CIBIL રિપોર્ટ માં નેગેટિવ ફ્લેગ્સ તરીકે આવી જાય છે ત્યારે એની ભૂમિકા તમારા CIBIL સ્કોર ને ઓછો કરવાની હોય છે. જ્યારે તમે તમારી કોઈ લોન કે ક્રેડિટ કાર્ડ ને સેટલમેન્ટ (ઓછા રૂપિયા ભરી ને) માં

CIBIL સ્કોર ને સુધારવા માટે ની ટિપ્સ

300   850

- તમારા ક્રેડિટ કાર્ડ ઉપયોગ 50% થી ઓછો કરવો
- તમારા CIBIL રિપોર્ટ ની ભૂલો ને ઠીક કરો.
- સમયસર હપ્તા/વ્યાજ ની ચુકવણી કરો.
- ભૂતકાળ ની બેંક ની બાકી ની રકમ ચૂકવો.

સારું ક્રેડિટ મિક્સ રાખો

- જો તમને જરૂર ના હોય તો નવી લોન કે ક્રેડિટ કાર્ડ ની અરજી કરશો નહિ.
- નિયમિત રીતે તમારા CIBIL રિપોર્ટ ને તપાસો.
- વધુ પડતી નવી લોનની ઇન્કવાયરી ટાળો જે પણ સિબિલ સ્કોર પર અસર કરે.

બંધ કરાવો છો અથવા તમારી બેંક તમારી લોન કે ક્રેડિટ કાર્ડ ને રાઈટ ઓફ (લોન ના રૂપિયા ની ચુકવણી બાકી હોવા થી) કરે છે અથવા તમે બેંક દવારા કરાયેલા

કાનૂની દાવા નો સામનો કરી રહ્યા હોવ છો અથવા તમે તમારી ચુકવણી ચુકી ગયા છો અથવા તમે ઇરાદાપૂર્વક તમારા EMI ચુકવવા તૈયાર નથી અથવા તમારું

જૂનું કોઈ બેલેન્સ તમારા CIBIL રિપોર્ટ માં દેખાય છે વિગેરે તમારા CIBIL સ્કોર ને ઓછો કરવા માં અસર કરે છે. તમારો CIBIL સ્કોર એ તમારી લોન અને ક્રેડિટ કાર્ડ ને પુનઃ ચુકવણી કરવાની તમારી આદતો જ તમારી ક્રેડિટ હિસ્ટ્રી કહેવાય છે એનું પરિણામ છે.

હવે પ્રશ્ન એ છે કે આ જે નેગેટિવ ફ્લેગ્સ છે એને દૂર કરવા શું કરવું જોઈએ? CIBIL સ્કોર સુધારવા માટે આ નેગેટિવ ફ્લેગ્સ દૂર કરવા જોઈએ કે નહિ? આનો જવાબ હા જ છે કારણ કે જ્યાં સુધી તમે આ નેગેટિવ ફ્લેગ્સ દૂર નહિ કરો ત્યાં સુધી CIBIL સ્કોર સુધરવાની શક્યતા ઓછી છે. નેગેટિવ ફ્લેગ્સ દૂર કરવાની પ્રક્રિયા માં જો બેંકની ચુકવણી બાકી હોય તો સૌ પ્રથમ બેંક ની નીતિ પ્રમાણે એ કરવી જોઈએ. એકવાર તમારા CIBIL રિપોર્ટ માંથી આ નેગેટિવ ફ્લેગ્સ દૂર થઈ જશે, ત્યારે તમારા CIBIL સ્કોર ઉપર એની હકારાત્મક અસર જોવા મળશે.
(લેખક : અપૂર્વ ફાઉન્ડેશન-ક્રેડિટ બ્યુરો કન્સલટન્ટ્સના ફાઉન્ડર છે)

અમદાવાદ 08-08-2022

MSME માટે સિબિલ રેન્ક-કંપની ક્રેડિટ રિપોર્ટનું લોન લેવા માટે મહત્ત્વ

એક વ્યવસાયિક હોવાને કારણે, તમે હંમેશા તમારા વ્યવસાય ને વિસ્તૃત કરવા માટે પ્રયત્નશીલ રહેતા હશો અને નાણાં વિના કોઈ પણ વ્યવસાય ને વિસ્તૃત કરવું મુશ્કેલ છે. જો તમે સરકારી લોન અથવા અન્ય કોઈ બેંક લોન લેવાનું વિચારી રહ્યા છો, તો એ માટે એક સારો CIBIL Rank હોવો એ મહત્વપૂર્ણ છે. તમારી કંપનીના ક્રેડિટ રિપોર્ટ માં ભૂતકાળ માં તમારી કંપની દ્વારા લેવામાં આવેલી લોન, તેની વર્તમાન ક્રેડિટ જવાબદારીઓ, તેના ક્રેડિટ નો ઉપયોગ તેમજ બેંક એ તમારી કંપની ની ક્રેડિટ હિસ્ટ્રી વિશે

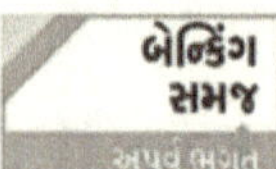

કરેલી પૂછપરછ ની સંખ્યા જેવી માહિતી ઉપલબ્ધ હોય છે.

તમારા કંપની ક્રેડિટ રિપોર્ટ પરથી CIBIL Rank મેળવવા માં આવે છે જે 1 થી 10 વચ્ચે નો કોઈ એક અંક હોઈ શકે છે. અને 1 ને શ્રેષ્ઠ CIBIL Rank માનવામાં આવે છે.

તમે હાલ લોન લેવા માટે વિચારી રહ્યા છો કે નહિ, પરંતુ જો તમારે કોઈ ભાગીદાર કંપની છે, કોઈ માલિકી ની કંપની છે, પ્રાઈવેટ લિમિટેડ કંપની છે અથવા તો તમે કોઈ એલએલપી હેઠળ આવો છો, તો તમારે વર્ષમાં ઓછામાં ઓછો એક વખત તમારી કંપનીનો ક્રેડિટ રિપોર્ટ તપાસવો આવશ્યક છે.

કેટલાક પરિબળો જે તમારા કંપની ક્રેડિટ

રિપોર્ટ અને CIBIL Rank ને પ્રભાવિત કરે છે.

- લાંબી ક્રેડિટ હિસ્ટ્રી
- ક્રેડિટ ઉપયોગ નો ગુણોત્તર
- લોન ચુકવણી ની હિસ્ટ્રી
- બાકી દેવું
- કંપની નું કદ

CIBIL Rank ની ગણતરી કરતી વખતે ભૂતકાળ ની લોન ની ચુકવણી ની વર્તણૂક અને તમારો ક્રેડિટ ઉપયોગ આ બે મુખ્ય પરિબળો ધ્યાન માં લેવાય છે.

- નેગેટિવ ફ્લેગ્સ જેવા કે,
- જૂનું કોઈ બેલેન્સ
- બાકી રકમ/ સિલક
- ખોટી જાણ કરેલી લોન અથવા તો ઓવરડ્રાફ્ટ સુવિધા

ડુપ્લીકેટ એન્ટ્રી

બંધ લોન એકાઉન્ટ નું હજુ પણ ચાલુ સ્થિતિ માં હોવું વિગેરે

આ જે નેગેટિવ ફ્લેગ્સ છે જે તમારા CIBIL Rank ને 7 થી 10 સુધી પાછળ લઈ જઈ શકે છે જે લોન મેળવવા માટે અનુકૂળ નથી.

સુવ્યવસ્થિત વ્યૂહરચના અને પ્રયત્નો સાથે, આ નેગેટિવ ફ્લેગ્સ ને દૂર કરી શકાય છે અને CIBIL Rank સુધારવા પર કામ કરી શકાય છે, જો કે, એ ભૂલવું ના જોઈએ કે આ એક સમય લેતી પ્રક્રિયા છે તેથી તેને વિલંબિત કરવું અથવા જ્યારે જરૂર હોય ત્યારે જ કરવું એ તમને ઇચ્છિત પરિણામ આપશો નહીં. વધુમાં, CIBIL Rank હવે રૂપિયા 50 કરોડ સુધીની વર્તમાન ક્રેડિટ ધરાવતી કંપનીઓ માટે ઉપલબ્ધ છે. પરંતુ CIBIL Rank ની ઉપલબ્ધતા ના હોવી એ નકારાત્મક બાબત નથી.

આનો નિષ્કર્ષ એ છે કે, વેપારીઓએ સમજવું જોઈએ કે મજબૂત CIBIL Rank અને કંપની ક્રેડિટ રિપોર્ટ જાળવવો એ ઝડપી અને મુશ્કેલી વગર લોન લેવા માટે મહત્વપૂર્ણ છે કારણ કે સૌથી અનુકૂળ CIBIL Rank બેંકો અથવા ધિરાણકર્તાઓને કોઈપણ વ્યવસાયને ઝડપી અને સસ્તું ધિરાણ પ્રદાન કરવાનો વિશ્વાસ આપે છે. વધુમાં, શ્રેષ્ઠ CIBIL Rank વેપારીઓ ને બેંકો સાથે વ્યાજ દરો ઓછા કરાવા ની વધારે તકો આપે છે.

(લેખક :અપૂર્વ ફાઉન્ડેશન-ક્રેડિટ બ્યુરો કન્સલટન્ટના ફાઉન્ડર છે)

અમદાવાદ 29-08-2022

કેડિટ સ્કોર ઘટવાના ડરથી ચિંતિત છો, તો તમારે ચિંતા કરવાની બિલકુલ જરૂર નથી

જેમ સ્વાસ્થ્યની તપાસ જરૂરી તેમ નાણાકીય સ્ટ્રેન્થ માપવા સિબીલ જરૂરી

મારામાંથી ઘણા લોકો CIBIL રિપોર્ટ અને CIBIL સ્કોર વિશે જાણતા હશે પરંતુ શું તમે જાણો છો કે CIBIL રિપોર્ટ શા માટે તપાસવો અને સમજવો જોઈએ? તમારા થી, બેંક થી અથવા ક્રેડિટ બ્યુરો ની ભુલ થી થયેલી કોઈપણ ખામી ને ઓળખવા માટે તમારે CIBIL રિપોર્ટ તપાસવો જોઈએ. યાદ રાખો કે તમારો CIBIL રિપોર્ટ એ માત્ર કાગળનો ટુકડો નથી પરંતુ તમારી સમગ્ર નાણાકીય સુખાકારી માટે એક મહત્વપૂર્ણ પરિબળ છે.

આપણા સ્વાસ્થ્યને સમયાંતરે તપાસની જરૂર છે; તેવી જ રીતે આપણા નાણાકીય સ્વાસ્થ્યને પણ સમયસર તપાસની જરૂર છે. તેથી, તમારે દર ત્રણ - ચાર મહિને એક વખત CIBIL રિપોર્ટ અને સ્કોર તપાસવાની જરૂર છે. જો તમે તમારા ક્રેડિટ સ્કોરના ઘટવાના

બેન્કિંગ સમજ
અપૂર્વ ભગત

ડરથી ચિંતિત છો, તો તમારે ચિંતા કરવાની બિલકુલ જરૂર નથી કારણ કે, જ્યારે તમે તમારો ક્રેડિટ રિપોર્ટ ક્રેડિટ બ્યુરો ના પોર્ટલ પરથી તપાસો છો ત્યારે એની અસર તમારા ક્રેડિટ સ્કોર પર થશે નહિ કારણ કે આને એક સોફ્ટ ઇન્કવાયરી ગણવામાં આવે છે.

■ માસ્ટર ક્રેડિટ રિપોર્ટ એ ક્રેડિટ બ્યુરોના પોર્ટલ પર થી તપાસતા નીચેના ફાયદાઓ થાય છેઃ

■ સારા CIBIL સ્કોર ને ફરી થી બિલ્ડ કરવા અને જાળવવા માં તે એક મહત્વપૂર્ણ પગલું છે.

■ તમારા અંગત નાણાંનું સંચાલન કરવાનો એક મહત્વપૂર્ણ ભાગ છે.

■ તમને ચોક્કસ ના લાગે તેવી કોઈપણ માહિતીને સુધારવા માટેનું તે પ્રથમ પગલું છે, જે તમને ભુલ-મુક્ત અને સચોટ રેકોર્ડ જાળવવામાં મદદ કરે છે.

■ તમારી નાણાકીય સ્થિતિ જાણવામાં મદદ કરે છે.

■ તમારી લોન અથવા ક્રેડિટ કાર્ડના નિયંત્રણમાં રહેવામાં મદદ કરે છે.

■ તમે વધુ સારી લોન અથવા ક્રેડિટ કાર્ડને લાયક છો કે નહિ એ જાણવામાં તમને મદદ કરે છે.

■ લોન અરજીનો અસ્વીકાર ટાળવામાં મદદ કરે છે.

■ ઓળખની ચોરી (આઈડેન્ટિટી થેફ્ટ) સામે રક્ષણ આપવામાં મદદ કરે છે.

■ નાણાકીય અને આર્થિક જવાબદારી સમજવામાં મદદ કરે છે.

■ તમારી ક્રેડિટ હેલ્થને વધારવામાં મદદ કરે છે.

CIBIL રિપોર્ટને વારંવાર તપાસવાનો વિચાર સારો છે કારણ કે જ્યારે તમે ભવિષ્યમાં લોન લેવાનું વિચારી રહ્યા હશો અને તે સમયે જ્યારે તમે તમારા CIBIL રિપોર્ટ ની સમસ્યાઓનું નિરાકરણ લાવવાનું વિચારશો ત્યારે તમે એકદમ જ એને સુધારી નહિ શકો કારણ કે, CIBIL રિપોર્ટ ની ખામીઓ ને સુધારવાની પ્રક્રિયા ઓછામાં ઓછા 30 - 90 કામકાજના દિવસો (કિસ પ્રમાણે સમય અલગ હોઈ શકે છે) લેતી હોય છે.

ટૂંકમાં, તમારો CIBIL રિપોર્ટ સારા નાણાકીય જીવન માટે મહત્વપૂર્ણ ઘટક છે તેથી, ભુલ-મુક્ત અને સચોટ CIBIL રિપોર્ટ જાળવવો મહત્વપૂર્ણ છે.

(લેખક :અપૂર્વ ફાઉન્ડેશન-ક્રેડિટ બ્યુરો કન્સલટન્ટના ફાઉન્ડર છે)

અમદાવાદ 12-09-2022

ઘણાં લોન લેનારાઓ ક્રેડિટ બ્યુરોની નબળી સેવાના કારણે મુશ્કેલીમાં

ભારતીય રિઝર્વ કરશે તમારી ક્રેડિટ બ્યૂરો સંબંધિત ફરિયાદનું સમાધાન

બેંકો અને ક્રેડિટ બ્યુરો દ્વારા થયેલી ખામી ના લીધે દર 4 ક્રેડિટ રિપોર્ટ માંથી એક ક્રેડિટ રિપોર્ટ ભૂલભરેલી અથવા ખોટી અથવા અપૂર્ણ માહિતીથી ભરેલો હોય છે અને તેને સુધારવા માટે ઘણા લોન લેનારાઓને ક્રેડિટ બ્યુરોની નબળી સેવાને કારણે અથવા બેંકો ની ખામી ના લીધે ઘણી મુશ્કેલીનો સામનો કરવો પડે છે અથવા યોગ્ય જવાબ/ઉકેલ મળતો નથી. પરંતુ હવે આ સ્થિતિ રહેશે નહીં કારણ કે, RBI ની દેખરેખ હેઠળની ફરિયાદ નિવારણ પદ્ધતિ થી તમે કોઈ પણ ક્રેડિટ બ્યુરો સામે ફરિયાદ કરી શકશો.

ક્રેડિટ બ્યુરો એ ક્રેડિટ ઇન્ફર્મેશન કંપની (CIC) તરીકે પણ

બેન્કિંગ સમજ
અપૂર્વ ભગત

ઓળખાય છે, તે એક કેન્દ્રિય સંગ્રહ સ્થાન છે, જે વ્યક્તિગત અને વ્યાપારી સંસ્થાઓની ક્રેડિટ અને લોન સંબંધિત માહિતી એકત્રિત કરે છે, સંકલિત કરે છે અને જાળવે છે એ માહિતી જે તેઓ બેંકો, ક્રેડિટ કાર્ડ કંપનીઓ અને અન્ય નાણાકીય સંસ્થાઓ પાસેથી મેળવે છે. જો કે, એવી શક્યતાઓ રહેલી છે કે ક્રેડિટ બ્યુરો પાસે ઉપલબ્ધ માહિતી ખોટી અથવા અપૂર્ણ હોઈ શકે કારણ કે કાં તો ક્રેડિટ બ્યૂરો તેમનું કાર્ય યોગ્ય રીતે ના કરતા હોય અથવા બેંકો યોગ્ય રીતે ડેટા/માહિતી મોકલતી ના હોય અને પરિણામે લોન લેનારનો ક્રેડિટ સ્કોર ઓછો થઈ જાય છે. બેંકોની જેમ ક્રેડિટ બ્યુરોએ પણ 30 દિવસની અંદર કોઈ પણ ફરિયાદ નો ઉકેલ લાવવો પડશે. હવે પછી જો 30 દિવસની અંદર આ ક્રેડિટ બ્યૂરો તરફની ફરિયાદ નો કોઈ ઉકેલ ન આવે, તો લોન લેનાર ક્રેડિટ બ્યૂરો

દેશની ક્રેડિટ ઇકોસિસ્ટમમાં સુધારો થશે

01મી સપ્ટેમ્બર 2022થી TransUnion CIBIL, Equifax, Experian અને CRIF High Mark જેવા ક્રેડિટ બ્યુરો ને સંબંધિત સમસ્યાઓ ધરાવતી કોઈપણ વ્યક્તિ/કંપની સીધી RBI માં ફરિયાદ નોંધાવી શકશે. આ પહેલ વ્યક્તિગત અને કંપનીઓ માટે તેમની ખોટી માહિતી જે ક્રેડિટ રિપોર્ટ માં આવે છે એને સુધારવા માટે ફાયદાકારક છે જે તેમને સમયસર નાણાકીય સાધનોનો ઉપયોગ કરવામાં અને તેમની નાણાકીય બાબતો ને નિયંત્રણમાં રાખવા માટે મદદ કરી શકે છે. વધુમાં તે દેશની ક્રેડિટ ઇકોસિસ્ટમમાં સુધારો કરશે અને બેંક અથવા નાણાકીય સંસ્થા વધુ લોકો ને ક્રેડિટ/લોનની સુવિધા આપવામાં મદદ કરી શકશે. એ સાથે MSME પણ પોતાની ક્રેડિટ સમસ્યાઓ ને RBI ની ફરિયાદ નિવારણ પદ્ધતિ થી દૂર કરી પોતા ને વિસ્તૃત કરવા માટે સરકારી યોજનાઓ અથવા બેંક લોન નો લાભ લઈ શકશે.

વિરુદ્ધ RBI માં ફરિયાદ નોંધાવી શકે છે.

તમામ ક્રેડિટ બ્યુરોને RBI ની સંકલિત લોકપાલ યોજનાના કાર્યક્ષેત્ર હેઠળ લાવવાનું પગલું ખરેખર સારું છે, જે ફરિયાદ માટે સમયસર ઉકેલ આપશે. વધુમાં, ક્રેડિટ બ્યુરોને ફરિયાદ નિવારણ ને મજબૂત કરવા માટે પોતાનું આંતરિક લોકપાલ માળખું હોવું જરૂરી રહેશે.

credithelp@apoorvaa.co.in

અમદાવાદ 10-10-2022

સામાન્ય લાગતી ભૂલો, લાંબા ગાળે તમારા ક્રેડિટ સ્કોર પર ભારે અસર કરે

ક્રેડિટ સ્કોરને લગતી કઇ ભૂલો ટાળવી જોઈએ

ટલીક નાની અને સામાન્ય લાગતી ભૂલો, લાંબા ગાળે તમારા ક્રેડિટ સ્કોર પર ભારે અસર કરે છે. આજે તમને એ માત્ર એક નાની વસ્તુ લાગશે પરંતુ ભવિષ્યમાં તેની ઊંડી અસર પડશે. તમને જો એવું લાગતું હોય કે થોડા દિવસો મોડા લોન ના હપ્તા ચુકવવાથી કંઈ ફરક નહિ પડે તો એ એક વહેમ છે કારણકે, તે તમારા ક્રેડિટ રિપોર્ટમાં DPD (Days Past Dues - ચુકવણી ની તારીખ થી મોડા ચુકવેલ હપ્તા ના દિવસો) તરીકે બતાવશે જે તમારી ચુકવણીની આદત દર્શાવે છે અને તમને આગળ લોન લેવામાં તકલીફ કરશે.

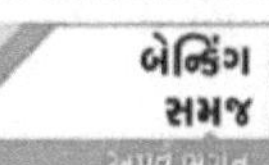

તેથી, આવતીકાલે વધુ સરળતા થી લોન મેળવવા માટે આપણે નાણાકીય શિસ્તતા જાળવવી જોઈએ.

- ચાલો જાણીએ ક્રેડિટ સ્કોર ની ભૂલો જેને તમારે ટાળવી જોઈએ.
- ક્રેડિટ મર્યાદા વધારવા માટે વારંવાર તપાસવું નહિ
- તમારા ક્રેડિટ રિપોર્ટ ને બેંક માંથી ના તપાસવો જોઈએ
- રિવોર્ડ્સ મેળવવા વધુ પડતો ક્રેડિટ કાર્ડ નો ઉપયોગ ના કરવો

ક્રેડિટ કાર્ડમાંથી રોકડ ના ઉપાડવી

વધુ પડતી ક્રેડિટનો બિલકુલ ઉપયોગ કરવો નહી

વધુ સારું નાણાકીય જીવન મેળવવા માટે આ સામાન્ય ભૂલોને ટાળવી જોઈએ. તમારો ક્રેડિટ સ્કોર જાળવવા માટે, તમારી નાણાકીય બાબતો પર નજર રાખવી અને સમયાંતરે તેમાં સુધારો કરવો જરૂરી છે.

ધ્યાન આપવા જેવી માહિતી જો તમને ક્રેડિટ રિપોર્ટમાં આ બાબત જણાય

- ખોટા લોન ખાતા નંબર
- ખોટું બેંક નું નામ
- તમે ઓળખતા નથી તેવા લોન ખાતા
- ચૂકવણીની અચોક્કસ સ્થિતિ અથવા મોડી ચૂકવણીની ઘટનાઓ
- બંધ ખાતા હજુ પણ ખુલ્લા તરીકે નોંધવામાં આવ્યા હોય
- સમાન ખાતાના ડુપ્લિકેટ એન્ટ્રી
- ખોટી ક્રેડિટ મર્યાદા

પરિબળો કે જે તમારા ક્રેડિટ સ્કોરને અસર કરતા નથી : મોટા ભાગ ના લોકો ક્રેડિટ સ્કોર ની બાબતે ચોક્કસ માહિતી ધરાવતા નથી અને કયા કારણો થી ક્રેડિટ સ્કોર ઘટે છે તે પણ જાણતા નથી. પરંતુ કેટલાક પરિબળોનો ક્રેડિટ સ્કોર સાથે કોઈ સંબંધ નથી. તેથી તેમને ધ્યાનમાં રાખવું કે નહીં તે તમારા ઉપર છે. ચાલો એવા પરિબળો જોઈએ કે જેની તમારા ક્રેડિટ સ્કોર પર કોઈ અસર પડતી નથી.

- તમારો પગાર
- તમે ક્યાં રહો છો
- તમે જે બાહુ ચૂકવો છો
- તમે જ્યાં કામ કરો છો
- તમારું બેંક બેલેન્સ
- તમારા યુટીલીટી બિલની ચૂકવણી
- તમારા વીમા નું પ્રિમીયમ
- તમારા ડેબિટ કાર્ડનો ઉપયોગ

જુઓ આ તમામ પરિબળો તમારા ક્રેડિટ સ્કોર અથવા ક્રેડિટ રિપોર્ટને અસર કરતા નથી, પરંતુ તેનો અર્થ એ નથી કે તમારે આને અવગણવા જોઈએ કારણ કે, તે તમારા જીવનના અન્ય વર્ટિકલ્સમાં મહત્વપૂર્ણ હોઈશકે છે. તેથી, આ પરિબળો પર નજર રાખવાથી તમારા નાણાકીય જીવનને મુશ્કેલી વગર જાણવા માં એક વધારાનો ફાયદો થશે.

અંતમા, જો તમને તમારા ક્રેડિટ રિપોર્ટમાં કોઈ ખોટી, અધૂરી અથવા કપટપૂર્ણ માહિતી દેખાય છે, તો તમે ક્રેડિટ બ્યુરો સાથે વિવાદ નોંધાવી શકો છો.

(લેખક : અપૂર્વ ફાઉન્ડેશન ક્રેડિટ બ્યુરો કન્સલટન્ટના ફાઉન્ડર છે. credithelp@apoorvaa.co.in)

દિવ્ય ભાસ્કર અમદાવાદ 24-10-2022

શું થશે? જો હોમ લોનના સળંગ ત્રણ હપ્તા ના ભરાય તો...ક્રેડિટ નબળી પડે

મારામાંથી ઘણા લોકો ને ઘર લેવાનું સપનું હશે. જો કે, ઘર લેવું સરળ નથી જેટલું એ લાગે છે અને તેના માટે હોમ લોનની જરૂર છે. યાદ રાખો, હોમ લોન એ લાંબા ગાળા ની પ્રતિબદ્ધતા છે, જેમાં તમારે ઓછા માં ઓછા 15-20 વર્ષ માટે હપ્તા ચૂકવવા ની જરૂર છે. જો તમારા હપ્તા ટ્રેક પર છે, તો તે એક સરળ બાબત છે, પરંતુ કોઈપણ હપ્તા ભરવા માં નિષ્ફળતા તમને મુશ્કેલી તરફ દોરી શકે છે. હોમ લોન ડિફોલ્ટ એ તમારી વર્તમાન અને ભવિષ્યની નાણાકીય સ્થિતિ પર ગંભીર અસર કરે છે. તે તમારી ક્રેડિટ પાત્રતા ને અસર કરે છે અને ભવિષ્યમાં તમારા માટે લોન લેવાનું મુશ્કેલ બનાવે

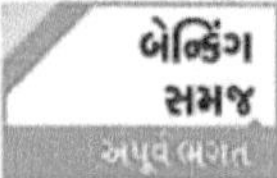

છે. જ્યારે તમે સતત ત્રણ હપ્તા અથવા 90 દિવસ માટે ડિફોલ્ટ કરો છો, ત્યારે બેંક લોનને નોન-પર્ફોર્મિંગ એસેટ તરીકે ગણી લે છે અને બાકીની રકમ વસૂલવાની પ્રક્રિયા શરૂ કરે છે. તે પહેલાં, તેઓ તમને રીમાઈન્ડર્સ, ઈમેઈલ્સ અથવા કોલ્સ મોકલવાનું શરૂ કરે છે.

જ્યારે તમે પ્રથમ હપ્તો ડિફોલ્ટ કરો છો, ત્યારે બેંક ચુકવણી રીમાઈન્ડર મોકલશે અને તમને લિંક દ્વારા અથવા રૂબરૂ આવી ચૂકવણી કરવા માટે નિર્દેશિત કરશે અને આ ક્ષણે બેંક બાકી હપ્તા સાથે બાકી લોનની રકમ પર 1-2% વિલંબિત દંડ બેંક ના નિયમ મુજબ વસૂલ કરી શકે છે.

બીજો હપ્તો ડિફોલ્ટ કરવા પર, બેંક તમને ચેતવણી આપે છે અને તમને પેનલ્ટી ચાર્જ સહિત તાત્કાલિક હપ્તા ની ચુકવણી માટે દબાણ કરે છે. જો કે તમને તમારી નાણાકીય પરિસ્થિતિના આધારે ચૂકવણી કરવા માટે થોડો સમય આપવામાં આવી શકે છે, બીજા હપ્તા નો ડિફોલ્ટ બેંક ચેતવણી રૂપે લે છે અને ત્રીજો હપ્તો વિલંબ અથવા બાઉન્સ થવાના કિસ્સામાં કાનૂની કાર્યવાહી શરૂ કરી શકે છે. આને દૂર કરવા માટે, તમારે તાત્કાલિક 2 હપ્તા ની ચુકવણી કરવાની જરૂર છે.

સળંગ ત્રીજા હપ્તા નો ડિફોલ્ટ બેંક તરફથી વધુ રીમાઈન્ડર્સ તરફ દોરી જશે; જો કે, 90 દિવસ અથવા ત્રણ મહિના પછી, બેંક બાકીની વસૂલાત માટે તમારી મિલકતની હરાજી કરવાની કાર્યવાહી શરૂ કરી શકે છે.

મહેરબાની કરીને યાદ રાખો, હોમ લોન એ ફાઇનાન્સનો સુરક્ષિત મોડ છે, અને કોલેટરલ એ મિલકત છે. તેથી, ફક્ત બેંક ત્રણ પગલાંઓ અનુસરે છે, કાનૂની સૂચના, મિલકત ટાંચ માં લેવી અને તેની હરાજી કરવી.

એકવાર તમે સળંગ ત્રણ હપ્તા ચૂકી ગયા પછી, બેંક આને નોન-પર્ફોર્મિંગ એસેટ્સ તરીકે જાહેર કરી દેશે, જેના કારણે તમારા ક્રેડિટ સ્કોરમાં ભારે ઘટાડો થશે. તમારી બેંકને તમારી નાણાકીય કટોકટીની જાણ કરવી એ એક સારો વિચાર છે જેથી તેઓ તમને ચુકવણી માટે કેટલાક વૈકલ્પિક વિકલ્પો આપી શકે જેમ કે, ગ્રેસ પીરિયડ, તમારી લોનનું પુનર્ગઠન અથવા લોન સેટલમેન્ટ. આવી અણધારી પરિસ્થિતિઓને ટાળવા માટે, તમારે પર્યાપ્ત ઇમરજન્સી ફંડ જાળવવું જોઈએ. વધુમાં, તમે હોમ લોન વીમાનો પણ વિચાર કરી શકો છો, જેથી મુશ્કેલ સમય ને ટાળવા માં એ તમને મદદરૂપ થઈ શકે છે જેના લીધે તમારા લોન ના હપ્તા વિલંબિત થતા અટકી શકશો.

અંતમાં, તમારે તમારા નાણાકીય અને ક્રેડિટ સ્કોર પર કોઈ નકારાત્મક અસર ટાળવા માટે હોમ લોન લેતા પહેલા પ્લાનિંગ કરવું જોઈએ.

લેખક :અપૂર્વા ફાઉન્ડેશનના ફાઉન્ડર છે.
credithelp@apoorvaa.co.in

અમદાવાદ 14-11-2022

સાવધાન! ઓનલાઇન ફિનટેક લોનની બીજી બાજુ જે તમે ક્યારેય નથી જાણતા

ટેક્નોલોજી એ એક વરદાન છે જેણે નવા સ્ટાર્ટઅપ્સને વેગ આપ્યો છે અને ફિનટેક કંપનીઓ પાસેથી કોઈપણ પેપર વર્ક વિના અથવા ઓછા પેપરવર્ક થી નાની લોન મેળવવાનો માર્ગ સરળ બનાવ્યો છે. ટેક્નોલોજીના વિકાસ સાથે, પ્રારંભિક/જલ્દી પગાર લોન, ખરીદો-હમણાં-પછી-પાછળથી ચુકવણી કરો અથવા અમુક સરળ કાર્ડ્સ સહિત નિર્ધારિત મહિનામાં પાક્કા લોન ના પૈસા ચુકવવાની સરળતા સાથેની કોઈપણ નાની સાઈઝની લોન સૌથી અનુકૂળ વિકલ્પો છે, જે તમને મનગમતી પ્રોડક્ટ ખરીદવા માટે ઝડપી લોન આપે

છે. આ ભંડોળ મેળવવા માટે અથવા મિનિટોમાં રોકડની પ્રવાહિતા આપવા માટે ઝડપી છે.

જો કે, આ સેવાઓમાં નાની રકમ છે એટલે ચુકવણીની અવગણના કરવી એ બિલકુલ અનુકૂળ નથી. કારણ એ છે કે આ નાની નાણાકીય સેવાઓ તમારા ક્રેડિટ રિપોર્ટમાં નવી લોન તરીકે સૂચિબદ્ધ થાય છે. આ લોન ફક્ત તમારા ક્રેડિટ રિપોર્ટમાં લોન એકાઉન્ટ તરીકે જ સૂચિબદ્ધ નથી થતી, પરંતુ તમારા ક્રેડિટ સ્કોરને પણ પ્રભાવિત કરે છે. મહેરબાની કરીને યાદ રાખો, તમારે પુનઃચુકવણી કરતી વખતે ખૂબ જ કાળજી રાખવાની જરૂર છે, કારણ કે અન્ય લોનની જેમ આની પણ પુનઃચુકવણી ની હિસ્ટ્રી અને ક્રેડિટ સ્કોર ને ગણતરીમાં ધ્યાન માં લેવામાં આવે છે.

દરેક વસ્તુના ફાયદાની સાથે તેના ગેરફાયદા પણ

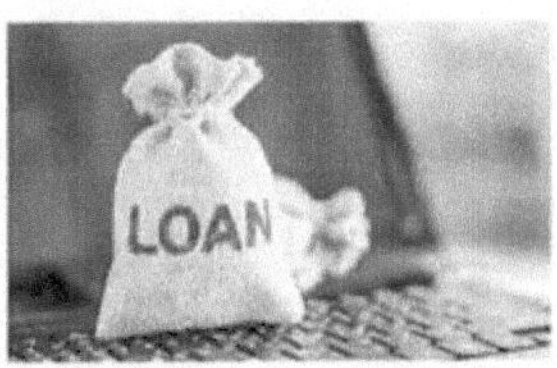

હોય છે, અને આ લોન અપવાદ નથી કારણ કે, આ એપ આધારિત લોન છે, જ્યાં તમારે વધુ સાવચેત રહેવાની જરૂર છે. જ્યારે તમે ચુકવણી કરવાનું ચૂકી જશો ત્યારે શરૂઆતમાં એ લાગે છે તેટલું તે ભવિષ્યમાં સરળ રહેશો નહીં. અહીં એપમાંથી લોન લેતી વખતે એક વધારાનો સાવચેતીભર્યો અભિગમ રાખવો જોઈએ, કારણ કે ભારતીય રિઝર્વ બેંક (RBI) શોધ્યું છે કે લગભગ 1100 ડિજિટલ લોન પ્રદાતાઓમાંથી અડધાથી વધુ ગેરકાનૂની રીતે કામ કરી રહ્યા છે. કોરોના કાળ દરમિયાન, ઝડપી રોકડનું વચન આપતી એપ્લિકેશનો મશરૂમ ની જેમ ઊઠવી હતી. ઘણા ઉધાર લેનારાઓની સાક્ષરતાના અભાવનો લાભ ઉઠાવી, વાર્ષિક ધોરણે 500% જેટલો ઊંચો વ્યાજ દર વસૂલ કરે છે અને કેટલાક કિસ્સાઓમાં સખ્ત રીતે વસૂલવાની યુક્તિઓનો ઉપયોગ કરે છે, જે આત્મહત્યા તરફ દોરી જાય છે. ઓનલાઈન લોનની દુનિયામાં ફસાવવાની સરળ પ્રક્રિયા એ છે કે, કોઈ અજાણી વ્યક્તિ તમારા મોબાઈલ પર એક લિંક મોકલીને લોનની લાલચ આપે છે, જેમાં ફસાઈ ગયા પછી લોન મળી જાય

છે, પણ ચૂકવ્યા પછી પણ પૈસા માંગે છે.

ટૂલ જે પૈસાને એક્સેસ કરતી વખતે શરૂઆતમાં અનુકૂળ લાગે છે, તે વાસ્તવમાં સારા કરતાં વધુ નુકસાન કરે છે. ઓનલાઈન લોન એપ્સને હેન્ડલ કરતી વખતે કેટલાક મુદ્દા ધ્યાનમાં રાખો;

- તમારા મોબાઈલ પર આવેલી અજાણી લિંક પર ક્લિક કરશો નહીં
- અજાણી એપ્લિકેશનો મોબાઈલ માંથી કાઢી નાખો
- ફિશિંગ કોલ્સ, SMS અને ઈમેઈલ્સથી સાવચેત રહો
- તમારી અંગત માહિતી ખાનગી રાખો
- તમારો ક્રેડિટ સ્કોર ટ્રેક કરો – TransUnion ના પોર્ટલ પરથી જ
- લોન આપનાર ની વિશ્વસનીયતા ચકાસો
- ફાઈનલ પ્રિન્ટ વાંચો અને સમજો
- સંશોધન કરો, મૂલ્યાંકન કરો અને પછી બુદ્ધિશાળી પસંદગી કરો
- એક સમયે અનેક લોન લેવાથી દૂર રહો

તમે એ ક્યારેય જાણતા નથી કે લોન મેળવવાની આ સરળતા તમારા માટે ક્યારે અભિશાપ બની જશો. તેથી સાવચેત રહો અને જો તમે આવી એપ છેતરપિંડીનો શિકાર બન્યા હોવ તો સાયબર ક્રાઈમ વિભાગમાં અથવા ભારતીય રિઝર્વ બેંક (RBI) લોકપાલ માં જઈને ફરિયાદ નોંધાવવામાં શરમાશો નહીં.

લેખક :અપૂર્વા ફાઉન્ડેશનના ફાઉન્ડર છે.
credithelp@apoorvaa.co.in

અમદાવાદ 28-11-2022

બેન્કિંગનાં કોઈ પણ માધ્યમોનો ઉપયોગ કરતી વખતે સાવચેત રહેવું જોઈએ
સુરક્ષિત બેન્કિંગ માટે શું કરવું અને શું ના કરવું

ટેક્નોલોજીમાં પ્રગતિ એ ખરેખર એક આશીર્વાદ છે, પરંતુ જ્યારે ટેક્નોલોજીને એક્સેસ કરવાની વાત આવે છે ત્યારે ખાસ કરીને ઓનલાઈન બેંકિંગ મોડ્સને હેન્ડલ કરવા માટે દરેકે સલામતીના પગલાં ભરવા જોઈએ. ટેક્નોલોજીના આ યુગમાં હોવાથી, બેંકિંગના કોઈપણ માધ્યમોનો ઉપયોગ કરતી વખતે સાવચેત રહેવું જોઈએ, તેમ

છતાં જો તમે કોઈ છેતરપિંડીની પ્રવૃત્તિ અથવા આઈડેન્ટિટી થેફ્ટ નો શિકાર બન્યા હોવ, તો ખચકાટ વિના સાયબર ક્રાઈમ વિભાગમાં અથવા ભારતીય રિઝર્વ બેંક (RBI) લોકપાલ માં જઈને ફરિયાદ કરો. (લેખક :અપૂર્વા ફાઉન્ડેશનના ફાઉન્ડર છે. credithelp@apoorvaa.co.in)

શું કરવું જોઈએ

- હંમેશા બેંકો/સેવા પ્રદાતાની અધિકૃત વેબસાઈટ પર જ જાઓ અને એવી સુરક્ષિત વેબસાઈટનો જ ઉપયોગ કરો જે ઉદા. https:// - જ્યાં 's' એ સુરક્ષિત વેબસાઈટ માટે વપરાય છે.
- જો તમને ટેક્નિકલ ખામીઓનો સામનો કરવો પડી રહ્યો હોય અથવા એપ્સ ડાઉનલોડ કરતી વખતે સમસ્યા આવી રહી હોય તો તમામ પેમેન્ટ/ફાઈનાન્શિયલ એપ્સ ને તમારા મોબાઈલ/લેપટોપ/પીસી માંથી લોગ આઉટ કરો.
- છેતરપિંડી થી બચવા માટે બેંકો અથવા ઈ-કોમર્સ પ્લેટફોર્મ જેવી બનાવટી અને ભળતા દેખાવ જેવી વેબસાઈટને ટાળવા માટે એક્સેસ કરવામાં આવતી વેબસાઈટ/યુઆરએલ (URL) ના સ્પેલિંગ તપાસો.
- ઈમેઈલ્સ અધિકૃત સરનામાંઓથી છે કે નહી તેની ખાતરી કરવા માટે પ્રાપ્ત થયેલ ઈમેઈલ્સ ના સ્પેલિંગ અને હેડર તપાસો.
- SMS/ Whatsapp/ ઈમેલ પ્રાપ્ત થયેલા ટૂંકા URL/ Google પર ક્લિક કરતી વખતે સાવચેત રહો.
- બેંકો/ઈકોમર્સ/સર્ચ એન્જિન વેબસાઈટની લિંક્સ પ્રદાન કરતા સ્પામ મેઈલને તપાસો.

શું ના કરવું જોઈએ

- SIM કાર્ડ અને મોબાઈલ નંબરની વિગતો શેર કરશો નહીં અથવા ATM કાર્ડ પર પીન લખશો નહીં અથવા વેબસાઈટ્સ/ડિવાઈસ/પબ્લિક લેપટોપ/ડેસ્કટોપ પર વિગતો સેવ કરશો નહીં.
- બેંકો, વીમા, સરકાર વગેરેના કોલ સેન્ટર એજન્ટ તરીકે ઓળખ આપતી વ્યક્તિઓની ઓફરો માં ફસાઈ જશો નહીં અને યુઝરનેમ, પાસવર્ડ, કાર્ડની વિગતો/પીન/સીવીવી/ઓટીપી, જન્મ તારીખ, આધાર નંબર, પરિવારના સભ્યોના નામ વગેરે શેર કરવા માટે દબાણ કરે તો પણ આ જાણકારી આપશો નહીં.
- અજાણી/અચકાસાયેલ લિંક્સ પર ક્લિક કરશો નહીં અને અજાણ્યા લોકોની સલાહ પર વણચકાસાયેલ સ્રોતોમાંથી એપ્લિકેશન્સ ડાઉનલોડ કરશો નહીં.
- તમારા બેંક એકાઉન્ટ્સ/એટીએમ(ATM) કાર્ડને કમિશન માટે અન્ય લોકો ને ઉપયોગ કરવાની મંજૂરી આપશો નહીં, જેના કારણે નાણાં લેવડ-દેવડ કરવા માટે બેંક એકાઉન્ટના દુરુપયોગને કારણે પોલીસ તપાસ થઈ શકે છે.
- અવિશ્વસનીય લોટરી ઓફર પર વિશ્વાસ ન કરો અને આવા ઈમેઈલ/કોલ્સના જવાબમાં તમારા ઓળખપત્રો શેર કરશો નહીં.

દિવ્ય ભાસ્કર

અમદાવાદ 12-12-2022

સંયુક્ત હોમ લોન લેવાનું આયોજન કરી રહ્યા છો? તો તેના ફાયદા-ગેરફાયદા જાણી લો

લોન પર ટેક્સલાભ માટે કો-એપ્લીકેન્ટસ રહો

ઘર હોવું એ વ્યક્તિના જીવનનું સૌથી મહત્વપૂર્ણ સ્વપ્ન છે. જો કે, ડાઉન પેમેન્ટ મેનેજ કરવાથી લઈને લોનની પાત્રતા સુધી રોકાણ અને જવાબદારીઓ અનિવાર્ય હોઈ શકે છે. જ્યારે કોઈ વ્યક્તિ હોમ લોનની જરૂરી રકમ મેળવવામાં નિષ્ફળ જાય છે અથવા પાત્રતાના માપદંડોને પૂર્ણ કરતી નથી, ત્યારે આ કિસ્સામાં, મોટાભાગના નાણાકીય સલાહકારો

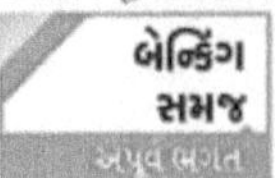

સંયુક્ત હોમ લોન લેવાનું સૂચન કરે છે.

તમે તમારા પરિવારના સભ્યો અથવા નજીકના સંબંધીઓ જેવા કે માતાપિતા, જીવનસાથી, પુરુષ બાળક, અપરિણીત સ્ત્રી બાળક અથવા સાથે રહેતા ભાઈઓ એટલે કે સીધી લીટીના વારસદારો સાથે સંયુક્ત રીતે લોન લઈ શકો છો. વ્યક્તિએ સમજવું જોઈએ કે હોમ લોન માટે કો-એપ્લીકેન્ટ થનાર વ્યક્તિ મિલકતનો સહ-માલિક બની શકતો નથી. પરંતુ ટેક્સ નો લાભ મેળવવા માટે બંને કો-એપ્લીકેન્ટસ મિલકતના સહ-માલિક હોવા જોઈએ.

જો કે આ વિકલ્પ લોન લેવાની ક્ષમતામાં વધારો કરી શકે છે, પરંતુ વ્યક્તિએ તેના ફાયદા અને ગેરફાયદા તપાસવા જોઈએ.

(લેખક : અપૂર્વા ફાઉન્ડેશનના ફાઉન્ડર છે, credithelp@apoorvaa.co.in)

લોન લેનારમાં કો-એપ્લિકેન્ટ્સ મહિલા હોય તો લોન સરળ બને

સંયુક્ત હોમ લોનના ફાયદા

- સંયુક્ત હોમ લોન લેવાથી હોમ લોનની વધુ રકમ મળવાની શક્યતા વધી શકે છે.
- સંયુક્ત હોમ લોનમાં, કો-એપ્લીકેન્ટ મિલકતના સહ-માલિક હોય, તો કો-એપ્લીકેન્ટ લેનાર પણ નિર્ધારિત મર્યાદામાં સેક્શન 24 અને 80c હેઠળ ટેક્સ નો લાભ મેળવી શકે છે.
- જો કો-એપ્લીકેન્ટ લેનારમાંથી એક મહિલા હોય, તો નીચા વ્યાજ દર પર બેંક લોન આપવાનું વિચારી શકે છે.
- જો આપનો ક્રેડિટ સ્કોર ખુબ સારો હોય તો પણ આપણે બેંક માં નીચા વ્યાજ દર માં લોન મળી શકે છે. (દરેક બેંક ના નિયમ મુજબ)

સંયુક્ત હોમ લોનના ગેરફાયદ

- જેમ કોઈપણ નાણાકીય ઉત્પાદનોના ફાયદા અને ગેરફાયદાને નકારી શકતા નથી, તેમ સંયુક્ત હોમ લોનમાં કેટલીક ખામીઓ પણ છે.
- જો કો-એપ્લીકેન્ટ હોમ લોન EMIs સમયસર ચુકવવામાં નિષ્ફળ જાય, તો તે બંનેના ક્રેડિટ સ્કોરને અસર કરશે.
- કો-એપ્લીકેન્ટ વચ્ચેના વિવાદના કિસ્સામાં, તે ચુકવણીને અસર કરી શકે છે અને ડિફોલ્ટનું કારણ બની શકે છે.
- જો પતિ-પત્ની દ્વારા લોન લેવામાં આવી હોય, તો છૂટાછેડાના કિસ્સામાં, તે કાનૂની વિવાદમાં પરિણમી શકે છે.

ભવિષ્યમાં કોઈપણ અણધારી પરિસ્થિતિને ટાળવા માટે મદદરૂપ સાબિત થાય

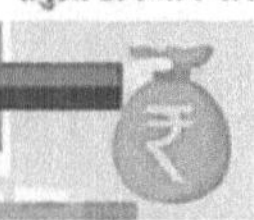

સંયુક્ત હોમ લોન નો વિકલ્પ ફાયદાકારક છે, પરંતુ તેની સાથે સંકળાયેલ જોખમોથી બચવા માટે સાવચેતીનાં પગલાં લેવાં પણ એટલા જ જરૂરી છે. વધુમાં, વ્યક્તિગત સંબંધો અને હોમ લોનની ચુકવણીના સંદર્ભમાં પછીના તબક્કે કોઈપણ પરિણામને ટાળવા માટે યોગ્ય કો-એપ્લીકેન્ટ હોવું મહત્વપૂર્ણ છે. સંયુક્ત હોમ લોનના નિર્ણયમાં પ્રવેશતા પહેલા, વ્યક્તિએ તમામ પાસઓ ને ધ્યાનમાં લેવા જોઈએ, અને બંને કો-એપ્લીકેન્ટસ એ હોમ લોન સાથે સંકળાયેલા નિયમો અને શરતો ને જાણવી જોઈએ. જેઓ સંયુક્ત હોમ લોનનો લાભ લેવાનું આયોજન કરી રહ્યા છે, તેઓએ ભવિષ્યમાં કોઈપણ અણધારી પરિસ્થિતિને ટાળવા માટે બંને કો-એપ્લીકેન્ટ માટે અલગ ટર્મ ખ્લાન લેવાનું જરૂર થી ધ્યાન માં લેવું જોઈએ.

દિવ્ય ભાસ્કર — **અમદાવાદ** 26-12-2022

બેરોજગારી, માંદગી-અન્ય કેટલાક કારણોથી લોન ચુકવણીમાં અસમર્થ છો ત્યારે

તમારા ક્રેડિટ સ્કોર પર લોન સેટલમેન્ટની કેવી અસર પડી શકે તેની સમજ કેળવો

જેઓ લોન લે છે તેઓએ લોન ના નિયમિત હપ્તા ચૂકવવા પડે છે. પરંતુ કેટલીક પરિસ્થિતિઓ તેમને હપ્તા ચૂકી જવા તરફ ખેંચી જાય છે, અને એના સમાધાન તરીકે જ્યારે તેમને લોન ના હપ્તા ની વસુલાત ટાળવા માટે બૅંક તરફથી વન-ટાઈમ સેટલમેન્ટની ઓફર કરવામાં આવે છે, ત્યારે તેઓ ઉતાવળિયે જ પગલાં ભરી ને લોન સેટલમેન્ટ કરી નાખે છે. જો કે, તેઓ સેટલમેન્ટ ના પરિણામો જાણતા નથી હોતા, અને તેઓ અજાણતા તેમના ક્રેડિટ સ્કોર ને ઓછો કરવામાં ભાગ ભજવી લે છે. આ ઉપરાંત, ઘણા લોકો અજ્ઞાનતા ના લીધે અથવા પુરી જાણકારી ન હોવા ના લીધે લોન ક્લોઝર અને

લોન સેટલમેન્ટ ને એક જ સમજે છે. પરંતુ આ બંને એક નથી. જ્યારે તમે તમારા તમામ હપ્તા સમયસર ચૂકવો છો, અને લોન કાર્યકાળ પૂર્ણ કરો છો, ત્યારે બૅંક લોન ખાતું બંધ કરશો અને "લોન ક્લોઝ" તરીકે અપડેટ કરશો.

લોન સેટલમેન્ટ એટલે શું?

એવી પરિસ્થિતિનો વિચાર કરો કે જેમાં તમારી પાસે લોન ચાલુ છે, અને તમે બેરોજગારી, માંદગી, ઈજા અથવા અન્ય કેટલાક કારણોને લીધે ચુકવણી કરવામાં અસમર્થ છો. તો આ કિસ્સામાં, તમે અને બૅંક વન-ટાઈમ સેટલમેન્ટ તરીકે ચુકવણી કરવા માટે અમુક રકમ પર નિષ્કર્ષ કાઢી શકો છો, અને એ રકમ ભર્યા પછી લોનની સ્થિતિ "સેટલ" તરીકે રેકોર્ડ કરવામાં આવે છે.

આવી સ્થિતિ માં બૅંક શું કરે છે?

જો લોન લેનારને લોન પર ચૂકવણી ન કરવાની વાસ્તવિક સમસ્યાઓ હોય તો બૅંકો વન-ટાઈમ સેટલમેન્ટ વિકલ્પ ઓફર કરે છે જો તમે અણધારી પરિસ્થિતિને ધ્યાનમાં રાખીને 6 મહિના ના હપ્તા ચુકવવામાં નિષ્ફળ ગયા હોવ ત્યારે બૅંક

તમારી સાથે ચર્ચા કર્યા પછી, વન-ટાઈમ સેટલમેન્ટ રકમ નક્કી કરે છે તે તમારે ચુકવવી પડે છે અને ચુકવણી પછી તે લોન "સેટલ" તરીકે પ્રતિબિંબિત થાય છે.

લોન સેટલમેન્ટ તમારા ક્રેડિટ સ્કોરને કેવી રીતે અસર કરે છે?

જ્યારે તમારી લોનને "સેટલ" તરીકે ઓળખવામાં આવે છે, ત્યારે બૅંક ક્રેડિટ બ્યુરોને અપડેટ કરે છે અને તે જ તમારા ક્રેડિટ રિપોર્ટમાં નેગેટિવ માર્ક તરીકે પ્રતિબિંબિત થાય છે જે લોન લેનારની નકારાત્મક ક્રેડિટ વર્તણૂક દર્શાવે છે અને તેના ક્રેડિટ સ્કોર પર નકારાત્મક અસર કરે છે.

તેથી જ્યારે તમે ભવિષ્યમાં લોન અથવા કોઈપણ પ્રકારની ક્રેડિટ માટે અરજી કરો છો, ત્યારે તેને ગેરલાયક ઠેરવવામાં આવે છે કારણ કે બૅંક ને તમારા હપ્તા ની ચુકવણી ની ક્ષમતા અને ક્રેડિટ સ્કોર વિશે શંકા હોઈ શકે છે અને ભૂતકાળના બિનચુકવણીના ઇતિહાસને કારણે લોનને નકારી શકે છે.

આવી સ્થિતિ માં તમારે શું કરવું જોઈએ?

એક ખોટું પગલું તમને તમારી ક્રેડિટના સંદર્ભમાં લાંબા સમય સુધી પરેશાન કરી શકે છે. જો તમારી પાસે અન્ય કોઈ વિકલ્પ ન હોય તો જ વન-ટાઈમ સેટલમેન્ટની ઓફર સ્વીકારો. જ્યારે તમને કોઈ પણ પરિસ્થિતિને કારણે તમારા હપ્તા ચુકવવામાં મુશ્કેલીનો સામનો કરવો પડે છે, ત્યારે પ્રથમ તક તરીકે લોન સેટલમેન્ટમાં ન જશો. યાદ રાખો, લોન સેટલમેન્ટ તમારા ક્રેડિટ સ્કોરને નુકસાન પહોંચાડી શકે છે અને તમારી ક્રેડિટ રિપોર્ટને બગાડી શકે છે. આ પહેલા, તમારા નાણાકીય પોર્ટફોલિયો અથવા કેટલીક સંપત્તિને લિક્વિડેટ કરવાનો વિકલ્પ શોધો. જો આ એવો વિકલ્પ નથી કે જેને તમે ધ્યાનમાં લઈ શકો છો, તો તમારા પરિવાર અને મિત્રો ની મદદ લઈ શકો છો, પરંતુ લોન સેટલમેન્ટ ટાળવાનો પ્રયાસ કરો. (લેખક :અપૂર્વા ફાઉન્ડેશનના ફાઉન્ડર છે credithelp@apoorvaa.co.in)

બેન્કિંગ સમજ — અપૂર્વ ભગત

Awards and Recognition

Under Advocate Apurva Bhagat's leadership, Apoorvaa Foundation was appreciated with many prestigious awards and achievements:

- Super Indians Award for Pioneer in the Most Admired and Innovative Credit Rectification Service in India 2024, presented by the Honorable Chief Minister of Gujarat, Mr. Bhupendrabhai Patel organized by Bharat 24 – Vision of a New India.

- Appreciation from the Surat Branch of WIRC of ICAI for Credit Bureau Awareness Seminar 2024.

- Appreciation from the Navsari Branch of WIRC of ICAI for Credit Bureau Awareness Seminar 2024.

- Appreciation from The Southern Gujarat Chamber of Commerce and Industry for Credit Bureau Awareness Seminar 2024.

- National Legal Excellence 2023 organized by The Associated Chambers of Commerce & Industry of India (**ASSOCHAM**) for NGO of the year.

- Appreciation from the Bhilwara Branch of CIRC of ICAI for Contributing in Anant National Conference 2023.

- Appreciation from the Bhavnagar Branch of WIRC of ICAI for Credit Bureau Awareness Seminar 2023.

- Appreciation from the Bhuj Branch of WIRC of ICAI for Credit Bureau Awareness Seminar 2023.

- Appreciation from the Akola Branch of WIRC of ICAI for Credit Bureau Awareness Seminar 2023.

- Appreciation from the Amravati Branch of WIRC of ICAI for Credit Bureau Awareness Seminar 2023.

- Blindwink Business Excellence Award 2022 for Pioneer in Credit Repair Business and Risk Governance Services in India.

- 2nd Innovators' Excellence Awards 2021 by The Associated Chambers of Commerce & Industry of India (**ASSOCHAM**).

- GTF Business Excellence Conclave 2021 Award for Best Unique Business – Credit Improve Services – Banking and Finance.

- The 2021 Global Choice Awards for Most Promising Credit Rectification Service Provider in India.

- Global Startup up Summit & Awards 2021 for Excellent Customer Service in Credit Rectification.

- GTF World Business Summit 2020 Awards for Best Credit Rectification Service – Banking & Finance.

- Achievers Icon Awards 2020 Entrepreneurial Excellence in Finance & Credit Rectification Services.

- Pride of Indian Leadership Awards 2020 for Best Credit Rectification Services in India.

- Pride of Indian Leadership Awards 2020 for Best Credit Bureau Counselors in India.

- 4th Global Business Awards by Unit Asian-African Chamber of Commerce & Industry.

- Appreciation E-Certificate from Unified Brainz of India.

- Best Excellence Awards 2019 for Best Credit Expert & Counselors in India.

- India Excellence Awards 2019 for Best Credit Analysts & Counselors in India.

- Appreciation from the Organization of Bank Officers, BMS Unit – TJSB Sahakari Bank Ltd.

- Appreciation from the ICAI Circle, Vadodara for Sponsoring WIRC Sub Regional Conference in 2018.

- Memento of Appreciation from MPGB Bank Indore 2017.

- Received maximum appreciation certificate from all leading Banks to appreciate our Credit Awareness Seminars.

- We have taken the initiative to conduct Credit Awareness Seminars.

Super Indians Award for Pioneer in the Most Admired and Innovative Credit Rectification Service in India 2024, presented by the Honorable Chief Minister of Gujarat, Mr. Bhupendrabhai Patel organized by Bharat 24 – Vision of a New India.

National Legal Excellence 2023 organized by The Associated Chambers of Commerce & Industry of India (**ASSOCHAM**) for NGO of the year.

Proud Moment with CA. Aniket Talati – President ICAI

Proud Moment with Mr. Satish Marathe – RBI Director

Resources

The following is a summary of sources which are used as a raw material for compiling this book.

- The Indian Credit Reporting System
- Improove Your Credit Health
- www.cibil.com
- https://www.credit.com/credit-repair/what-is-the-difference-between-a-credit-counselorandacreditanalyst
- https://www.bankrate.com/financing/credit/what-is-the-difference-between-a-creditcounselorandarepairconsultant
- https://www.creditcards.com/credit-card-news/credit-counseling-for-people-with-bad-credit.php
- https://www.investopedia.com/articles/investing/032915/how-to-start-a-counselingbusiness.asp
- The Credit Information Companies (Regulation) Act, 2005
- Wikipedia.org
- investopedia.com
- www.equifax.com
- www.experan.com
- www.crifhighmark.com
- The Ultimate Guide to Starting a Credit Repair Business
- Some Genuine Internet Sources

Disclaimer

The opinions and views provided in this book are for educational and informational purposes only. Many writings in this book have online references and sources. We cannot claim that following all these practices will surely impact your credit score or not because it is not in our hands. All the credit reports and credit scores are managed by credit bureaus, and data is provided by creditors or lenders. We cannot even claim that following all points of this book, you can generate lots of income through credit counseling and repair as it depends on individual capacity, how you take up the business, how hard you work, how much effort you put in, and so on.

All the content and information in this book belong to Apoorvaa Foundation and are protected under Copyright Law. Kindly do not copy or reproduce our content without our prior explicit permission. The names used in illustrations do not have any correlation with any person – living or dead, and are only used for informational purposes. Some technical definitions are typical in nature and hence have been taken from trustworthy online and offline sources, but the unique format and narration of the book exclusively belong to Apoorvaa Foundation. All the resources are mentioned in the resources part of the book, and hence we do not claim information sourced from other materials to be ours.

– Apoorvaa Foundation

309/B, Hare Krishna Complex
B/H City Gold Cinema
Ashram Road
Ahmedabad – 380009
Gujarat, India
Website – www.apoorvaa.co.in
Email – ceo@apoorvaa.co.in